DATE DUE

MAY 17 05			

DEMCO 38-296

GENDER, FAMILIES, AND STATE

GENDER, FAMILIES, AND STATE

Child Support Policy in the United States

Jyl J. Josephson

ROWMAN & LITTLEFIELD PUBLISHERS, INC.
Lanham • Boulder • New York • London

ROWMAN & LITTLEFIELD PUBLISHERS, INC.

Published in the United States of America
by Rowman & Littlefield Publishers, Inc.
4720 Boston Way, Lanham, Maryland 20706

3 Henrietta Street
London WC2E 8LU, England

British Cataloging in Publication Information Available

Library of Congress Cataloging-in-Publication Data

Josephson, Jyl J.
    Gender, families, and state : child support policy in the United States / Jyl J. Josephson.
    p. cm.
    Includes bibliographical references and index.
    ISBN 0–8476–8371–0 (cloth : alk. paper).—ISBN 0–8476–8372–9 (paper : alk. paper)
    1. Child support—Government policy—United States. 2. Child support—Government
policy—Maryland—Prince George's County. 3. Child support—Government Policy—
Texas—Lubbock County. 4. Family policy—United States.
5. Women heads of households—United States. I. Title.
HV741.J67   1997
362.7'1—dc20   96–33119
                                            CIP

ISBN 0–8476–8371-0 (cloth : alk. paper)
ISBN 0–8476–8372-9 (pbk. : alk. paper)

Printed in the United States of America

♾™ The paper used in this publication meets the minimum requirements of American
National Standard for Information Sciences—Permanence of Paper for Printed Library
Materials, ANSI Z39.48–1984.

Contents

List of Tables

Acknowledgments

In taking on a project of this magnitude, one acquires many debts. The first and most obvious debt is to the women and men who agreed to speak with me regarding their experiences with the child support system. Their willingness to discuss their encounters with child support enforcement is what has made this project both possible and rewarding. Many thanks also to the administrators who shared generously of their time and knowledge; I gained a great deal from the information and insights offered by those who know child support policy from the inside out.

The Department of Government and Politics at the University of Maryland and the Political Science Department at Texas Tech University provided material assistance with the costs of mailing the survey to custodial and non-custodial parents. The Graduate School of the University of Maryland also provided travel expenses for attendance at a conference for the presentation of a preliminary version of chapter 5. The Women's Studies Program at the University of Maryland provided an early opportunity to present the research in their annual research forum.

This project began as a doctoral dissertation under the direction of Stephen Elkin, who encouraged me to pursue this project when it seemed an unlikely prospect and whose commitment to getting the argument right has helped to make this a more coherent book. Thanks to the probing questions and very helpful suggestions of the other members of my dissertation committee, as well, this is an improved product: William Galston, Ronald Terchek, Robin West, and Linda Williams. Linda Williams also provided helpful suggestions on the focus group questions. Additional thanks are due to Michael Gusmano, John Penn, and Valerie Johnson, who volunteered their time and skills to help conduct the interviews reported in chapter 4. Thanks also to those who helped me gain access to the court records discussed in chapter 4, especially Richard Olsen of Patuxent Abstracts, and the staff at the Lubbock County court archives.

Two students provided me with the opportunity to supervise their internships at child support agencies—Adam Weisblatt with the federal Office of Child Support Enforcement, and Natalie Atallah with the Texas Child Support Division—and I thank them for the valuable information and insights this offered.

A great number of friends and colleagues provided encouragement and read and commented on various versions of this project. Lori Joy Eisner first introduced me to child support law in Maryland. Virginia Haufler gave very early stage encouragement. The Gender and Politics discussion group at the University of Maryland provided many opportunities to explore the ideas out of which this project grew. My intellectual and personal debts to Cynthia Burack are great: it is hard to imagine how I would have completed the project without her friendship, encouragement, and mentorship. James Nelson carefully read and meticulously and intelligently edited the entire manuscript. Without his attention to detail and continuing support, this would be a much poorer venture. Sue Tolleson-Rinehart provided useful final stage encouragement. Many friends and colleagues, including Chuck D'Adamo, Patricia de los Rios, Bonnie Thornton Dill, Kathy Doherty, Michael Gusmano, John Hindera, Barbara Hopkins, Valerie Johnson, Karin Johnston, Manabi Majumdar, Al Melchior, Mary Beth Melchior, Todd Perry, Suzanne Samuels, Stacy Van-Deveer, Iris Young, and Diana Zoelle made valuable comments on various aspects of the work in progress. The comments of an anonymous reviewer helped greatly with the organization and clarity of ideas. And Donna Barnes cheerfully helped me to finalize preparation of the manuscript. Of course, all of the usual caveats apply: the errors are mine.

Many of the ideas in this book took shape in my courses on feminist theory at the University of Maryland, on women and social welfare policy at Georgetown University, and on social welfare policy at Texas Tech University. I would like to thank these institutions for the opportunity to teach these courses, and my students for making each course an interesting learning and teaching experience.

Several friends—Tommie Robinson, Al and Mary Beth Melchior, Todd Perry and Pam Goddard, Valerie Johnson, Cynthia Burack, Stacy VanDeveer, Michael Gusmano and Kate Blodgett, Diana Zoelle, and Leah Schafer and Ned Fredrickson—also quite cheerfully provided that most valuable resource: child care. The encouragement of Patricia, Barbara, Anne, Gilda, Pepper, and Kathy, as well as the community of St. Peter's, was invaluable.

Finally, I would like to acknowledge the support and encouragement provided by my parents, David and Betty Josephson, and by my son, David Foster. Without them, this project would not have been possible.

1

Families and the State in a Liberal Republic

In the United States, as in most industrialized liberal democracies, families and family policy and law have changed greatly in the past thirty years. Most especially, the rapid demographic changes in American families during this period have received attention from both academics and the general public. The statistics cited are familiar: rising rates of child poverty and divorce, the growth of out-of-wedlock births, and the concomitant rise in single-woman headed families.

While there is general agreement that families and households in the United States have changed, there is great disagreement about both the causes of and the appropriate responses to these changes. Some argue families are changing because of economic shifts, domestically and internationally; others attribute the changes in families to moral decline, changes in women's roles within and outside of families, or feminism and the women's movement.

Proposals for responding to these changes in families depend upon whether the changes are seen as positive. To some, alteration of families creates great potential for human freedom and self-expression (Stacey 1990). For others, changes in families are cause for alarm and should be reversed if possible (Blankenhorn 1995; Elshtain 1994). Corresponding public policy proposals range from reinvigorating traditional values to the elimination of the Aid to Families with Dependent Children (AFDC) program for single parents to the provision of a universal child benefit and more child-friendly tax and workplace policies.

The changes in families cited above are not the only contemporary challenge to traditional understandings of the families-state relation. The women's movement and the large body of feminist scholarship on gender,

1

race, class, sexual orientation, and family life have also seriously strained understandings in political thought regarding the nature of the families-state nexus. Thinking and rethinking this relationship is crucial not only for those concerned with gender equality in families, but for political theorists and public policymakers as well.

Amidst these differing views regarding changes in families, one public policy that seems to receive widespread support among political leaders as well as the general public is enforcement of the child support obligations of absent parents. Across the political spectrum, child support is seen as at least part of the solution to some of the problems listed above, especially the problem of child poverty and of poverty in single-parent families.

Partly as a result of this consensus, the United States has, since 1974, developed and implemented a comprehensive federal child support policy. But what kind of a "solution" is this system of child support enforcement, and to what problem? Answering these questions is at the heart of this book.

Public policies do not come from nowhere: they take place in a particular historical, political, and institutional context. Policies are shaped by ideas, as well as by the historical developments that bring them about and the institutional structure of the state of which they are a part (Skocpol, Weir, and Orloff 1988). Contemporary child support policy constitutes a relatively direct and focused state intervention in particular kinds of families, thus providing a lens for viewing the families-state relation in practice. Given that policies are shaped by ideas as well as by institutions, we might expect child support policy to reflect ideas about the families-state relation, the form it should take, and what kind of state action with respect to families is appropriate and justified, as well as ideas about those aspects of family life where state action is not warranted. These ideas regarding the families-state relation are in turn shaped by ideas about the state itself or about what might be termed the political theory of the regime.

Thus, child support in the contemporary United States takes place in the context of ideas about the regime. In order to understand child support policy, it is important to understand the ideas, institutions, and historical context that help to shape this policy. Therefore, although this is a book about child support policy, our discussion begins with the context of this policy in a particular kind of political regime.

This chapter focuses on ideas about the families-state relation, beginning with ideas about the kind of political regime that the United States is and providing a theoretical basis for understanding the ideas that have shaped child support policy.

The United States as a Liberal Republican Regime

Political institutions in the United States, and the justifications for those institutions, have historically been (and continue in the present to be) shaped by multiple theoretical traditions (Ceaser 1990; Elkin 1987; Smith 1993). As Ceaser points out,

> The names that political analysts usually employ to identify the dominant form of government in the West, especially when striving for a degree of precision, are compounds. The list of these names, which is remarkably long, includes *liberal democracy, constitutional republic, democratic republic, constitutional democracy, representative democracy,* and *representative republic.* (6, emphasis in original)

This is not accidental, per Ceaser; rather it is because regimes such as the United States are the institutional and historical product of more than one tradition in political thought. Thus, in order to achieve some degree of precision, one must attend to these multiple traditions.

For Ceaser, the compound terms always refer to two ideas: one having to do with limited government and protection of rights; the other with rule by the people. He refers to the United States as a liberal democracy. Elkin describes the United States as a "commercial republic": a regime that combines a particular organization of economic life and a tradition that emphasizes individual rights with popular government. Smith is discussing the persistence of what he calls "ascriptive traditionalism" in the United States, coexisting with both liberal and republican traditions. For Smith, both liberalism and republicanism have shaped American political thought and political development, although they have existed alongside traditions inimical to the aspirations of, most especially, liberalism. Stephen Holmes also argues that "[l]iberalism and republicanism are not opposites" (1995, 5), but are rather compatible in both theory and practice, bound together in part by a common commitment to constitutionalism.

For the purposes of the present analysis of families-state relations in the United States, the compound "liberal republic" seems the most apt, for several reasons. First, in terms of the history of law and constitutionalism in the United States, the discussion of traditions has usually been about whether the United States is a liberal or a republican regime. Thus, scholars such as Louis Hartz argued that liberalism was and is the dominant feature of American government (Hartz 1955; de los Rios 1994). On the other hand, historians such as Gordon Wood and Joyce Appleby argue that republicanism was the dominant feature of the regime the Constitution's framers were forging (Appleby 1992, Wood 1969).

A second reason to analyze the families-state nexus utilizing an understanding of the American regime as both liberal and republican is because both traditions are especially relevant to the relationship between families and state, though in different ways. Each tradition has a slightly different construction of the relation between families and the regime. Each tradition has shaped historical understandings of what families are and how families are to be treated in both family law and social welfare policy. In addition, each has had important implications for the relationship between men, women, and children in family life and family law.

Third, current debates over changes in families, and some of the conflicts over the purposes of social policies such as child support, reflect some of the contradictions both between liberal and republican thought and within each tradition. The latter is reflected to some extent in the recent liberalism-communitarianism discussions in American political thought. The modern communitarian turn in political thought draws on the tradition of republicanism in American thought and law. Some communitarians are primarily engaged in a critique of liberalism, especially of the possessive individualism that is seen as central to liberal political thought, and therefore they are not articulating a clear and independent political philosophy. Other communitarians, however, invoke ideas of citizenship and of civic virtue that are in keeping with modern republicanism.

This being said, however, a few caveats are in order. First, it is not my intention to engage the discussion of whether the United States is liberal or republican; both traditions have shaped law and policy. What is most interesting for understanding the families-state nexus is how both traditions interact to shape family policy. Further, it should be noted that the American versions of both republicanism and liberalism are distinctive, drawing on the larger traditions in political thought but taking their own particular form.

Nor is this to say that there are not other traditions or institutional features that shape the families-state relation in the United States. Especially important is the structure of economic life and the relation between families, state, and economy. In addition, the democratic or egalitarian impulse in American thought has shaped political aspirations regarding the meaning of one's family origin in relation to political life (Fishkin 1983) as well as feminist aspirations for a more egalitarian life within families. Also, the ascriptive traditionalism that Smith discusses plays a role in the history of family relations as well as in contemporary concerns regarding the recent changes in family life.

Finally, it must be noted that contemporary feminist scholarship calls into question both liberal and republican understandings of family life and the families-state relation. Feminist scholarship calls for a rethinking of our understanding of the families-state relation, to which this book contributes. But rethinking the families-state relation requires an understanding of how it actually functions *now* and must start from there, not from some hoped-for reality. Thus, the most useful theorizing about how things might be is grounded in how things are. Reconceptualization is most usefully done within the context of the political traditions and practices of the regime under discussion—and the strongest traditions with respect to families in the American regime are liberalism and republicanism. In the following section, some feminist critiques of both liberal and republican understandings of the families-state relation are discussed.

Thus, the goal here is not to argue for an unreconstructed liberalism or republicanism. Rather, understanding the liberal republican impulses that have shaped contemporary understandings of the families-state nexus will help to both understand the kind of families-state relation that shapes contemporary public policy, and, in the end, reconstruct a more egalitarian and inclusive approach to families and family life.

Families in a Liberal Republic

Families[1] stand in a complex relation to the liberal republican regime. Liberal thought, defined by its distinctions between matters that are public and matters that are private, has for most of its history enforced and justified the patriarchal, heterosexual family as the sphere of private relations and defined the relations within that family (in theory, though not in practice) as beyond the reach of the state. Republican thought rests upon distinctions between public and domestic and has generally assigned women to the domestic sphere, often valuing women for their "difference" and for the service that their domestic labor provides to the republic. Both liberal and republican theorists have historically paid very little attention to women, generally finding the problem of inequalities based on gender, race, class, and sexual orientation of very little moment. Further, the role of markets, the economy, and the structure of wage labor in mediating the families-state relation is rarely directly addressed in either liberal or republican thought. Yet both theories depend upon the work performed by women in families.

Further, in the United States, the very definition of "family" rests upon legal regulation of the types of private relationships that are and are not recognized as families. In the United States it was never the case, in practice, that the state "stayed out" of the "private" realm of families. The state created the legal entity known as the family, defined the parties eligible to form families through regulation of the marriage contract, defined the terms of this contract, and regulated the dissolution of families as well as the obligations among the members of legally recognized families and former families. Laws prohibiting racial intermarriage were in place in most states until *Loving v. Virginia* (388 U.S. 1 [1967]). State law defines the terms under which divorce is permitted. No state permits same sex couples to marry. Clearly, the state has historically enforced the heterosexual family by defining it as natural, and to a large extent it continues to do so; the state has been legally constructing this family, while denying its own role in this construction. As Martha Minow states,

> Rather than marking a boundary limiting state intervention in the family, laws governing the family define the kinds of families the state approves.(1990, 276)

This contradictory stance of liberal republics, simultaneously viewing families in theory as naturally private while in practice regulating their formation, dissolution, and functioning, makes thinking about families, gender, and the relationship between families and the state difficult. The problems presented, both in theory and in practice, are multiple and complex. Further, thinking about families brings forth an entire range of presuppositions and assumptions of which we are rarely fully cognizant: assumptions about gender, race, class, and sexual orientation; about what human beings are like; about the nature of human connection; about the place of affective life in human life and in the life of a polity, just to name a few. Thinking about families is at root a normative, as well as empirical, project. Thus, clear thinking is crucial.

In the most general sense, then, I am concerned in this book with the relationship between public and private in liberal republics, and the public-domestic as an instance of that relationship. In general, it is my contention that in liberal republics, the contradictory construction of the heterosexual family as "natural" and "private" has served purposes that are deeply connected to how liberals and republicans describe the nature of political life. Because of the way in which assumptions about families and family life are embedded in liberal and republican thought, as well as in liberal republican practice, rethinking the role of families requires much more than minor adjustments to understandings of liberal republican thought and practice. To make this point clear, it will be useful to briefly outline the nature of public-domestic relations in liberal and in republican thought.

Liberalism comes in many varieties, and contemporary scholars who self-identify as liberals have very different ways of understanding liberalism. Nevertheless, most scholars would agree that certain features are necessary to any liberal political philosophy: a commitment to individual rights, to toleration among various conceptions of the human good, and to limits on the scope or extent of state action with respect to citizens. Each of these rest to some extent on the liberal distinction made between matters that are public and matters that are private. In liberal thought, public and private have been seen historically as utterly separable spheres (Benn and Gaus 1983). In liberal theory, the state is set off as distinct from civil society, which is in turn separate from the private life of individuals.[2] It is fundamental to liberalism that the power of the state is limited. Moreover, liberals have historically pointed to a variety of tangibles—private property, fundamental rights, "the family"—as prior to or more valuable than the political or public sphere, and thus as "natural" limits to the reach of state power. Thus, the private family serves as one means for demonstrating, via a specific social institution, the limits of state power.

Though liberals of differing views may draw the public-private line in different ways, families and family life have generally been seen by liberalism as very much in the arena of that which is private. The idea of a natural, private family, existing in a realm that is out of state reach, has been useful to liberal theorists for purposes of identifying and maintaining the boundary between public and domestic. This private sphere limits the reach of the state: it limits the actions that a state may take in relation to its citizens. The idea of the private sphere, occupied by families (historically represented in liberalism's public sphere by male heads of households), provides a basis for arguments about individual rights as limits to state power. The idea of "the private" gains legitimacy as a limit by virtue of being, or at least seeming, "natural." Thus, when families seem to be a natural, not a human, construction, the privacy of these families can be seen as a right that exists before the invention or intervention of government.

However, this construction of the private, natural family has come under increasing strain. As Linda Nicholson has pointed out, the family that early liberals such as Locke discussed was historically specific; yet in subsequent liberal thought the categories "family" and "state" became reified, leaving behind the historical context in which they were first articulated (1986, 131). The scholarship of feminist historians has shown that families have changed significantly over time, in response to economic transformations as well as state law and policy; families also vary among different racial, ethnic, and socioeconomic groups (Collins 1991; Coontz 1992; Weston 1991). Indeed, the public-private distinction has been much more a part of heterosexual white middle-class experience than has been true for working-class women, women of color, and lesbian women (Hurtado 1989; Law 1988; Weston 1991).

Further, placing families in the theoretical realm of the private did not mean that families were not subject to public power. The terms of the marriage contract were, from the beginning of the American republic, set out in state laws, and those terms included specific roles for husband and wife (Phillips 1991, ch. 2). Gender roles in families, and the rights and obligations of family members, were thus structured and enforced by the political and legal power of the state. Antimiscegenation laws and slave law made black and white Americans subject to different legal rules with respect to family life; poor law distinguished between the laws that applied to poor or indigent families and the civil law of families, which applied to all other families (tenBroek 1964–65). Thus, although families were definitionally private, they were not by any means exempt from state power, nor was the state neutral with respect to the practice of family life or to life in different sorts of families.

The separation of public and private, and public and domestic, in liberal political thought and practice has been criticized by a wide variety of scholars. Feminist scholars such as Carole Pateman, Susan Okin, Martha Minow, and Frances Olsen have argued that the construction of a public-domestic relationship in the form taken by liberal political theory and practice not only excludes women from public life, but also disadvantages women in the domestic sphere (Minow 1990; Okin 1989, 1991; Olsen 1983; Pateman 1983). Feminist arguments also point out the ways in which families, the market, and the state are not separate, but deeply intertwined (Abramovitz 1988; Barrett 1988; Folbre 1994; Olsen 1983).

The public-private divide has been criticized in other arenas as well. For example, political economists argue that the "private" arena of markets and ownership of the means of production deeply affects and shapes the public life of the regime (Bowles and Gintis 1986; Dahl 1985; Elkin 1987; Lindblom 1978). Political theorists such as Alan Ryan and Jennifer Nedelsky argue that property in liberal regimes has both public and private dimensions (Nedelsky 1990a; Ryan 1987). Philosophers such as Benn and Gaus argue that the public-private divide in liberal thought rests on two contradictory sets of assumptions about human beings and social life. (Benn and Gaus 1983, 31–65). They term these "individualist"—shaped by Locke, Hobbes, and Bentham—and "organic"—derived from Rousseau and Hegel, and they argue that no single model of public and private can encompass liberalism's view of the public-private relation.

Crucial to these critiques is their challenge of liberal ideas of public and private. Diverse family forms and the idea that families are socially, not naturally, constructed challenge the basis of the liberal distinction between public and private. If neither families nor private property are natural formations in the sense that early liberals held them and if liberal political practice (as well as contemporary family law and social welfare policy) has proven them to be subjects of constant negotiation that are still deeply defined and constrained by the state, then in what sense and by what means can state power be limited?[3] Without a bounded private sphere, how can individual rights be secured? What is to prevent the state from taking whatever action it chooses?

Republicans, ancient and modern, also separate public from private, but they tend to place more value on the activities of the public sphere. Republicanism is based on the ideas of representative self-government, civic virtue, selves who are situated in traditions and communities, with a distinction between public and domestic life (Smith 1993).[4] In the modern republican tradition, families are private, but have dimensions that are recognized as important to public life, especially in terms of the cultivation of citizen virtue in children.[5] For republicanism, the virtues of citizens are essential to the public life of the regime. Citizens must make decisions about public life that are in keeping not merely with their own self-interest, but with the common or public good.

Yet, as feminists have pointed out, in both ancient and modern republicanism, the public life of the male citizen is deeply dependent upon the activities of women, slaves, and male noncitizens in the "private" sphere (Okin 1979; Pateman 1988b). Republican theory thus generally assumes the naturalness of the patriarchal, heterosexual family and denies that inequality in the "natural family" is a political problem. In fact, women's virtues are extolled as necessary and valued by the republic. Yet if women had equal access to the public sphere, they would not possess these indispensable virtues. Women's subordination, as well as their domestic labor, is thus crucial to the founding and sustenance of the republic.

This is evident in a variety of ways in American republican thought, especially as it relates to families and to women's role in family life. In the late eighteenth century at the time of America's founding, "republican mothers" held a special role in the life of the republic, accomplishing their political role in the private realm of families and child care (Kerber 1980). Further, the cult of domesticity (Cott 1977) and arguments for "republican motherhood" (Kerber 1980) illustrate the extent to which republican thought in American history rested on a sharp division of gender and racial roles, on the confinement of white women to the domestic sphere, and on the simultaneous devaluing of women of color. White women's domestic labor, necessary to the economy and to the well-being of their husbands and children, was viewed as simultaneously virtuous and demeaned, necessary and unimportant. Black women's low-paid domestic labor was appropriated to support the cult of domesticity for white women, and, while black women were simultaneously demeaned by white culture, black men and women created their own meanings and values with respect to their familial arrangements (Dill 1994). Arguments were made both for and against women's suffrage based upon women's role in domestic life, and race played a significant role in the women's suffrage movement (Giddings 1984). While many feminists have argued for a revaluing of care (Gilligan 1982) and of women's role in family life (Elshtain 1981), scholars such as Joan Williams argue convincingly that it is not possible to claim the positive aspects of domesticity without the negative aspects attached (1991). Thus, "republican motherhood" is in many ways a racialized, double-edged sword.

The idea of republican motherhood did not end in the nineteenth century, but is evident, for example, in the maternalist politics of white women's advocacy of mother's pensions, the precursors to the modern Aid to Families with Dependent Children program (Gordon 1994; Ladd-Taylor 1994; Mink 1995). White maternalist advocacy of mother's pensions for single mothers in the early part of this century was motivated in part by an effort to "Americanize" immigrant families. Advocates argued that these pensions (and classes in proper parenting) were necessary in order to ensure that single immigrant mothers were properly socializing their children into American citizenship (Mink 1995, ch. 2). As Linda Gordon has shown, black women activists had a somewhat different vision of social provision: it was maternalist, but focused more on equal rights and on universal provision than on special programs for women (Gordon 1994, ch. 5). Thus, in American republicanism, the role of women in family life has been celebrated as a source for the socialization of children into citizenship, even while women have been excluded from political life.

The communitarian critique of liberalism in political thought and the emergence of a set of scholars who self-identify as communitarians constitute in some senses a revival of American republicanism. Communitarianism emerged primarily as an intellectual movement involving a critique of liberal individualism and value neutrality. However, some communitarian intellectuals have become increasingly activist, arguing for specific policy positions, especially in relation to such issues as contemporary families and family life. In some senses, communitarian and feminist criticisms of liberalism share common characteristics (see Frazer and Lacey 1993, 117–129). But there are important differences, as well, and many communitarian impulses are inimical to feminist concerns (Burack 1994; Frazer and Lacey 1993, 130–162; Friedman 1990). This is especially true in relation to families and family life, where communitarians seem to call on traditionalism and a revival of family life without a sufficient critique of gender inequality in families (Etzioni 1993; Elshtain et al. 1991). The tradition of republicanism in American history is thus fairly specific about gender roles in families and the importance to the republic of the work of mothers in traditional families. This republicanism, and its modern revival in communitarianism, thus shares some common elements with traditionalism, and brings with it a troubling legacy of sex- and race-based inequality. Republicanism values public life, but requires a private sphere in which certain virtues are cultivated. The challenge to contemporary republicans is to find a way to value both public and private without the ascriptive inequalities republicanism has often sustained in American political thought and history.

Thus, both liberal and republican theory and practice have historically separated public and domestic life in ways that assumed that the division of labor within the heterosexual patriarchal family is natural and that women's place in families is not only natural but does not raise any *political* questions. Both have historically found no place for women as individuals in the polity and have assumed that the organization of life as it has existed within families is separate from and prior to the organization of the polity.

But critiques, especially feminist critiques, of both liberal and republican understandings of the families-state relation make it clear that the relationship between public and private and, most especially, between public and domestic in liberal republics is more complicated than the metaphor and ideology of separate and separable spheres would imply. Yet it is not enough to simply say that family, state, and market are intertwined. What is crucial is to understand *how* families and the state are connected, institutionally and normatively.

The Normative Functions of Family Law

Current scholarly discussions regarding family law in the United States provide a useful starting point for understanding the normative dimensions of the families-state relation. Historically, as has been noted, the state has been very much involved in defining the terms of family life, especially through family law. Despite what we would now call their discriminatory nature and intent, the distinctions made in American family law between different sorts of families and the enforcement through family law of rigid gender roles were seen as in keeping with state purposes with respect to family life. The political importance of the legal enforcement of the heterosexual family, for example, has been articulated as recently as 1986 in the *Bowers v. Hardwick* (478 U.S. 186 [1986]) decision. Yet, changes in family law in recent decades have altered the nature of state involvement in defining the terms of family life.

A number of legal theorists have argued that contemporary American family law has abandoned the enforcement of gender roles and distinctions between families based upon race and other factors, and in doing so family law simultaneously has become increasingly privatized (Hafen 1991; Schneider 1985; Singer 1992). As Singer argues, this privatization has occurred in both "substantive legal doctrines" and "preferred procedures for resolving family law disputes". Mary Ann Glendon has described these changes as constituting a tendency to treat family members as individuals, enforcing the values of equality, individual liberty, and tolerance (Glendon 1989, ch. 7). Schneider describes this transformation as one from the public moral ordering of family relationships and roles to a system of private ordering. Whereas courts and public bureaucracies had been setting out standards for appropriate conduct based on specific familial roles, individuals now form their own agreements or contracts regarding those arenas of human life that traditionally have been associated with families and family law. Milton Regan describes these changes as a transition from status to contract (Regan 1993).

Schneider identifies a number of arenas of family law that seem to have moved during the period since around 1965 from primarily public toward private ordering: divorce, reproduction, sexual relations, the law of nonmarital relations, and the law surrounding child abuse (1985, 1807–19). Specific examples include the recognition by courts of relationships established outside of marriage contracts (cohabitation, children born out of wedlock), the shift to no-fault divorce, and the use of mediation and private contracts in the process of divorce dispute resolution.

With respect to the role of family law in the polity, Schneider argues that family law has largely abandoned its role in articulating an aspirational morality for family life (1985, 1820). To be sure, Schneider is careful to point out that this shift from public to private moral ordering does not necessarily imply that the law (or the society, for that matter) is suffering from irreparable moral decay (1985, 1808). Schneider's argument implies, however—and some of these scholars specifically argue—that there is a need for some sort of publicly articulated "moral order" with respect to families. This concern is echoed by other legal scholars who cite the "waning of belonging," the rise of individualism,[6] and a legal system that seems to reinforce individual autonomy rather than familial relationships and obligations (Glendon 1989; Hafen 1991). Many contemporary republican and communitarian scholars voice similar concerns that Americans have abandoned community in the pursuit of individual goals (Bellah et al. 1985, 1991; Elshtain et al. 1991; Etzioni 1993).

Feminist scholars have also indicated that privatized decision making is not an unequivocal good with respect to gender equality because some such processes may also exacerbate pre-existing gender inequalities. The literature on the economic consequences of divorce, and on the use of mediation in divorce proceedings, indicates that women and men are in general not on equal terms in these proceedings. Therefore, mediation tends to benefit the more powerful spouse at the expense of the less powerful one (Bell 1988; Fineman 1991; Singer 1992; Weitzman 1985, 1987).[7] Some feminists have also argued that self-interested individualism does not describe women's experiences in families and that altering legal practices to make them more friendly to persons who care for young children (whether male or female) would require *greater* recognition of relationships in families (Minow 1990; Nedelsky 1990b, 1989; West 1988).

For those concerned about the possibility of substantive equality between men and women within and outside of families, however, the demise of legal enforcement of traditional marital roles must also be recognized as beneficial to women and necessary to the goal of gender equality in families as well as in the larger polity (Singer 1992, 1517–22). Until the last thirty years or so, the history of public ordering in family law in the United States consisted of enforcement of the patriarchal family and of racial segregation and inequality. The contemporary challenge, if we are to have some degree of public moral ordering of family life, is to find a kind of public ordering that does not discriminate against individuals or families on the basis of race, gender, class, sexual orientation, or family structure.

The choices, then, are not simple; leaving individuals in families to their own devices with respect to the nature of their relationships and obligations to one another may be desirable in some instances, but undesirable in others. When individuals are left "on their own" to engage in contractual family relationships, vulnerable persons may be irremediably harmed. Yet if history is any guide, when the state regulates family relationships, it seems likely to discriminate against some persons in undesirable ways. The choices are not simply between the "free exercise of families" (Minow 1991) versus "public moral ordering" (Schneider 1985). *However* the state acts with respect to families, it is engaging in *some* kind of moral ordering. For example, leaving families entirely to contractual relations could be described as a public moral order of private contract. And, especially in families, the "contracting" parties would rarely be on equal footing.

This discussion thus points out an important reality about the families-state relation: whatever form law that deals with families takes, such law will have normative dimensions. Rather than tell a story about a private family out of reach of state power, then, it seems much more helpful to identify state purposes with respect to families and to try to develop policy and law that accomplishes those ends (Galston 1991; Holmes 1995; Sunstein 1993). Family law and public policy that deals with families is by nature normative. Thus, engaging in state regulation of familial relations involves normative decisions that must be based upon some grounds. The question then becomes, on what principles might public ordering with respect to families be based?

Families are not simply private—they have public dimensions. Some aspects of family life are appropriately subject to the "public ordering" that states provide. The question of appropriate state action with respect to families thus touches on very fundamental questions about the relationship between the state and its citizens: about the appropriate, and inappropriate, uses of state power to coerce, encourage, discourage, or remain indifferent with respect to citizen behaviors and decisions; about the nature of state interests in citizen behaviors and decisions regarding their families and family life; about the nature of citizen claims on state power to protect their interests, needs, and rights with respect to families and family life; about the balance between individual and collective interests in what happens in families; and about the balance between different sorts of state interests in families.

So these questions about the public order established by the institutions of the families-state relation are regime questions—questions about the kind of political system under discussion. The form that the families-state relation takes thus cannot be understood without reference to the regime as a whole. This being the case, it seems clear that the principles that ought to guide analysis of the families-state relation in the contemporary United States should come from an understanding of the principles that guide the regime.

Regime Principles and the Families-State Nexus

Liberal republican regimes, then, have a particular construction of the families-state relationship. Historical understandings of the nature of this relationship have been subject to a great deal of criticism on the basis of gender inequality. Yet state policy with respect to families will always have normative dimensions. Given a liberal republican regime, what kind of interests might be reflected in the families-state relation? How will the interests of the state in families and family life be reflected in public policy? How should the interests of individuals in the family-related policies of the state be understood?

In order to analyze the extent and sort of public ordering of families and family life in a liberal republic such as the United States, it is necessary to know what is at stake. In the families-state relation, there are stakes and interests on both sides: the state has interests in some of the activities of families, and individuals have interests in state policy both as individuals and as members of families. To explore some of the "regime principles" involved in the families-state relation, we will look to each side of the equation: from the perspective of the state and from the view of families and individuals in families. To do so, we will look to several important features of the regime, including both liberal and republican thought, as well as the economy and aspirations regarding equality. The strands of these different traditions and institutional features are woven together in complicated ways, but for clarity's sake it may be useful to look at each separately.

State Interests

The Liberal tradition and families

Although the purpose of the public-domestic distinction in liberalism was to limit the reach of state power into the lives of its citizens, the critique of the patriarchal, heterosexual family cuts to the very root of liberal thought and practice. Liberal thought relies on "the family" to do more than enforce gender inequality. Critiques of the liberal stance toward "the family" undermine fundamental aspects of how liberalism understands itself. As William Kymlicka puts it,

> Liberalism expresses its commitment to modern liberty by sharply separating the public power of the state from the private relationships of civil soci-

ety, and by setting strict limits on the state's ability to intervene in private life.(1990, 251).

Given the above discussion regarding the critique of families as naturally private, the question of how liberty should be understood in relation to families and family life becomes crucial not only in understanding the families-state relation, but in understanding liberalism itself. Rethinking "the family" thus requires a fundamental reformulation of liberal thought in terms of how public and domestic are understood.

Yet this does not mean that any distinction between public and private, or public and domestic, should be abandoned. The value that liberalism accords to the private pursuits of citizens need not be rejected simply because the way that private and public are distinguished requires re-thinking. Rather, what is required is a way of distinguishing those aspects of families that are appropriately subject to state action from those aspects that are not. Given the importance that liberalism accords to limits on state action, public regulation and intervention in family life should be guided by connecting such action with specific state purposes. Thus, to the extent that the state has interests and purposes that require definite types of action regarding families, clear reasons must be given for such action.

A second principle can also be drawn from the liberal tradition's view of the families-state relation. In important ways, though a liberal state does have purposes that are deeply intertwined with, and dependent upon, families and family life, the value that liberalism accords to privacy, to individual rights, and to each individual's freedom to choose among ways of life requires that the exercise of state power with respect to families be limited. Thus, simply because there are state or collective interests in family life does not mean that all state action (or inaction) with respect to families is justified and justifiable. Any desirable liberal regime accords great weight to the principle that government should be limited in its powers with respect to individuals, regardless of whether a natural, prepolitical source can be found for those limits.

This stance—that privacy in relation to families is still valuable, despite feminist and other critiques of the incoherence and inconsistency of the public-private distinction in liberal thought—may seem to contradict some of the above discussion. However, as Elizabeth Frazer and Nicola Lacey point out, the feminist critique of the liberal public-private divide does not require a rejection of the idea of a private sphere:

> The feminist argument is that the private sphere is not beyond political critique: this does not imply any general prescriptive position on the aptness of state intervention in response to the critique. (1993, 75–76)

In fact, feminists have strong interests in maintaining ideas of a private sphere, especially as it relates to some aspects of families and family life, such as reproductive choice and decisions about family formation and dissolution.[8]

Therefore, simply abandoning the separation between public and private in liberal regimes, especially in relation to families and family life, is not a solution to the problems with this distinction discussed above. Some aspects of families are proper subjects of state power; some are not. In family law and social welfare policy, the difficulty is twofold: first, in distinguishing which aspects of family life are the proper subjects of state action and which are not and, second, in identifying proper state action to take in particular circumstances.

Thus, from liberalism we can draw two general principles with respect to families and the families-state relation: the need to identify (and defend, giving reasons) state purposes with respect to families, and the necessity that the use of state power with respect to families be both related to state purposes and limited. Both of these principles will be crucial in understanding contemporary child support policy.

The Republican tradition and families

As noted above, in the republican tradition, families are private, but have dimensions that are recognized as important to public life in terms of the cultivation of citizen virtue in children. For republican regimes to sustain (or reproduce) themselves, some modicum of responsible action on the part of citizens is required. Put simply, republican regimes require good citizens (Bellah et al. 1991; Elkin 1987; Galston 1991; Macedo 1990).[9] But good citizens do not "spring like mushrooms from the earth" as Susan Okin has put it (Okin 1989, 21).[10] Thus, republican regimes have an interest in the education and well-being of children, and, because some of this education and much of child well-being has to do with what happens in families, the republican tradition indicates that the state has an interest in what happens to children in families.[11]

Among contemporary liberal republican theorists concerned about the moral education of children, William Galston is notable for connecting the practices of families and family policy and law to the liberal republican regime as a whole. Galston states:

> My focus is on what must be a key objective of our society: raising children who are prepared—intellectually, physically, morally, and emotionally—to take their place as law-abiding and independent members of their commu-

nity, able to sustain themselves and their families and to fulfill their duties as citizens.(1991, 285)

Because families with children are "engaged in activities with vast social consequences"(286), the state has an interest in how these purposes are accomplished.

This concern for the moral education of children is shared by a variety of theorists: feminists, communitarians, conservatives, and liberals alike. As noted above, communitarian theorists such as Amitai Etzioni argue that children need two biological parents in order to be educated properly (1993). James Q. Wilson argues that human beings have an innate moral sense, but that it must be cultivated in children via proper parental teaching (1993). Susan Okin argues that families are indeed schools for the basic values of a regime and that principal among the things children ought to learn in families is the practice of justice (1989). Children, Okin argues, cannot learn this if their families are, in basic and obvious ways, unjust; and, she says, families in which there is gender inequality are unjust.

Okin's argument rests on the notion that the family is the school for whatever values/norms citizens may learn, that justice is an important—indeed crucial—norm and practice for the citizens of liberal regimes to learn, and that, if the family itself is unjust due to its reproduction of and participation in gender inequality, children cannot and will not learn what justice is or how to practice it. So the injustice in families is not only bad for women; it is bad for the regime. Despite the many disagreements between communitarianism and feminism, Okin's concern with respect to the education of children may not be incompatible with some of the related concerns of republicans.

Okin further argues that the practice of nurturing is itself a school for moral understanding; it helps us to understand others and therefore is crucial to the development of "a sense of justice"(1989, 18). Thus, Okin seems to be saying that the nurturing that takes place in families is a kind of moral education for adults. This argument suggests that a polity that offers citizens a balance between nurturing and competing would be desirable, as would be a social and political system that permitted people to do both without penalizing them for choosing nurturing. Although this point is merely suggested by Okin, other feminists have developed this idea in arguing for the importance of mothering or parenting, and of nurturing behavior, in the lives of adults and in the polity (Ruddick 1988; Held 1993). These arguments share some ground with communitarian scholars, such as Etzioni, Galston, and Elshtain, who argue that contemporary parents should devote more time to their children. Nevertheless, the sources of their concern are very different, as are their public policy prescriptions. And, insofar as contemporary communitarianism draws on traditionalism and "traditional values", it is incompatible with the goal of gender equality.

The republican tradition thus points out the importance of the care and education of children in the life of the regime. Further, this concern is not necessarily incompatible with feminist concerns regarding equality in families—although the form that this concern takes, especially in public policy, must be carefully addressed. If families are to remain the means by which such basic and crucial tasks are accomplished, it is necessary to examine how this can occur, given the realities of contemporary family life, especially if ascriptive gender inequalities are not seen as a solution to this problem.

For, if republican regimes require good citizens, and if such qualities are not innate but rather learned, someone must engage in the education of children in virtuous citizenship (or at least, minimally acceptable citizenship). Also, someone must care for those citizens unable to care for themselves: children, elderly persons, disabled persons. Historically families (that is, women) have provided the bulk of this labor. As families and the economy change, and conceptions of appropriate and acceptable family life change, we need to carefully consider how to combine commitments to gender equality with the care and well-being of children.

Families and markets

A third lens for viewing the families-state relation is through the economic traditions and practices of the United States. Fundamental to the liberal republican regime in the United States is a market-based economy with private ownership of the means of production, and this economic system shapes the form that the families-state relation takes.

Although there is a tendency in political thought to view families and the market as separate arenas, they are in fact deeply intertwined (Abramovitz 1988; Dill 1994; Folbre 1994; Olsen 1983). Historically, many changes in families, family structure, and family functions, including those changes cited at the beginning of this chapter, constitute the adjustments that families have made to changes in the economy. When there have been structural changes in the economy, families have responded by altering their division of paid and unpaid labor. By the middle of the nineteenth century, industrialization and the growth of factory-based production had moved the site of production out of the household. During the Depression of the 1930s, women's paid labor increased despite negative public opinion (Abramovitz 1988, 215–40). The rapid deployment of women into factory production during World War II (followed by their immediate dismissal after the war) is well known (S. Hartmann 1982). In fact, the family of the 1950s—the family to which contemporary families are most frequently compared—was historically unique in a number of respects (Coontz 1992; Minow 1991). Further, differences among different kinds of families at any particular point in history often reflect their different economic position and the economic opportunities available to family members (Dill 1994).

But a liberal republican state that has limited resources has an interest in limiting state economic support of families. As Valerie Lehr points out, the family that is encouraged in market-based systems is a family that forms an "autonomous economic unit" (Lehr 1994, 4). Thus, part of the concern about single parent families is that they are less likely than families with a male wage-earner present to be economically self-sufficient, at least in the most visible ways of requiring direct income transfers.

Some of this concern, however, ignores the fact that *all* families receive economic assistance from the government in one form or another. Tax policy is a means by which resources are redistributed; although we do not often think of homeowners' tax deductions, for example, as an income transfer, it is a form of government subsidy for particular types of households. Historically, income transfers to families have included direct grants of land to settlers in the nineteenth century, subsidies for suburban highways, tax credits or deductions (e.g. the Earned Income Tax Credit or deductions for home mortgage holders), as well as direct income transfers (e.g. social security, AFDC, and general assistance) (Coontz 1992, ch. 4; Gordon 1994, 1–13).

If we are to be honest about the families-state relation, then it is necessary to pay attention to how families, state, and the market are connected. In doing so, we need to pay attention not only to government transfer programs (the most obvious place where family, state, and the market meet), but also to the multiple aspects of this connection: tax policy, labor market policy, child and elderly care policy, health care policy, and housing policy, to name a few.

Nevertheless, in terms of state interests, liberal republican regimes with market economies have an interest in limiting their financial liabilities with respect to families. This is especially true for financial obligations that are highly visible and lack widespread public support, such as public assistance programs. This interest plays an especially important role in the development of child support policy, as chapter 2 will discuss.

Equality and Families

Within liberalism and within republicanism there are a variety of positions on the nature and importance of equality in the liberal or republican
polity. Although the Locke of *The Second Treatise* takes a more egalitarian
position on gender roles than Filmer, his commitments to gender equality
in families are at best limited (Pateman 1988b). Republicanism seems to
both venerate republican motherhood and denigrate women, or at least
consign women to a private sphere. Modern communitarianism has paid
little attention to the problem of gender equality in families. Nonetheless,
in terms of historical practice in the United States, both liberalism and
republicanism have fit nicely with the *in*egalitarian family and traditional
gender roles.

Throughout U.S. history contemporaneous families have been different
from one another, often along racial and class lines and often enforced
through law. There is a long history of gender, class, and racial discrimination in the legal relationship between families and the state. Slave law
made enslaved African-American families subject to an entirely different
legal system than white and free black families (Dill 1994). Economic and
political discrimination necessitated different practices for families of
color than for white families with respect to the division of paid and unpaid labor. Consequently, these different practices often led to innova-
tions in family form and functions, a necessity which continues to some
extent in the present (Baca Zinn 1994; Collins 1991; Dill 1994; Hurtado
1989; Stack 1974). Contrary to much public opinion, such adaptations
reflect not a weakness, but a strength of minority families (Baca Zinn
1994; Dill 1994).

Despite this history of gender inequality within families and racial, ethnic, and class differences in the legal treatment and economic opportunities afforded to different kinds of families, both liberalism and republicanism as political doctrines have egalitarian aspirations. Political equality is
intertwined with both liberalism and republicanism and certainly is part
of political aspiration in the United States, regardless of the history of
political practice.[12] Therefore, the benefits, privileges, and rights that are
distributed and enforced by the state in the public and domestic life of
families should not promote inequality along such lines as gender, race,
class, or sexual orientation. To the extent that contemporary family life
(in theory and in practice) makes these egalitarian aspirations impossible
to realize, it is necessary to rethink what we mean by families and the
families-state relation (Okin 1989; Young 1995).

In a liberal republic such as the United States, the state does have specific interests in families, especially in relation to the well-being of family members and the basic education and care of children. Yet a liberal republic with a market-based economy also has a strong interest in keeping the economic aspects of family life—including the support of children—as a matter of private or individual responsibility. In addition to this economic limit to state intervention in families, there is at least in principle a political limit to state intervention in families, as liberal republican regimes are defined in part by the value that is accorded to private life. And, state interests include a general interest in equality. So the state has crosscutting interests in families and family life.[13]

Clearly, there are deep conflicts between a liberal republic's economic and noneconomic interests in families. In practice, state interests in families, historically and at present, are conflicting and complex. As we examine any public policy, such as child support, we should expect to see these conflicting interests at work.

The Interests of Individuals and Families

On the other side of the equation, individuals, individuals as family members, and families as units also have some legitimate claims to state power and economic resources, and, in some instances, state protection. Governmental economic policy—from tax policy to labor laws to social welfare policy—sets the framework for the kinds of family life that are possible (and impossible). Adult individuals have some claim to choices about the formation and dissolution of their families. Families have some claims to privacy; individuals have some claims to privacy within their families. Individual family members have legitimate claims to state protection from abuse by other family members. The claims of family members may conflict or may change over time. The freedom of choice that one individual in a family exercises may deeply harm other family members.

Adult individuals have a liberty interest in the protection of their freedom to make decisions with respect to their intimate relationships (Struening 1996). In the contemporary United States, this includes decisions with respect to choosing a partner or choosing not to form an intimate partnership, as well as the freedom to choose to end an intimate partnership. Although the state has always regulated this process through domestic relations law, state interests in this regard may be more limited than the history of family law would indicate (Young 1995). Certainly, claims that there is a state interest in restricting legal recognition of intimate partnerships to heterosexual partners seem tenuous at best (Law 1988; Lehr 1994). And, as Mary Ann Glendon suggests in her discussion of divorce law, state interests in the dissolution of marriage are limited in cases where members of the couple are relatively equal and have no children (Glendon 1987, 1989).

Individuals also have an interest in freedom to choose whether, when, and under what circumstances to have children. Thus, individuals have an interest in the use of state power to protect rights to private decisions about family life. None of these liberty interests are absolute, or unencumbered: when individuals form a partnership or become parents, they take on a set of obligations to the other members of their family. Families then involve individuals in relationships that make them vulnerable to the needs and claims of other family members. In families where there is inequality—either due to gender role division or economic inequalities among members or because of the presence of children, who are by definition dependent on their caretakers—some members are more vulnerable than others. This becomes especially evident upon the dissolution of families, in economically marginalized families, and when some family members are physically harmed by other family members. Individuals as members of families thus have an interest in the use of state power to protect vulnerable family members from harm.

Families are also economic units; in a liberal republic with a market economy, families require social and economic conditions that make their economic survival possible. Because these conditions require state action, individuals as members of families have an interest in state provision of basic economic and social institutions that make family life possible and sustainable. Therefore, economic policy and decisions about the use of collective resources also involve decisions about families and family life.

This brief discussion makes it clear that, on both sides of the families-state relation, there are multiple and sometimes conflicting claims. The relationship between families and state is complicated; there is no bright line that separates the private life of families from the public life of the regime. This makes the formulation of public policy especially difficult, because it is not always clear on what basis policy should be made: families have both public and private dimensions, and the state has interests in both intervening in and limiting its intervention in families. Families and state are deeply intertwined, and yet distinctive.

Public-Domestic and Child Support

The changes that have occurred in family life in the United States since the 1960s have not occurred in isolation. They have been accompanied by changes in the economy, in social policy, and in family law. The causal connections between the demographic changes in families and changes in law, policy, and the economy are indeed the subject of a great deal of scholarly and public debate.

Two arenas of public policy in particular have elicited specific discussion by both scholars and public policymakers of family policy: family law and social welfare policy. It is in these particular arenas that state and family come in the most direct and observable contact. Thus, these areas provide fruitful ground for observing the institutional and normative features of public-domestic relations in the United States.

Child support sits at the nexus of family law and social welfare policy. The involvement of the federal government in child support policy has emerged in the past twenty years, at least partly in response to some of the changes in families cited at the beginning of this chapter.

When the state responds to changes in families by reforming law and policy, what kinds of policies emerge? This project addresses contemporary child support policy in the United States as a case study in the evolving relationship between families and the state. Child support is a public policy through which the thick border of the families-state relationship is evident.

Child support policy is interesting on a number of levels. First, as noted above, it constitutes a public policy that combines aspects of social welfare policy and of family law. Second, it constitutes federal involvement in family law, an arena traditionally reserved to state governments. Third, child support law has become increasingly bureaucratized, moving away, to some extent, from its traditional place in courts. Further, although the past several decades have been marked by a general trend toward privatization and less state ordering in family law, child support is an anomaly. Child support obligations have in fact been subject to increasingly centralized public ordering since the mid-1970s (Murphy 1991; Singer 1992, 1555). This policy also embodies a set of ideas about the families-state relation: the basis of this public policy is that the legal parents of a child are the primary source of the child's financial support. Thus, in a number of ways, contemporary child support policy constitutes a specific state intervention intended to alter the practices of separated families. What happens when the state designs and implements a policy with this sort of objective?

To examine this question, the overall project involves an examination of the federal law of child support, a comparative case study of child support programs in Maryland and Texas, collection and analysis of samples of child support cases from Prince George's County, Maryland and Lubbock County, Texas, and a survey of members of the sample. After looking carefully at this policy from several angles, the families-state relation is analyzed as it is revealed through this policy. Thus, this study looks carefully at both the normative and institutional dimensions of child support law.

Chapter 2 asks the following questions: What kind of public order is this? What kinds of values does the child support system reinforce? What is the institutional and historical context of child support policy? After examining the history of child support law and discussing the child support policy that has emerged since 1974, chapter 2 discusses the stated goals of the policy as well as recent scholarship that examines child support laws in practice.

Chapter 3 turns to the questions of how the system operates at the state level by examining child support law in Maryland and Texas. Chapter 4 examines the effect of child support law on individuals and families through an analysis of court data, surveys, and interviews from a sample of cases in Prince George's County, Maryland and Lubbock County, Texas.

Chapter 5 takes up normative questions again, with special attention to gender, asking whether this system alters power relationships within separated families and between different kinds of families. How does it affect relations between men and women in separated families? How does it affect different families, especially custodial women from different class and racial groups? How much does child support policy actually help children?

Chapter 6 summarizes the main conclusions of this study, and discusses some possible reforms of the child support system. It also addresses the general question of how child support policy sheds light on the actual relationship between families and the state in the United States. What conclusions can be drawn regarding the public-domestic relationship? How does this relationship need to be rethought, and remade?

In the end, child support policy also raises questions with respect to the scope of collective responsibility for the economic support of families. To what extent should collective resources be devoted to the economic support and well-being of children? To what extent should families be expected to "stand on their own two feet"? And, given the thickness and complexity of the families-state relation, what does it mean, what is required, for families to be independent economic units? Does this mean different things for different kinds of families?

It is difficult to have meaningful dialogue on this subject without looking to the multiple ways that families and state intersect in public policy:

tax policy, economic policy, labor laws—all deeply affect families. Child support policy is usually discussed in isolation from other policies. This has created policies that work well for some families, but work poorly or not at all for others.

When public policy focuses on only one part of the complex and multi-faceted families-state relation border, and does not attend to the other points of connection along that border, we may be led astray. To think that enforcing child support by itself solves the economic problems of all or even most separated families is to miss the multiple ways that families and state are connected, economically and otherwise: the multiple ways that public policy shapes family life. Thus, the project ends with some reflections on the limits of support enforcement in terms of its likely impact on child well-being and the economic resources available to single parent families.

Notes

1. Using "the family" to describe the multiple historic and contemporary forms that families take is misleading; therefore "families" will generally be utilized.

2. There are actually several different versions of this distinction; see Kymlicka (1990) and Olsen (1983).

3. It is this sort of concern that leads some liberals to believe that feminist scholars and advocates for women are calling for the elimination of privacy or of any separation between public and individual life. In fact, however, those groups that are most vulnerable have the greatest interest in limiting state power with respect to personal life, for in many ways their personal life, historically, has been the most subject to the coercive use of state power.

4. There is a very large literature on the place of republicanism in American history (cf., Wood 1969), and on the recent "liberal-communitarian debate" in political thought (Holmes 1989; Walzer 1990). Feminists have also commented on this discussion and its inattention to questions of women and gender (Burack 1994; Friedman 1990).

5. Both Rousseau and Wollstonecraft can be seen as modern republican theorists. Although Wollstonecraft is very critical of Rousseau's arguments regarding gender and the family, *A Vindication of the Rights of Woman* argues that women cannot be virtuous if not properly educated and, in turn, will not be able to properly educate their children. She does not argue for an abandonment of women's role in families or in the care and education of children.

6. It is interesting and not incidental to note that this rising concern with individualism coincides with women claiming individual rights in the public

sphere as well as in families (i.e., when women are beginning to have real opportunities to be individuals).

7. Jana Singer (1989) and Annemette Sorenson (1992) discuss some of the flaws in Weitzman's study and in any measure of the economic consequences of divorce. More generally, on the tendency of law that remains neutral (such as by allowing "private" bargaining) to reinforce existing inequalities, see Sunstein, 1993. Such arguments—which imply the need for protection of women from the vulnerability created by performing traditional roles—carry with them the usual dangers of policies that "protect" women because they are different (i.e. not men).

8. For an argument that feminists should protect a private sphere as it relates to "lifestyle experimentation," see Struening, 1996.

9. Certainly the point is not uncontroversial, but to argue it here is beyond the scope of this project.

10. Okin is paraphrasing Thomas Hobbes here.

11. Of course, this interest was the foundation of the theorists and activists who advocated "republican motherhood" and were discussed above.

12. Equality is certainly a greatly contested concept, but it cannot be settled here. For the moment, I am simply saying that in a *desirable* liberal republic, and in the liberal republican regime in the United States, equality is a core value.

13. There will also be ongoing political controversy over these interests, and some questions with respect to the interests of the individual, families and the state may never be entirely resolved. But to understand how states and families are connected, it behooves us to put on the table all of the questions that are actually being discussed when we talk about family policy. For this reason, it is necessary to look at the contesting interests of state, individuals, and families.

2

Federal Child Support Law and Policy

Public policies take place not only in the context of a particular political regime, but in a specific historical and institutional framework as well. This chapter discusses the basic features of contemporary child support law and policy, including the historical background of child support policy; the emergence of a federal policy of child support since the mid-1970s; the purposes of this policy; and several measures of the success of child support enforcement efforts.

Given the conflicting state interests in liberal republican regimes with respect to families, discussed in chapter 1, public policy toward families is likely to have conflicting goals and purposes. This is especially true of a program such as child support, which has been shaped not only by the multiple interests that the state has in families, but also by the institutional structure of social welfare policy. This chapter shows both how child support policy reflects some of the state interests discussed in chapter 1, as well as the goals of this policy.

A Brief History of Child Support

As discussed in chapter 1, child support policy grew out of both family law and social welfare policy. The obligation to provide support to minor children evolved differently, historically, in family law than it did in poor law. The general obligation to support one's minor children was present from the beginning of poor law in the colonies during the seventeenth century, and developed especially in the nineteenth century in family law; however, contemporary child support as a matter of public policy grew out of social welfare policy, and particularly through the Aid to Families with Dependent Children (AFDC) program. Thus, though the obligation

29

to support one's children derives from law and the courts, the public policy of child support is situated institutionally in the social policy administrative agencies of the executive branch.

Family Law and the Child Support Obligation

Historically, the federal government had little role in the realm of family law; such matters were left to states. Though divorce, for example, was initially available in the English colonies (as in England) only by legislative enactment in particular cases (Friedman 1973, ch. 4; Phillips 1991), throughout most of U.S. history domestic relations has been a matter handled at the state and local level by courts.[1] Though state court systems vary a great deal, a good deal of consistency across states had emerged by the nineteenth century, such that it was possible to say that a state-based family law system existed (Grossberg 1985; Reeve 1862; Vernier 1932).

The history of the child support obligation, however, is not entirely clear. The two primary authoritative sources that were utilized by nineteenth-century judges and scholars of family law disagreed as to whether a father's obligation to support minor children was a moral or a legal duty.[2] Blackstone asserted that it was a moral but not legally enforceable duty; Kent argued that this duty was indeed enforceable by law. Thus, in the civil law of domestic relations, the legal basis for any duty of a father to support his legitimate minor children during marriage as well as after divorce was uncertain (Krause 1981, 3; Schuele 1989, 809–816; tenBroek 1964, 300–301).[3] On the other hand, poor law clearly indicated the obligations of parents, children, and grandparents, to economically support their relations (tenBroek 1964–65), and bastardy law was concerned with the problem of paternal support (Grossberg 1985). Institutionally, therefore, there were different systems of law with respect to support obligations, depending upon whether the parties were subject to poor law, as well as upon the marital status of parents.

To the extent that the obligation to support dependent children existed, it seems to have emerged out of bastardy law and poor law, and at common law out of claims of third parties. TenBroek documents how poor law was intended to reduce local expenditures for the poor by imposing duties of support on relatives and restricting the mobility of those who had support obligations and those who might become subject to poor laws. He further argues that the civil law of the family and the law of the poor were developed in distinctively different ways, constituting a 'dual system of family law'.[4] Grossberg notes that in bastardy proceedings there was a clear emphasis on paternal support (1985, 215). The problem of child support enforcement originated, thus, out of a concern for containing local government costs for aid to the poor and to children born out of wedlock.[5] As will become clear, this same concern is reflected in the contemporary child support enforcement program, originating as it did as an effort to contain AFDC costs.

TenBroek notes that cases involving the enforcement of a support obligation under common law generally involved a third party supplier, recovering costs for the provision of goods or services (1964–65, 302–304). He further notes that when the common law was first codified in New York, poor law and bastardy law were codified under the law of criminal procedure, while the law of domestic relations (family law) was part of the civil code (1964–65, 309).

Historically, in cases of divorce, the support obligation and the custody decision were generally considered together by the courts. It is well known that up until the nineteenth century in cases of divorce, fathers were generally awarded custody of children (Mason 1994, ch. 2). Nonetheless, even in the late eighteenth century some women did obtain custody of children upon divorce. These decisions apparently were made on the basis of whether the father was at fault in the divorce, some emerging notion of the 'best interests of the child', and the mother's demonstrated ability to support the child (Schuele 1989, 817–820). By the end of the nineteenth century, women were generally awarded custody unless deemed unfit, and most states had enacted divorce codes that required courts to determine questions of both custody and support of children (Grossberg 1985; Mason 1994; Vernier 1932).

There was no guidance, however, regarding the amount of support required; this matter was left entirely to judicial discretion (Schuele 1989, 835).[6] A common judicial practice, up until the adoption of child support guidelines in the 1980s, was to set the support award below what the judge actually believed sufficient, under the theory that this would decrease the noncustodial father's hostility toward the obligation and increase the likelihood that he would actually make the payments (Maryland Judicial Conference 1990, 51; Schuele 1989, 836, 839).[7]

Yet even when a support award was granted by a court, whether in cases of divorce or of illegitimacy, there was little to ensure that the support obligation was actually paid. If a support obligation was not paid, the custodial parent would be required to petition the court again to request enforcement. In some states, courts did have the authority to hold obligors who did not pay in contempt of court, or to order imprisonment, but this was apparently infrequently used (Schuele 1989, 838). At any rate, for such enforcement to be effective, the obligor had to be located, and to have some assets or income.

Clearly, the system as described here was not designed in a way that would ensure reliable economic support for custodial parents and their children. Some states were more concerned about the problem of child support than others. In general, until the very recent involvement of the federal government in child support enforcement, the child support system was not really a 'system'. In fact, in most cases the state-based child support system was unlikely to provide adequate or reliable economic support for children with absent parents. Prior to 1974, there was some federal attention to the problem of child support enforcement, notably the Uniform Reciprocal Enforcement of Support Act (URESA) and the Social Security Acts of 1965 and 1967. However, federal laws were generally ineffective, contained few mandated practices, and were poorly enforced (Krause 1981).[8]

The Institutional Transformation of Child Support Enforcement

Child Support as Social Welfare Policy

Family law has undergone extensive changes in the past several decades, partly as a result of demographic changes and changes in gender role expectations. Though scholars describe these changes differently, the trend in the United States toward no-fault divorce laws, the use of mediation in divorce (Singer 1992), and the increased recognition of the rights of children born out of wedlock (Zingo and Early 1994) have all meant a decrease in the legal enforcement and regulation of familial relationships. In this respect, child support policy is an anomaly: this aspect of family law has been subject to increased public regulation and scrutiny (Murphy 1991). The federal policy itself was created as part of the AFDC program, and is linked to this social welfare program. The institutional features of child support, as well as its purposes, are thus more in keeping with the U.S. social welfare system than with the tradition of family law. To understand the context of child support policy requires an understanding of the institutional features of social welfare policy in the United States.

Scholars have provided a variety of explanations for the historical development and institutional structure of U.S. welfare policies. Some see grass-roots social movements as the impetus for the development of New Deal and Great Society programs (Piven and Cloward 1977). Others see a continuous history, from the poor laws of the seventeenth century to the public assistance and social insurance programs of the present, which divide the poor into deserving and undeserving, and provide services on that basis (Katz 1989; tenBroek 1964–65). Still others see the development of social welfare provision as part of the process of state-building, beginning in the late nineteenth and early twentieth century, and taking new form with the New Deal (Skocpol, Weir, and Orloff 1988; Skowronek 1982).

Although scholars disagree about the historical explanation for the particular institutional structure of the U.S. welfare state, they tend to agree that social welfare policy in the United States is unique, and is different from welfare states in other industrialized democracies. The historical development of the U.S. welfare state should be understood on its own terms (Skocpol, Weir, and Orloff 1988). It is useful, however, to know that it developed later, and consists generally of less generous and less universal programs than welfare states in countries with similar political and economic systems.

Welfare programs in the United States generally take one of two forms: social insurance or public assistance. Social insurance, or contributory programs, provide benefits to workers or former workers on the basis of contributions made by them or on their behalf. These programs include Old Age Insurance (popularly known as social security), Medicare, and unemployment benefits. Public assistance, or means-tested programs, provide benefits to individuals from general tax revenues based upon individual need. Both types of programs were present in the Social Security Act of 1935, which created both Old Age Insurance and Aid to Dependent Children. In general, however, there is much wider public support for social insurance programs than for public assistance programs (Cook 1992; Marmor, Mashaw, and Harvey 1990; Skocpol, Weir, and Orloff 1988). Social insurance benefits are widely seen as an earned benefit to deserving recipients (despite the fact that most recipients collect a great deal more in benefits than they paid into the programs), whereas public assistance benefits are viewed as government handouts to mostly undeserving individuals.

The program that created the impetus for federal child support policy is the Aid to Dependent Children (ADC) program, renamed Aid to Families with Dependent Children (AFDC) in 1962. ADC replaced the mothers' pension or mothers' aid programs that had been created in most states in the early part of the twentieth century to provide assistance to deserving single mothers and their children (Gordon 1994; Ladd-Taylor 1994; Mink 1995; Nelson 1990; Skocpol 1992). The state-level programs came about as a result of the advocacy of women activists and reformers, and served as the model for the ADC program of the Social Security Act of 1935. The basic logic of the programs, both as mothers' pensions and as ADC, was to provide support for children of single mothers (particularly widows). While the grant was not enough to substitute for a breadwinners' wage, it did provide some relief.

Whereas Old Age Insurance was and is a federally established and administered program, AFDC, like most other social insurance and public assistance programs in the United States, involves federal-state cooperation. The federal government provides a portion of the grant and sets basic guidelines for implementation, and states provide the remainder of the grant and administer the program. States are free, within fairly minimal bounds, to set their own standards of need and other eligibility criteria as well as the grant level provided. From its formation in 1935 through the time of this writing, the ADC/AFDC program was an entitlement program: anyone who met the eligibility criteria was entitled to receive the grant.[9]

For a variety of reasons, participation levels in the AFDC program remained relatively low until the 1960s. Many people who were eligible for the program did not seek this assistance. In the late 1960s and early 1970s, however, a variety of factors converged to rapidly increase participation in the AFDC program, including the growth of divorce and of out-of-wedlock births, as well as the civil rights and welfare rights movements. In turn, program expenditures nearly doubled from 1965 to 1973, as did the number of participants, and this helped to place child support enforcement squarely on Congress' agenda (DiNitto 1995, 186–187).

The Beginnings of a Federal Family Law

In 1974, the federal government ventured into the arena of family law by establishing a federally-mandated, state-implemented child support program. The point of entry into family law for the federal government was the AFDC program. Congress was concerned not only about the expansion of the AFDC rolls, but also with the fact that many custodians and children who were receiving AFDC were in need of support not because of the death of the former partner or spouse of the custodian, but because of the absence of a living partner or spouse. Thus, they established a program intended to collect child support for custodial parents on AFDC; custodians not on AFDC were also to be provided the services of child support agencies.[10] This program, established by the Social Services Amendments of 1974, and greatly expanded since that time, was "directed at the goal of achieving or maintaining economic self-support to prevent, reduce, or eliminate dependency" (P.L. 93-647, Part A, Sec. 2001).[11]

There are three major federal legislative initiatives: The Social Services Amendments of 1974 (P.L.93–647), the Child Support Enforcement Amendments (CSEA) of 1984 (P.L. 98–378), and the Family Support Act (FSA) of 1988 (P.L. 100–485).[12] The Social Services Amendments established Title IV-D of the Social Security Act—the child support enforcement provisions of the AFDC program—and established federal and state offices of child support enforcement. CSEA and FSA extended the scope of child support enforcement, requiring new and strengthened practices in the arenas of paternity establishment, the enforcement of support orders, and the collection and disbursement practices of child support enforcement agencies.

Federal child support enforcement law is innovative in several respects. First, it constitutes federal involvement in a realm of law that has traditionally been reserved to the states—family law.[13] Second, it provides some common elements and requirements, as well as continuing distinctions, across the different systems of family law which are embodied in the AFDC program and the family/civil court system of divorce law. This raises the related question of whether child support law is social welfare policy or family law or some combination thereof. Third, it constitutes legislative- and executive-centered public ordering, as opposed to (historically) judicially-centered public ordering. The pervasive use of administrative/bureaucratic mechanisms for locating parents, establishing paternity, establishing support orders, and enforcing payments has altered the institutional structure of support enforcement. Fourth, the use of mandatory child support guidelines and enforcement mechanisms constitutes the establishment of fixed rules for determining child support obligations in a realm of law that has traditionally been governed by discretion (Glendon 1986; Murphy 1991). The child support enforcement system also constitutes a trend toward greater public ordering of the behavior of family members, in contradistinction to the privatization that has occurred in other aspects of family law during the past thirty years in the United States.

The arguments utilized to justify this increased public ordering are related to state interests with respect to families: limiting public expenditures on children by reinforcing families as private economic units, and reinforcing a set of norms regarding family life.[14] Public documents (in legislation and documents produced by the Federal Office of Child Support Enforcement) regarding the justification for this federal policy identify several (sometimes contradictory) purposes: the first and foremost goal is fiscal savings. Child support payments are utilized to offset AFDC expenditures, and presumably, to prevent the necessity for AFDC for some single-parent families. Thus, the historic concern for limiting public liability and expenditures for children with absent parents is continued through child support enforcement. A second stated purpose relates to two aspects of child well-being: to promote some minimum level of child economic well-being, as well as some aspects of psychological and emotional well-being. Recent legislation that emphasizes paternity establishment is described as beneficial to a child's emotional well-being, since this establishes some connection to the father (and implicitly, thereby provides some sense of identity). Some legislators and policy-makers also believe that absent fathers are more likely to remain involved with their children if they are required to pay support.[15] Child support policy is thus intended to provide some link between absent fathers and their children. The assumption is that this link is clearly beneficial.[16] Finally, child support enforcement is seen as promoting 'parental responsibility', and enforcing the premise that children are primarily the financial responsibility of their biological parents and not of the state.[17]

Federal child support law and regulation mandates or encourages state laws and practices aimed at establishing and enforcing child support by providing federal matching funds and performance incentive payments (varying from 66–90 percent) for state administrative expenditures and censures, including fiscal penalties, for non-compliance. Federal law conditions AFDC payments to states on compliance with the provisions of Title IV-D of the Social Security Act; all states have chosen to participate. The child support program was intended originally as a cost-saving measure for the federal and state governments. However, due to the structure of incentive payments, the child support program has in recent years cost the federal government while providing additional revenue to state and local governments. States are not required to funnel federal reimbursements and incentive payments into the AFDC program or back into their child support program; they can go to the state's general fund. Some states administer the program directly; in others it is administered by local governments under the supervision of a state office. Thus, some reimbursements go to local government as well.

The federal requirements have several general features: they provide fiscal incentives to the states for establishing effective mechanisms for child support enforcement. Child support agencies have available to them increasingly strengthened means for enforcing support, with provisions for wage garnishment, liens on property, credit reporting of child support debts, and federal and state tax refund withholding. The Family Support Act of 1988 requires that states establish, implement, and regularly evaluate mandatory child support guidelines that provide a numerical support award. Federal law mandates that states have automated record-keeping systems, and makes available the use of state, federal, and local information and data banks for purposes of locating absent parents and their places of employment.

The FSA also provided incentives to encourage states to pursue cases in which biological paternity needs to be established; these incentives include coverage of most administrative costs for establishing paternity, as well as performance incentive payments. This emphasis has been expanded through the child support related provisions of the Omnibus Reconciliation Act (OBRA) of 1993, which requires the establishment of administrative processes for paternity acknowledgment, including procedures for doing so in the hospital at the time of birth.

Thus, in the course of twenty years, a federal administrative system with a wide array of responsibilities, mechanisms, and powers for establishment and enforcement of child support obligations has emerged. As noted above, this new federal policy has multiple interesting features; what follows is a discussion of the transition from court-centered to administratively-centered policy-making.

From Judicial Discretion to Fixed Rules (from Court to Bureaucracy) in Child Support Law

... the choice between fixed rules and discretion not only involves the proper allocation of functions between courts and legislatures, but, more importantly, it determines the balance between official decision-making and private ordering.(Glendon 1986, 1167)

One way of characterizing this institutional transformation is as a move from judicial discretion in child support law toward fixed rules implemented through bureaucracies. Thus, as family law generally was becoming more privatized (Schneider 1985; Singer 1992) child support law was becoming more centralized and uniform. As indicated, one criticism of the child support system as it existed prior to federal intervention was that judicial discretion led to great inequalities and inequities. As Glendon points out in the above quotation, even a system centered on judicial discretion needs to be based upon some underlying principles—principles that were sorely lacking in the practice of child support law until federal legislative involvement. The system of judicial discretion in the awarding and enforcement of child support resulted in vastly different monetary

awards for similarly situated persons; in general it did not provide for
adequate awards based on the actual cost of children, it did not provide
for regular enforcement, and it failed to adequately consider the disadvantages most custodial parents faced and continue to face in the labor market. Thus, the system of judicial discretion in this particular aspect of
family law worked to the detriment of custodial parents and their children. As Murphy argues, the assumption that discretion led to just treatment was indeed a myth (Murphy 1991). That some judges continue to
have unrealistic notions regarding the adequacy of child support awards
has been documented by the studies of gender bias in state court systems
(Czapanskiy 1990; Maryland Judicial Conference 1990).

As the child support enforcement system has moved from judicial discretion toward fixed rules, discretion has not been eliminated by any
means—exceptions are allowed to most requirements, though generally a
written statement of the reason for the deviation is required. Generally,
court decisions on cases challenging various aspects of the child support
system have upheld child support law, deferring to legislative intent and
confirming the legitimacy of state and federal intervention in child support enforcement.[18] Courts have affirmed the legitimacy of federal
involvement in child support law, and have enforced Congress' intent
(stated specifically in the Child Support Enforcement Amendments of
1984) to provide child support services to all custodial parents who apply
for services. In several cases that have been brought on behalf of AFDC
recipients who have received child support services, courts have held that
the primary intent of the law is to provide public cost savings, not to
provide services to custodial parents or their dependent children (Hirsch
1988; Harris 1988).

Courts have also upheld the constitutionality of the use of guidelines
to establish the amount of child support an absent parent is required to
pay. The suitability of fixed rules as a form of public ordering in child
support has been challenged, however, especially with respect to child
support guidelines. In *Blaisdell v. Blaisdell* 492 N.E. 2d 622 (Ill.App.
1986), the obligor (absent parent) argued that mandatory child support
guidelines were unconstitutional in that the legislature had usurped judicial authority. The court held, however, that this was not the case, due to
the possibility of exceptions and the existence of legislative mandates in
other areas of law, such as mandatory sentencing guidelines. Obligors
have also challenged the applicability of guidelines in their particular circumstances. Courts have responded by limiting the conditions under
which deviations from the guidelines are permissible (OCSE 1992a, 102–
104). Nevertheless, deviations from the guidelines are typically down-

ward, making guidelines in effect an upper limit on support awards (Erickson 1992).

Congress has also encouraged states to develop administrative mechanisms for procedures still accomplished through courts, such as paternity establishment. Even before the enactment of OBRA of 1993 required such programs, some states had experimented with programs that provide for voluntary acknowledgment of paternity in hospitals at the time of birth. Voluntary acknowledgment is not the same as paternity establishment, but does create a presumption of paternity (OCSE 1993c). States may choose to make the acknowledgment convert to establishment after a certain period of time.

Given the extent to which important and conflicting rights and obligations of family members are involved in child support related policies, courts and court-based proceedings are likely to remain an important part of the support enforcement process. Administrative procedures seem unlikely to entirely replace the role of courts, at least not without a major federal legislative overhaul of the current system. However, the clear trend, even with the current administrative structure, is toward increased bureaucratization and reduced court discretion, and the use of administrative procedures wherever possible.

Basic Case Processing

With these broad characterizations of the present child support system in mind, it may be useful to describe in general terms how this system functions from the viewpoint of children and their custodial parents, and from the viewpoint of non-custodial parents. A case is initiated when a custodial parent applies for support enforcement services to their local child support agency. This may occur either as part of an application for AFDC through the local social services office, or by application of a non-AFDC recipient seeking child support services. In the latter case custodial parents apply directly to the child support agency, and pay a small application fee. Depending upon their state of residence, the non-AFDC custodial parent may also be charged a fee for the specific services required, such as paternity establishment or parent location. The custodial parent, however, may never be required to appear in court, depending upon the particular services required and upon whether the jurisdiction in question utilizes administrative processes. In all proceedings, the child support agency provides legal representation before the court on behalf of the child.

This process for seeking child support—when it works well—is much simpler for the custodial parent to pursue than child support prior to the establishment of child support agencies. In most states, the costs to the custodial parent are minimal, and there is no need to hire an attorney or go through the process of filing for support. All of this is handled through the support agency.[19]

Many additional services related to support are provided by the child support agency. These include the location of absent parents through the use of various government and private information banks, location of the absent parent's employer, paternity establishment, support establishment, establishment of health benefits for the child (if available through the non-custodial parent's employer), and support enforcement. Support establishment and enforcement can be provided across state lines when necessary. Thus, if the custodial parent does not know where the absent parent is or where he or she is employed, child support agencies can provide assistance. Further, and perhaps most importantly, if the non-custodial parent does not pay support, child support agencies have a number of enforcement mechanisms available, including wage garnishment, tax refund intercepts, and reporting arrears to credit reporting institutions, as well as the threat of incarceration for contempt of court for failure to pay. Some states also have mechanisms such as Maryland's lottery intercept program, which garnishes the lottery winnings of obligors, and Texas' license suspension law, which provides for the suspension of professional, recreational, and drivers' licenses for obligors who are seriously behind in their support payments.

Child support services were made available to non-AFDC families on a temporary basis in 1974, and on a permanent basis in 1980. Thus, child support services are available to AFDC and non-AFDC families alike. However, support that is collected and distributed through the Title IV-D agency is treated differently depending upon the AFDC status of the custodial parent. Beginning in 1967, custodial parents who applied for AFDC were required to assign their child support benefits to the state in which AFDC benefits were received in order to reimburse federal and state AFDC costs. Until 1984, any child support benefits collected on behalf of the child and custodial parent were retained by the state and federal government.[20] Beginning with the Deficit Reduction Act of 1984, custodial parents are required to include all children in applications for AFDC—even those receiving regular child support—and the child support is counted as income for purposes of calculating the AFDC benefit.[21] So that custodians in these circumstances can keep some portion of that child support, all AFDC beneficiaries are permitted to keep the first $50 per month of child support, if the support is paid in the month in which it is due.[22] If the child support award amount exceeds the monthly AFDC award amount, the custodial parent is also paid the excess up to the monthly award amount. Any excess paid beyond this is utilized to reimburse any arrears owed the state.[23]

For non-AFDC custodial parents, once a support order is established, collections are made through the child support agency. The non-custodial parent either pays directly to the agency, or the parent's garnished wages are paid to the child support agency. Non-AFDC recipients then receive the entire amount of the support collected. Payments are first credited to current payments and then to arrears, if any, and may also be credited to future payments if a payment exceeds current debts. As noted by Paula Roberts (1991), the main problem for non-AFDC custodial parents whose support is actually collected has been timeliness of distribution. In response to this problem, the Family Support Act established time frames for the distribution of funds received in these cases, as well as requirements that receipts and payments be regularly reported to non-custodial and custodial parents. Non-AFDC custodial parents who do not use child support agencies to establish support (for example, those whose support is established in a divorce proceeding) may also request that support payments be made through the child support agency. This provides for regular accounting of payments, and also makes the enforcement mechanisms of child support agencies available to these families.

In AFDC child support cases, most of the funds collected are utilized to reimburse federal, state, and local governments for their AFDC expenditures. Nationwide, more than 10 percent of annual AFDC expenditures have been recovered through child support payments since fiscal year 1989; in fiscal year 1993 this figure reached 12 percent (OCSE 1995a, 69). For the past ten years, however, the fastest growing portion of the caseload of child support agencies has been non-AFDC custodians, and increased collections are due primarily to this portion of the caseload.

From the perspective of the non-custodial parent, and again depending upon the jurisdiction and the particular services required, the process begins when he or she receives notice that a support case has been filed and is asked to respond. This may be handled administratively, or the non-custodial parent may be asked to appear before a judge or master. If paternity has not been established, the alleged father will be asked whether he admits paternity. Most men do in fact admit paternity, and the entire case, including the establishment of a support award, may be handled at one proceeding by consent. However, the alleged father has the opportunity to contest paternity, in which case a blood test will be ordered. If his paternity of the child or children is excluded, the state pays the cost of the blood test. If he is found to be the father, he is generally charged for the cost of genetic testing. The paternity test by itself does not establish paternity, but, given the accuracy of current testing methods, the paternity test does shift the burden of proof to the father. Thus, most men whose paternity tests are positive consent to paternity establishment.

Once paternity is established, a support order is then established based upon the state's child support guidelines.[24] The guidelines are a rebuttable presumption, meaning that they are presumed correct unless there is a specific finding that they should not be applied to a particular case. The non-custodial parent may request a deviation from the guidelines due to his or her particular circumstances. The support order establishes the amount, effective date, and payment method for support payments. Under the Family Support Act, as of January 1, 1994, wage garnishment of support payments was required in all new support cases. If payment is not made, the non-custodial parent (now the obligor) will be required to appear in court again, and may eventually be held in contempt or even jailed for failure to pay. Obligors are required to notify the court and the child support agency if they move or change jobs, and their employers are also required to provide notice of termination if this occurs. Employers who fail to comply with wage garnishment orders may also be held in contempt or fined. Obligor parents who fail to pay may thus eventually find the full force of the law utilized to require them to meet their obligation.

From the perspective of those individuals affected by it, then, the child support process works very differently now than it did prior to the establishment of federal child support law. Chapter 4 will provide some evidence as to how custodial parents and non-custodial parents view the child support system and their experiences with it. I now turn to an examination of the basic goals of the child support program.

The Public Goals of Child Support Enforcement

Since the beginning of congressional attention to this arena of law, strengthened child support provisions have in general received fairly widespread, bipartisan support. The 1984 child support amendments were passed unanimously; there was also wide bipartisan support for the Family Support Act of 1988.

Why this widespread support? Child support enforcement has elements that appeal to both political conservatives and political liberals. Attention to reducing costs of AFDC, emphasis on parental responsibility, increasing the financial support of poor children and decreasing the economic vulnerability of custodial parents—each of these goals has aspects that appeal to people across the political spectrum.

Students of public policy point out that most public policies have multiple goals. This is especially true of policies that are the result of compromise among groups with different sets of political beliefs and values. Further, the several goals of a policy may be in conflict with one another. Marmor, Mashaw and Harvey point out that scholars often engage in an almost formulaic criticism of public policies on the basis of their multiple and conflicting goals (1990, 222–28). However, they argue that such conflict is inevitable when policies are the result of political compromise. In fact, multiple goals may be desirable in the arena of social welfare policy, since they often respond to the policy preferences of the coalitions supporting the policy (ibid., ch. 2). If it is the case that most social welfare policies are the result of multiple and conflicting goals, how do the multiple goals of this particular policy play out in practice? Which goals take priority, and what are the consequences of this prioritization?

Given its institutional and historical context, it is not surprising that child support policy has multiple and conflicting goals. Not only is the program linked to social welfare policy through the AFDC program, it is also a policy that deals with the relationship between families and state. As outlined in chapter 1, there are multiple interests at work on the part of both families and state, and these multiple interests are likely to be reflected in public policies that deal with families. Therefore, because child support policy is linked to social welfare policy, because it is a policy supported by liberals and conservatives alike, and because it is a policy that deals with families and familial relationships, we should expect it to be a policy with multiple goals. The stated goals of federal involvement in child support enforcement are threefold: fiscal savings, child economic well-being, and a version of public enforcement of parental responsibilities.

Fiscal Savings

As noted, the basis and authority for federal legislative involvement in the arena of family law is the federal AFDC program. The basic goal of the child support program as it was instituted in the 1974 Social Services Amendments was to reduce the cost of AFDC programs. Congressional concern over the rising costs of the program was coupled with concern that the existence of government support for single parents promoted or caused single parenthood and promoted "irresponsibility" on the part of non-custodial (usually male) parents (Krause 1981, ch. 7). Further, according to a General Accounting Office study requested by Representative Martha Griffiths, many of these non-custodial parents had enough earnings to comfortably pay child support, and yet did not do so (as cited in Krause 1981, 282–85). The spectre of non-custodial parents easily avoiding financial responsibility for their children, while taxpayers bore an increasing burden to support the AFDC program, led Congress to create the current child support program. The program was intended to require the non-custodial parents to reimburse taxpayers for expenditures on AFDC by paying child support, which was collected by the state on behalf of the child. It was also believed that many families would no longer need AFDC if child support obligations were paid (Harris 1988).

Parental Responsibility

The clearest norm evident in the child support enforcement system is the emphasis on the financial responsibility of legal parents, whether biological or adoptive, to support their children. The system clearly emphasizes that it is a child's legal parents who are primarily responsible for providing financial resources for the child's care, and that the state's role is first of all to enforce this obligation, and secondarily to provide state funds when the resources of the parents are not adequate. This is the case even if the parents have no ongoing relationship with one another and the absent parent is not involved at all in the child's life and has no interest in the child. This is the meaning of "parental responsibility" in child support policy. The clear message of the system is that individual parents are the primary contributors to the economic needs of children, and that collective responsibility for the economic needs of children begins only when the economic resources of parents are insufficient. Thus, individual, private provision for children is emphasized over public provision.

It should be noted that there are at least two different aspects to this emphasis on parental responsibility: responsibility before conception and responsibility after conception. One way to view child support policy is by saying that the enforcement of the financial responsibility of child support may deter people from having children if they cannot afford to support them. The second aspect is that, once a child is conceived, regardless of the circumstances of that conception or the marital status of the parents, the child is the financial responsibility of both parents.

Child Well-Being

As the federal OCSE puts it,

Concern for the well-being of children who live with only one parent and a desire to promote self-sufficiency for these families prompted the establishment of this program.(OCSE 1990b, 1)

The economic problems faced by women who are single parents are well-known. Child support enforcement is therefore intended to improve the economic well-being of children in these families by ensuring that absent parents contribute financially to their support. Certainly, the economic benefits—to the child(ren) and the custodial parent—of regular and reliable child support payments are clear. But Congress and OCSE also claim that there are additional benefits of the support enforcement program in terms of other aspects of child well-being.

A recent OCSE annual report cites the following possible benefits of child support enforcement, in addition to the economic benefits: a sense of heritage for children, enhanced self-esteem for children, the creation of a bond between father and children, the promotion of family well-being, and the enhancement of family self-sufficiency (OCSE 1993a, 6). With respect to the emerging emphasis on the legal establishment of paternity, benefits cited include the establishment of the child as a legal heir, therefore making the child eligible for inheritance and social security benefits. The establishment of paternity is also claimed to have a positive effect on non-economic aspects of child well-being; thus, ". . . establishing the father-child relationship fosters a sense of self-esteem, identity, and social structure for the child" (OCSE 1990b, 12). OCSE also cites medical and psychological benefits from establishment of biological paternity, regardless of whether the father establishes a relationship with the child (ibid., 13).

All of these claims may in fact be true, though they are, as OCSE itself terms it, "intangible." They are assumed to be secondary, beneficial, consequences of child support establishment and enforcement mechanisms, especially of paternity establishment. The mechanisms of the program itself, however, are not designed to have any direct effect on children's emotional or psychological well-being, their self-esteem, their identity, or their relationship with either parent. The mechanisms of the child support program are economic and legal, and program success is measured in those terms. Thus, despite these references to a richer sense of child well-being, the effects of the program on child well-being, given its current structure, are measured only in economic terms.[25]

Purposes in Conflict

These multiple purposes are not necessarily compatible. Most especially, a *substantive* version of child well-being is likely to conflict with
the goal of short-term fiscal savings for the state. These conflicting goals
might be described in general terms as the difference between a public
policy with the social welfare goal of promoting well-being and a policy
that emphasizes the enforcement of rights and obligations. As noted
above, the impetus for this program comes from social welfare policy. In
practice, the primary goal of this policy is to redistribute private funds in
separated families, recover some of the costs of AFDC, and to provide
AFDC cost-avoidance by redistributing the economic resources of separated families. The meaning of parental responsibility is economic responsibility; child support policy emphasizes the primacy of private provision
of economic resources for children. The goals of this policy are in accord
with the goal of limiting state expenditures on families by maintaining
families as independent economic units. In terms of the institutional
structure of contemporary child support law, the policy is focused on the
first goal: fiscal savings for the state. At best, this law attends to other
aspects of state interests in families—including substantive child well-
being—only indirectly.

Data and Studies of Child Support

How well is the child support system that has been briefly described here
working? There are three sources of data on the child support system:
data from the federal Office of Child Support Enforcement, census data
that has been collected since 1979, and direct collection of data from
sources such as court records of child support cases, public opinion surveys, and surveys of parents subject to child support laws.

Data from OCSE

The federal Office of Child Support Enforcement provides an annual
report to Congress based upon data reported by state child support agencies. The data gives a sense of the rapid growth in this program, in terms
of the size of the caseload (including the growth in the non-AFDC caseload) as well as the total dollars collected (table 2.1).[26]

OCSE's reports also offer several measures of the program's efficiency,
including cost-effectiveness ratios, the percent of total cases in which a

TABLE 2.1
Total Child Support Collections and Caseload

	FY81	FY86	FY91	FY92	FY93
Collections: (in billions)					
AFDC	$0.67	$1.2	$1.98	$2.26	$2.42
Non-AFDC	$0.96	$2.0	$4.9	$5.7	$6.49
Total	$1.63	$3.2	$6.88	$7.96	$8.91
Caseload: (in millions)					
AFDC	5.11	7.22	8.03	8.71	9.6
Non-AFDC	1.15	2.5	5.39	6.46	7.47
Total	6.26	9.72	13.42	15.17	17.07

Source: OCSE Annual Reports to Congress, various years

collection is made, and the percent of AFDC expenditures recovered through child support collections (table 2.2).[27] Table 2.2 shows that total collections have risen markedly since 1981. However, the percent of cases in which there is a collection in a given year has remained relatively steady. It should be noted, however, that the figures reported in table 2.2 are totals for both arrears (support uncollected from previous years) and current obligations for all cases, including those cases for which no support order has been established. This provides a somewhat distorted picture of collections on two counts. First, although there has been marked improvement nationwide in terms of the establishment of support orders, in FY 93 only 55.4 percent of OCSE child support cases had a support order. Since no collections can be made until a support order has been established, measuring collections in terms of the total caseload reflects the percentage of *potential* cases in which a collection could be made, not *actual* cases in which support is owed. Second, collection rates are much higher in cases of current support than in cases of back support. In FY 93, for example, a total of $13.04 billion dollars was owed in current support, and $6.87 billion of that was paid (52.7 percent). By contrast, in that same year, $26.9 billion in back support was owed, and only $2.02 billion of that was paid (7.5 percent) (OCSE 1995a, tables 68 through 71). Thus, on current support obligations, OCSE collects more than half of the dollars owed.

OCSE data also shows that in terms of overall expenditures and receipts, the federal child support program no longer provides overall cost savings. Because of the structure of federal incentive payments, the costs

TABLE 2.2
OCSE Efficiency Measures

	FY81	FY86	FY91	FY92	FY93
Collections per dollar of administrative cost:	$3.18	$3.45	$3.82	$3.99	$3.98
Percent of cases with collections:	13.9	15.7	19.3	18.7	18.3
Percent of AFDC expenditures offset by collections:	5.2	8.6	10.7	11.4	12.0

Source: OCSE Annual Reports to Congress, various years

of the program are borne by the federal government, while states receive income from the program. Administrative expenditures began exceeding AFDC collections in FY 89. The marginal costs remain quite low: in FY 93, collections totalled $8.9 billion while administrative costs exceeded AFDC collections by $278 million, or 3.1 percent of total collections. Although the original goal of cost savings is no longer being realized, the child support program certainly serves legitimate public purposes, and the costs of the program are small in comparison to the financial benefits to children in single-parent families. Nevertheless, the child support program is not likely to generate overall cost savings in the future unless the collection rate increases significantly because the duties of child support agencies have continued to expand.

Census Bureau Data

In 1979 the Census Bureau began collecting data on child support, with subsequent studies in two-year intervals. These studies originally included women who are custodial parents and are eligible for a child support award (whether or not they actually have a support award); more recent studies have included both women and men who are custodial parents.[28] According to the most recent report available at the time of this writing, which includes data from 1991, 56 percent of women and 41 percent of men eligible for child support actually have a support award, for an overall rate of 54 percent. Of those custodial parents due support, 76 percent of women and 63 percent of men receive some payment. About 49 percent of custodial parents due support received the entire amount, and another 24 percent received a partial payment (U.S. Bureau of the Census 1995, 6). Thus, OCSE cases have a lower collections rate than is the case overall. This is likely due to the fact that custodial parents with more difficult cases—in which paternity needs to be established, the absent parent located, or in which the absent parent is unable to pay—are more likely to utilize child support agencies.

The most extensive examination of the Census Bureau data is Andrea Beller and John Graham's study (1993) of the studies conducted from 1979 through 1986, which provides a comprehensive analysis of the economic effects of federal and state child support laws during that period. Through detailed examination of the data, they conclude that, though the aggregate figures on collections during that period reveal little change, some changes did occur as a result of federal and state child support laws (1993, 6).

Beller and Graham conclude that one of the major problems with the child support system has been the failure to update support awards. Until the Family Support Act, regular review of the support award amount was not required, and in some states it was difficult for a custodial parent to request a review without showing a substantial change in circumstances (Roberts 1991). As a result of inflation, low initial awards, and the increasing financial needs of older children, many custodial parents who were owed child support during the period studied found that their child support award had decreased significantly in value (Beller and Graham 1993, 111–24).

To test the effectiveness of enforcement mechanisms, they utilized information on state laws in place at the time of each survey, and analyzed differences in collection rates among states with procedures such as earnings withholding, tax refund intercepts, and criminal penalties for nonsupport (1993, ch. 6). They found that earnings withholding, liens on property, and criminal penalties all appeared to increase receipts (1993, 174). Income tax intercepts did not have a statistically significant effect on receipts, and expedited processes seemed to have a negative effect, though the reasons for this were not clear (1993, 176). They also come to the counterintuitive conclusion that during the period studied, increased government expenditures had no impact on receipts (183).[29] Nevertheless, the existence of enforcement mechanisms did have a positive effect on receipts for all custodial parents, and especially for black women (188).

In terms of the effect of child support guidelines, Beller and Graham found that guidelines did increase average award amounts for non-black, ever-married mothers, but had a negative effect in terms of awards and receipt rates for black and never-married mothers (190–195). These conclusions are tentative, however, since guidelines were not made mandatory by the federal government until after the period studied. Also, for three of the four survey years, the guidelines affected less than 30 percent of the sampled population (188). Measuring the actual effects of guidelines will require study of guidelines law in practice, as well as more recent Census Bureau survey data.

While this study provides a great deal of detailed and careful analysis of census data, it has the limitation of using data only through 1986. Many aspects of child support law have changed since that time, including the use of mandatory guidelines and wage liens. To determine how the system works at present, it is necessary to examine more recent data.

An additional limitation in the use of census data is the absence of several types of information. First, no information is collected directly from non-custodial parents. Thus, Beller and Graham are forced to make inferences about fathers from the characteristics of the mothers (1993, 12). Second, while the Census Bureau survey does ask respondents whether they utilized state and local child support agencies to establish and enforce their support award, they do not report results (collections) by use or non-use of support enforcement agencies. Without further analysis of the data there is no way to know whether there are differences in the success rates in awards and collections for these different means of case processing. Third, the information on the award itself is limited; there is no way to know the date of the award, the number of children included, or the actual amount awarded (as opposed to the amount due, which may include arrears) (1993, 12).

Other Studies

Irwin Garfinkel and colleagues engaged in a decade-long study of child support in Wisconsin, made possible in part because of a collaborative relationship between the Institute for Research on Poverty and the Wisconsin Department of Health and Social Services (Garfinkel, McLanahan, and Robins, eds., 1992). The study involved the collection of several sets of data in Wisconsin during the period 1980–1988, including data from court records, paternity records, and a study of absent parents' income (ibid., 9–10). They also used national studies such as the Panel Study of Income Dynamics and Census Bureau data. In addition, they conducted a public opinion survey of Wisconsin residents about child support, including a proposed child support assurance system (ibid., ch. 14).

The studies asked a wide variety of questions regarding child support, including the ability of absent parents to pay support, the relationships among support, custody and visitation, the barriers to paternity establishment, and the costs and benefits of a child support assurance plan such as the one proposed, but not entirely implemented, in Wisconsin.[30] Also studied were the effects of mandatory wage withholding on collections, on AFDC participation and cost, and on labor participation by custodial parents; and the effects of child support on the remarriage rates of single mothers.

In a more recent volume, Garfinkel and colleagues have studied the effects of child support on various aspects of child well-being, as well as various facets of child support law in practice (Garfinkel, McLanahan, and Robins 1994). The studies use a wide range of data sources, including census data, other national surveys, and OCSE demonstration projects.

Combined with Garfinkel's *Assuring Child Support* (1992), the studies constitute a comprehensive analysis of the child support system in Wisconsin during the 1980s. The studies also have another purpose: Garfinkel and his colleagues argue for a system of child support assurance. Child support assurance involves the payment of a minimum level of child support by the government regardless of whether a support collection is made.[31] The authors conclude that, though there are unanswered questions about such a system, the benefits of a system of child support assurance outweigh potential costs.

One advantage of a study such as those done by Garfinkel and colleagues is the availability of a wider and more detailed range of data on individual cases than in either the Census Bureau studies or the OCSE reports. In particular, this set of studies is able to provide more information about absent parents based on actual data (as opposed to extrapolation). The use of multiple sources of data, including court and administrative records as well as a survey of the general public, provides a richer base of data for analysis. This study attempts to emulate the Garfinkel studies to the extent that multiple sources of information are utilized.

Both the Garfinkel et al. and the Beller and Graham studies analyze the aggregate effects of child support policy. One factor missing from these studies, however, is an analysis of what child support policy means in the lives of individuals and families. Further, in these studies policy outcomes are often analyzed as desirable or undesirable with little connection to the purposes the policy serves, or to why the outcomes are valued in the way that they are. For example, both Garfinkel et al. and Beller and Graham study the effects of child support on the remarriage of single mothers. Neither study addresses the effect of child support on the remarriage of absent fathers. Nor is it ever clearly articulated *why* the remarriage rate of single mothers should be studied; the studies assume that remarriage (of women who are single parents) is desirable, and imply that if child support payments delay women's remarriage rates, this is a deleterious side effect.

This study is designed to address these two gaps in the child support literature. I examine the operations of two state child support programs through several lenses: the views of its administrators, the data collected and reported as well as the studies conducted by various state agencies in two state programs, the records from a sample of court cases in each state, a survey of parents who have been through a child support case, and a small number of interviews with these parents. These various means provide a relatively comprehensive view of the operations of two state programs for child support enforcement. Most especially, this study provides more information about how individuals who are subject to child support law are treated by the child support system, in what ways the system succeeds and fails for them, and how they think the system ought to be changed.

The other aspect of this project attempts to ground child support policy in the larger context of the regime as a whole. I analyze child support policy in light of the purposes it serves, fails to serve, or ought to serve. The next chapter discusses the child support systems in Maryland and Texas. Some of the details outlined there illustrate and highlight the themes of this chapter. Chapter 4 will provide more information about child support policy at 'street level', in the lives of individual citizens.

Notes

1. Phillips (1991, ch. 2) notes that among the first changes enacted by some of the colonies once they became independent from England were provisions for divorce.

2. Generally only fathers had a duty to support their children (both those who lived with them and those who did not); it was not until the twentieth century that mothers were also subject to child support obligations.

3. It is also interesting that at least two principles of nineteenth-century family law seem to have grown out of cases brought by third parties, and were the result of the interaction of property and contract law with family law; Lawrence

Friedman suggests that the Married Women's Property Acts emerged this way (1973, 186) and tenBroek, Grossberg, and Schuele note that the duty to support children emerged from third party claimants.

4. Though he is specifically discussing California's system, tenBroek discusses the Elizabethan poor laws, as implemented in the colonies and retained by most of the states in some form, as the source of this dual system. His argument thus has general applicability to U.S. family law.

5. Under the poor law, local governments were responsible for providing for the poor within their jurisdiction.

6. Alimony and child support were often not distinguished from one another.

7. This implicitly values the autonomy of the non-custodial parent over the obligation to support the child, the well-being of the child, and the economic and other burdens imposed on the custodial parent. It is also noteworthy that in Maryland's report on gender bias, the perceptions of judges regarding the adequacy of child support awards were markedly different from the perceptions of family law attorneys (Maryland Judicial Conference 1990).

8. The Progressive Era was marked by some concern over 'deserters' (absent fathers) but did not result in widespread legal enforcement mechanisms, as in the current era; the emphasis was instead on private aid. See Tiffin, 1982, and Brandt and Baldwin, 1972.

9. As this book was going to press, Congress passed, and President Clinton signed legislation that will end the entitlement status of the AFDC program, and limits eligibility for this and other public assistance programs. This legislation was the conclusion of more than two years of efforts on the part of the Clinton administration and both the 103rd and 104th Congress to pass welfare reform legislation.

10. Many states were slow to implement the provision of services to non-AFDC custodians; see chapter 3.

11. It should be noted that there were several efforts to introduce child support prior to 1974, and in 1967, recipients of AFDC were required to assign their child support benefits to the state in which they received benefits. However, the extensive federal enforcement efforts did not begin until the Social Services Amendments of 1974 were enacted.

12. For a more detailed legislative history, see appendix A.

13. See Garfinkel 1992; Roberts 1991; and U.S. Commission on Interstate Child Support 1992, for similar statements of the revolutionary and anomalous aspects of child support enforcement.

14. These are the goals discussed more fully in chapter 1.

15. The National Survey of Children data indicates that there is a correlation between the absent parent's amount of contact with children and payment of support. It seems more likely that this is not a causal relationship between support and involvement, but rather that both involvement and support are the result of some other factor such as greater interest and concern for the child(ren) on the part of the absent parent (see Furstenberg and Cherlin 1991).

16. This is not to say that such links are *not* beneficial; in many cases they may be. The point is simply that such links are *assumed* in these documents to be beneficial in all or almost all cases.

17. For a discussion of the controversy over the child support enforcement program when it was first enacted, see Krause 1981, ch. 7.

18. This is in keeping with the general tendency of contemporary courts to defer to most policy and statutory decisions of legislatures and bureaucracies.

19. Of course, non-AFDC custodial parents may still establish support directly through courts, and many choose to do so.

20. Actually, if the child support benefit level exceeded the AFDC benefit, the custodian should have been permitted to keep the excess, although in most states this would have been counted as income and reduced the AFDC benefit. In practice, however, states did not have very good accounting mechanisms at that time, and federal regulations for distribution were nonexistent or unclear, so the entire support payment, if received, was frequently retained by states (Roberts 1991).

21. This requirement was challenged by AFDC beneficiaries, but was upheld by the Supreme Court. See *Bowen v. Gilliard*, 107 S.Ct. 3008 (1987).

22. The $50 is called a "pass through" because it is not counted as income, and is not paid except for the current month i.e. if all child support for a year is paid at one time (in one month), the custodial parent would only receive $50.

23. Arrears may also be collected in cases for which there is no current child support obligation because the children are no longer minors.

24. Guidelines will be discussed further in chapter 3.

25. Irwin Garfinkel and colleagues have attempted to measure the effects of child support on child well-being in a variety of ways and find that there are a number of positive effects (Garfinkel et al. 1994, 240–346).

26. A case would include all children who have the same two biological or legal parents. In cases where the custodian has two children with two different partners, separate cases are filed. Similarly, when a non-custodial parent has children by different custodians, separate cases would be filed. Cases are therefore not necessarily synonymous with custodian-child residential units.

27. There is a great deal of detailed information in the annual reports. The information offered here is not intended to be comprehensive, but to give the reader a general sense of the size and scope of the program. For more detailed information the reader is referred to the reports themselves.

28. The Census Bureau data is most often cited in press reports on child support.

29. This finding may be due to the fact that the Census Bureau data includes parties who do not utilize the services of child support agencies, while expenditures calculated were from OCSE data.

30. Originally, a child support assurance program was to have been implemented in Wisconsin. However, it has yet to be fully implemented. See Garfinkel et al. 1992.

31. There are a number of different designs for such a system, including the

Child Assistance Program (CAP) implemented in several counties in New York, the Wisconsin proposal, outlined in Garfinkel (1992), and the proposed system in the Downey-Hyde Child Support Assurance Act of 1992. (This latter bill died in committee, and is not likely to win passage in the near future).

3

Child Support in the States: Maryland and Texas

As has been outlined in chapter 2, contemporary child support policy is implemented through a federally-mandated and state-administered program, as is the case with many social welfare functions in the United States. There is some variation among the states in terms of administrative structure, and a great deal of variation among the states with respect to the effectiveness of their child support programs (Ebb 1994; Subcommittee on Human Resources 1991). To some extent, then, national summary data can be misleading, since it masks some of the detail of program implementation as well as the differences among state programs.

Further, one needs to see a program implemented to know how the multiple goals are prioritized. To understand which of the goals discussed in chapter 2 take priority in practice, it will be useful to see how states implement child support policy and the criteria by which their success is measured.

One way to examine how child support operates in practice is to conduct a comparative case study of state programs with differing administrative structures. This study examines two state programs, those of Maryland and Texas. These two states were chosen partly because they are quite different in terms of demographic characteristics as well in size and political culture. They also have contrasting child support programs: as will be discussed below, the programs are located in different administrative agencies and have contrasting structures in terms of the centralization of their child support programs.

The study of each state involved the use of public documents as well as the collection of original data through interviews with administrators. Documents included legislation related to child support, such as legisla-

57

tive reports and special committee reports; state and federal administrative documents; and other public documents regarding the child support program in each state. The study also included interviews with selected administrators in the state and local child support offices.[1] What follows is a discussion of each state's child support program, with attention to the questions raised in the first two chapters regarding the nature and purposes of this public policy.

The history and structure of the child support program in both states illustrate several of the themes of chapter 2. First, both state systems have been engaged in a gradual and as yet incomplete transition from judicially-centered case processing to administratively-centered handling of cases. This transition has not been without difficulty and controversy, as is illustrated in this chapter. The implementation of child support policy requires the cooperation of the judicial branch with child support agencies. In Texas this is facilitated by the location of child support services in the Office of the Attorney General. In Maryland, proactive statewide coordination of this cooperative effort has only occurred fairly recently. Nevertheless, in both states, a move toward administratively-centered child support law, while incomplete, has occurred. Second, the question of which of the multiple goals of child support should take priority has been a live issue at some point in both states. The primary question is whether child support law is and should be focused only on cost recovery, or should also focus on child well-being, parental responsibility, and service provision as an aspect of social welfare policy. The history of attempts by the Maryland legislature to limit access to the system and to charge fees for services to non-AFDC custodial parents partly illustrates this question. In Texas, the change in the administrative structure and location of the program in the early 1980s from the (then) Department of Public Welfare to the Office of the Attorney General evidences a change in focus from social welfare goals to cost savings. The philosophical orientation toward child support policy of the child support administrators interviewed also illuminates this issue.

Third, the history of social welfare policy in the United States in general demonstrates that, in federal-state cooperative programs, states are often slow to respond to new federal mandates and laws. This has been true of child support policy. Both states have had a variety of compliance difficulties. In Texas, child support performance was very poor prior to the centralization of the program under the Office of the Attorney General. Organizational difficulties have also caused some problems, especially an administrative reorganization in the early 1990s that separated legal functions from enforcement functions. Some of Maryland's problems in complying with federal law have reflected philosophical objections on the part of some legislators to the federalization and bureaucratization of child support law. The history of guidelines adoption in Maryland, in particular, illustrates some of the difficulties in the transition to a federally-mandated, state-implemented administrative system. Maryland was the last state to comply with federal requirements for guidelines adoption, in part due to the resistance of some legislators to accept federal mandates in the arena of family law.

The discussion that follows is in four parts. First, the transition from judicial to administrative processes is addressed by examining the institutional structure of child support agencies in each state. This includes an overview of the administrative structure of each child support system. Second, some of the implementation difficulties of each state are discussed: for Maryland, adoption and implementation of child support guidelines were controversial; in Texas, organizational difficulties, initial poor collections performance, and the politicization that comes with serving under an elected official have all affected the program. Third, interviews with child support administrators in both states provide the basis for a discussion of the conflicts between social welfare policy and cost savings in child support policy. Finally, the performance, in terms of collections and case processing, of these two child support systems are discussed.

Toward Administrative Ordering

Administrative Structure of Child Support in Maryland and Texas

The Social Services Amendments of 1974 require that each state establish a separate administrative unit to implement the child support program. However, states and territories may adopt either local or state administration and design their own administrative structure.[2] Forty-three states have opted to establish a state unit with local subsidiaries (OCSE 1993b). Nine states, however, have chosen to permit local administration, supervised by the state child support agency, and two states have a combination of county- and state-administered programs (ibid.). Further, since child support involves a number of functions appropriate to several different types of state agencies, states have opted to locate their child support programs in several different types of agencies. Most are located in the state social services agency, as in Maryland, but some are located in the state attorney general's office, as in Texas. A few states have recently moved their child support agency to the revenue or taxation department, seeing child support as primarily a process of collection and distribution of revenue.[3]

Maryland

The initial child support agency in Maryland was the Bureau of Support Enforcement, created in 1976 as a unit of the state Social Services Administration. In 1980, the support enforcement agency was renamed the Office of Child Support Enforcement and transferred to the Income Maintenance Administration. In 1984, the title was changed to the Child Support Enforcement Administration, and it became a separate administrative unit within the Department of Human Resources. Although Maryland is technically a centrally- (state-) administered program, in practice Maryland has administrative structures that vary by county. The child support agency in some counties operates out of the Department of Social Services office, in other counties this office is a subdivision of the circuit court,[4] and some of the smaller counties provide services through the Department of Social Services and contract with the state to provide legal services. In one of the more populous counties, the head of the county agency is directly supervised by the state office; in the other counties, the work of the agency is supervised by the state office, but the chief administrator reports to a local official within the county's executive office or within the court system.

Maryland consists of twenty-four jurisdictions: twenty-three counties and Baltimore City. Of these there are five large jurisdictions, together comprising 80 percent of the child support caseload in Maryland (Maryland CSEA 1992a). In these five large jurisdictions, three child support units operate out of the circuit court with slightly different administrative structures (Anne Arundel, Montgomery, and Baltimore County). The Baltimore City program originally operated out of the Department of Social Services, but since 1991 has had a consolidated office that coordinates all child support functions. The final jurisdiction, Prince George's County, has an executive-level agency that supervises all child support functions.

The smaller counties have one of two systems. In all of the smaller counties, child support services are provided by a division of the county Department of Social Services. Legal representation is provided in most counties by the State's Attorney's Office, under contract with the state Child Support Enforcement Administration. In two counties, the county office of the State's Attorney has elected not to provide these services;

here, the Maryland State Attorney General's office appoints special counsel to provide legal representation.

As this description makes clear, there is less uniformity between counties than one might expect in a state-administered system. This may have some advantages, including possibilities for innovative programs based on local circumstances. However, lack of uniformity also has some disadvantages: the difficulties for Maryland's child support agencies include problems in passing federal audits because of a lack of a statewide data bank of cases, and the failure of some localities to comply with federal requirements (Office of Child Support Enforcement 1992d).

Further, some jurisdictions, such as Baltimore City and Prince George's County, have organized or reorganized their child support systems in response to the new demands created by federal mandates. These administrative structures reflect a recognition of the ongoing administrative-judicial cooperation required by child support policy. In Prince George's County, court functions that have to do with child support, as well as social services functions that are child support related, fall under the same administrative umbrella. In Baltimore City and Montgomery County, consolidation has permitted administrative supervision of most court functions, since child support legal counsel are supervised by the child support agency. Other jurisdictions, such as Anne Arundel County, have retained the basic administrative structure that existed prior to 1974. In Anne Arundel County in particular, this reflects the retention of a more court-centered approach to child support policy. The transition to administrative case processing has thus been gradual and somewhat uneven. Nonetheless, regardless of administrative structure, the same services must be provided and federal mandates must be met.

For applicants who receive the services of child support agencies in Maryland, the process of receiving child support is very different than it would have been prior to the presence of child support agencies. Custodial parents apply to their local child support agency, either as part of their application for AFDC in the county social services office or, as a non-AFDC recipient seeking child support services, directly to the child support agency. Depending upon the particular county, the case may be handled entirely by consent. This means that both parties meet with a representative of the child support agency, agree to paternity (if necessary), utilize the guidelines to calculate the child support award amount, agree to this payment, and provide employment information to the support agency. Although these cases are signed by a judge, the parties never actually appear before the court. Legal representation before the court is provided on behalf of the child by the child support agency. Of course, any party can request a hearing before a judge or master if they do not agree with any aspect of the administrative procedure. Nevertheless, this process is decidedly different than child support proceedings prior to the establishment of child support agencies, which would have required the interested parties to deal directly with the court.

Of course, some custodial parents do not utilize the services of child support agencies, but have their cases processed directly through the court. Although it is difficult to estimate how many cases are processed in this way, the head of the Maryland child support office estimated that about half of all cases statewide are handled by child support agencies. In some counties with relatively efficient child support programs, such as Montgomery and Prince George's counties, the administrators estimated that close to 80 percent of all cases were handled through their agencies. Thus, in less than twenty years, a decentralized, court-centered system—with little in the way of enforcement mechanisms—has been transformed into a more administratively-centered system. This could not have occurred without some degree of cooperation on the part of courts.

Judicial-Administrative Cooperation in Maryland

Federal child support law and policy make the child support agency responsible for the implementation and effectiveness of the state child support program. The federal Office of Child Support Enforcement requires states to meet certain performance mandates, and program funding incentives are tied to that performance. For child support agencies to meet federal mandates, however, coordination and cooperation is required between courts and child support bureaucracies.

To encourage cooperation between courts and child support agencies, in 1991 the federal Office of Child Support Enforcement urged the Conferences of Chief Justices of each state judiciary to adopt a resolution emphasizing the need for greater coordination between state child support agencies and the judiciary. As a result, the Maryland Judicial Conference established a special Committee on Child Support Enforcement, which convened in January of 1992. This committee was charged with conducting a comprehensive review of paternity establishment and child support enforcement practices in Maryland courts and providing a report to the Judicial Conference.

The committee conducted a survey of all circuit courts with respect to their practices in various aspects of paternity and child support cases. This survey found rather diverse practices among courts, especially with respect to practices in paternity establishment cases (Maryland Judicial

Conference 1993, 11). Among the recommendations of the committee was to make practices more uniform throughout the state.

The committee also called for greater coordination between courts and child support agencies. The committee urged the circuit courts to coordinate with child support agencies and develop procedures with respect to the division of labor on all aspects of paternity establishment and child support enforcement (Maryland Judicial Conference 1993, 39). Also, as a means to facilitate statewide coordination between the judiciary and child support agencies, officials from the Maryland Child Support Enforcement Administration are regularly invited to attend meetings of the Committee on Child Support Enforcement. This committee, upon its recommendation to the Judicial Conference, is now a standing committee of the Conference.

Finally, at the request of the Maryland Child Support Enforcement Administration, the committee also considered and recommended the adoption of administrative processes in lieu of court-centered processes. With administrative processes, most aspects of child support would be handled though the child support agency staff; hearings, when necessary, would be conducted by administrative law judges. This would apply to both paternity and child support cases, and would make available the establishment of paternity by default. Modifications of child support orders would also be handled through administrative processes. The committee's report notes that a number of states have adopted administrative processes and seem to have higher rates of collection (Maryland Judicial Conference 1993, 43).[5] In addition, the committee argued that the adoption of administrative processes would likely be more cost-effective and provide for the more effective use of time by both courts and child support agencies. Thus, administrative process would streamline procedures and case processing, consolidate child support functions under the management of one agency, and reduce court dockets and expenditures (Maryland Judicial Conference 1993, 47–48).

The head of the Maryland Child Support Enforcement Administration stated that one of the biggest problems her agency faced was the extent to which the system in Maryland remains a court-centered (as opposed to administratively-centered) system. She stated that this was true despite the fact that the relationship between the agency and the judiciary was amicable. Thus, although some counties are in effect using administrative processes (such as establishing paternity and support awards by consent so that the parties themselves never go before a judge or master) all actions must be approved by the courts. The adoption of administrative process would make it possible to complete all aspects of a child support case without review by the circuit courts. Indeed, the state child support administration has been making efforts to move toward administrative processes, encouraging both the judicial branch and the legislature to consider adopting such procedures. The Judicial Conference report outlined above seems to constitute judicial branch support for a more administratively-centered child support system in Maryland. At the time of this study, however, the Maryland legislature had not approved any such changes beyond those mandated by federal law.

All county administrators interviewed reported an amicable relationship with the judiciary. Depending upon the administrative structure, however, there were different degrees of coordination between the child support agency and the court. Most counties have a particular judge or judges who handle child support cases; many have a Master of Domestic Relations who hears most cases. Only in Baltimore County was this not true; here, the fifteen circuit court judges rotate. Often, however, in counties where one judge was designated to hear domestic relations cases, the judge was the most junior: domestic relations are considered the least desirable assignment, despite the fact that domestic relations cases are a very large proportion of all circuit court cases. Some administrators noted that this was problematic, especially because judges may not have particular knowledge of, or interest in, domestic relations law. The Committee on Child Support Enforcement recognized this problem and the need for more judicial training on child support law in its report, and recommended the development of a training program by the Judicial Institute (Maryland Judicial Conference, 1993, 49).

Requirements for administrative-judicial cooperation in case processing have led both counties and the state to adopt formal mechanisms intended to facilitate cooperation between child support agencies and courts. Such coordination has not yet resulted in uniform practices among different counties. However, the transition to an administrative system is not complete, nor has it always been smooth, as will be clear in the discussion of child support guidelines in Maryland.

Texas

In Texas, child support was initially located as a division of the state's Department of Public Welfare. The Department contracted with each county to provide child support services (Texas House/Senate Joint Interim Committee on Child Support 1988, 4–5). In 1973 the Texas Legislature passed S.B. 709, which required the Department of Public Welfare to attempt to collect child support on behalf of applicants for AFDC.[6]

Legislation passed in 1975 established the Department of Public Welfare as the child support agency as required by the federal Social Services Amendments of 1974. Some counties also established child support divisions through their District or Domestic Relations Court. The Department of Public Welfare (DPW) utilized county-based administration, as was true of their other programs. Thus, the structure of the child support program under DPW (later changed to the Department of Human Resources) was very decentralized, with a great deal of local variation. In a state as large as Texas, with 254 counties, this made for an administratively complex child support system.

In 1983 in practice, and in 1985 by statute, child support was moved to a newly created Child Support Division in the Office of the Attorney General. Texas has a plural executive branch, with separate elections for the top executive offices, including the Office of the Attorney General. The Child Support Division is the largest division in the Office of the Attorney General. As such, child support enforcement has become a much more visible part of state government. Jim Mattox, the attorney general from 1983-1991, made child support enforcement a high priority, and enforcement efforts as well as results were improved under the new administrative structure (Texas Office of the Attorney General 1986, 1991). This improvement in collections has continued under the current attorney general, Dan Morales.[7]

The current administrative structure of the Child Support Division consists of central administrative offices located in Austin, eight regional offices throughout the state, and field offices which actually handle child support cases. The jurisdiction of a field office may consist of one or more counties, depending upon the population. However, child support is now entirely a state-based function, and all child support workers are state employees. The regional offices are supervised by an area manager, who may or may not be an attorney, assisted by a special counsel. Field offices are supervised by a managing attorney, with office managers who handle most of the administrative aspects of the child support program. Line authority flows from the Child Support Division Director through the Director of Field Operations to the area managers, and then to the managing attorneys (Texas Office of the State Auditor 1995, 43–45). Child support in Texas is administered through a truly statewide agency, with no county-based child support offices.

Texas also has a child support master program, and in many counties cases are heard by Title IV-D child support masters instead of by judges. Although funding is channeled through the Child Support Division, the masters are under the supervision of the State Office of Court Administration through a contractual relationship with the attorney general's office. Not all county courts have opted to utilize masters, although counties that do not meet performance standards are required to participate in the child support master program. Although still a judicially-based procedure, the use of masters generally provides for more timely case processing. In addition, in 1995 the Texas Legislature passed S.B. 793, which permits the use of administrative processes for more aspects of child support such as modifications, paternity establishment, and payments for retroactive support. Thus, these functions may now be handled entirely by the Child Support Division without any involvement on the part of courts.

Administrators from the Child Support Division generally indicated that their relationships with the judicial branch were quite cooperative. Several administrators, including some who had worked in child support when it was part of the Department of Public Welfare, noted that the placement of child support functions in the Office of the Attorney General provides for greater legitimacy in the relationship with the judicial branch, as well as in the eyes of the general public and of child support obligors. Being part of the office of the state's chief legal officer gave child support more "credibility," "authority," and "clout," in the words of these administrators. It also helped to provide a better ongoing relationship with the state legislature, since the attorney general's office has regular dealings with the legislature.

Several administrators noted that child support was simply one small division when it was located in the Department of Public Welfare. In addition to being much less visible than it now is, many administrators in the Department had disagreed with the fundamental purposes of child support enforcement, seeing it as contradictory to the role of providing assistance to needy families. It did not receive as much administrative support in the Department of Public Welfare as it now does in the Office of the Attorney General. Further, the move to the Office of the Attorney General facilitated a move to a more centralized administrative structure rather than a county-based program. In addition, as of 1989, the Texas Legislature permitted the Child Support Division to retain and reinvest the state income received from support enforcement, giving the Division more resources with which to operate.

Texas and Maryland represent two different ways of structuring a state child support system. Although both are technically state-operated programs, Texas has a more centralized administrative structure than does Maryland. In addition, Maryland's program, like most states, is located in a human services or social welfare department; Texas, like three other states, operates its program out of the Office of the Attorney General.

The two states offer two different models of how child support policy might be implemented.

Implementing Child Support Policy

Many public policies work differently in practice than intended or imagined by those who formulate the policy initiative. This is especially true of programs that require the cooperation of multiple levels and/or different branches of government. Thus, it might be expected that in child support policy, which requires coordination among federal, state, and local governments and between administrative agencies and courts, multiple implementation difficulties would occur. The following section examines some of the administrative and implementation difficulties that Maryland and Texas have had in putting in place a child support program that meets federal requirements.

Child Support Guidelines in Maryland

Perhaps the most direct means by which judicial decision-making has been curtailed with administrative processes and federal mandates is in the use of child support guidelines. As noted in chapter 2, the amount of child support awarded to a custodial parent was determined by judicial discretion until federal laws were passed that required states to adopt child support guidelines.

Child support guidelines provide a formula for determining the support award amount. Each state has adopted its own formula for establishing support awards; the most common types are the percentage-of-income model and the income-shares model. The percentage-of-income model calculates the support award based upon a percentage of the non-custodial parent's gross or net income. The percentage varies depending upon the number of children involved. The income-shares model is generally based on both parents' incomes, and requires that each parent contribute to the child's support based upon their share of the total income of both parents. Some states also consider expenditures in their formula, such as health care and child care. Texas utilizes the percentage-of-income model; Maryland uses an income-shares model.

Federal law required states to adopt advisory, and then mandatory, child support guidelines.[8] In some states, guidelines were already in use; in others, the adoption of guidelines was highly controversial and politicized. Although states have adopted different approaches to guidelines, all are in one way or another based upon economic studies regarding the estimated actual costs of raising children (Barnow et al. 1990), which adds an element of objectivity to the support award process.[9]

Establishing Guidelines

Maryland was the last state to establish both advisory guidelines, which were required by the Child Support Enforcement Amendments of 1984, and mandatory guidelines, required by the Family Support Act of 1988. By the time advisory guidelines were passed by the Maryland legislature in the 1989 session, the Family Support Act of 1988 had been passed by Congress, requiring that guidelines be mandatory as a rebuttable presumption by October 1, 1989. Although the legislature was advised of this requirement, they did not make the guidelines passed in 1989 mandatory. In the 1990 legislative session, emergency legislation was passed which made the guidelines mandatory, finally bringing Maryland into compliance with the federal law.

These delays were not, however, due to lack of effort on the part of the governor or the state child support agency. In compliance with the Child Support Enforcement Amendments of 1984, the governor appointed a commission to study the state's child support system; among their tasks were to study the guidelines question and provide recommendations. By late 1986, the Child Support Enforcement Advisory Council had developed a set of guidelines, based on the Melson (Delaware) formula. The council recommended to the Rules Committee of the Court of Appeals that these guidelines be adopted. However, the Rules Committee decided that guidelines were a matter more appropriately addressed by the legislature, since the guidelines were, in their view, more substantive than procedural. The Maryland Child Support Enforcement Administration requested legislation enacting the guidelines in the 1987 session (Maryland Senate Bill 706), but this legislation failed in the House Judiciary Committee. In order to comply with the federal law, the Child Support Enforcement Administration then notified the Maryland Senate's president of its intent to promulgate the guidelines for use by judges and masters as advisory guidelines. The Senate requested that they not do that, since guidelines would be taken up again in the 1988 session.

Although several guidelines bills were introduced in the 1988 session, the Maryland House and Senate could not agree on a guidelines bill and none passed. As a consequence, the federal Office of Child Support Enforcement disapproved the Maryland child support plan in 1988 for failure to comply with the guidelines law. Under threat of loss of its federal grant, the Maryland legislature finally passed a guidelines law in the 1989 session.

The guidelines that were passed in the 1989 session of the legislature, and made mandatory in the 1990 session, were very different from the advisory guidelines that had been proposed by the Child Support Enforcement Advisory Council. The Maryland guidelines are based on the income-shares model, which calculates child support based on the monthly gross incomes (before taxes) of both parents. Each parent is permitted deductions for health insurance payments for dependent children, and the non-custodial parent is permitted deductions for pre-existing child support awards that are currently being paid. After these deductions, the two incomes are added. The law provides a basic child support payment schedule amount based on this combined income figure. Any additional expenses, such as monthly child care or expenses for children with special needs, are added to this monthly child support amount. The total is the monthly child support amount. The non-custodial parent then pays the proportion of the total child support amount based on his or her proportion of the total earnings of the two legal parents. As required by federal law, the guidelines are a rebuttable presumption, meaning that any change from the child support obligation established by applying the guidelines formula must be justified in writing by the judge or master.[10]

Court Interpretations of Child Support Guidelines

The passage of guidelines raised a number of questions with respect to their implementation, especially regarding the modification of existing child support awards. As a result, several cases involving custodial and non-custodial parents with disputes over the transition to the use of guidelines, and the application of guidelines have come before Maryland courts. Court interpretations of guidelines cases illustrate the courts' acceptance of guidelines as an administrative, relatively fixed rule. However, courts in Maryland have also clearly retained their prerogative to interpret and deviate from the guidelines, and the transition to the use of guidelines raised some special questions.

Two cases in particular dealt with the application of guidelines to particular cases. *Voishan v. Palma* [327 Md. 318 (1992)] raised the question of the application of guidelines in cases where the income was above the amounts specified in the Maryland law.[11] In this case, a judge, applying the guidelines in a case where the combined income was higher than the highest amount indicated in the guidelines ($10,000 per month), increased the child support award for one child from $700 to $1550 per month. The combined income of the two parents in this case was $175,000, and the non-custodial father earned 83 percent of the combined earnings. The father appealed, arguing that the legislature had intended that the child support amount to be awarded for earnings above $10,000 per month be the same as if the earnings were $10,000 per month; in other words, he argued that the maximum amount in the guidelines was a cap on child support awards. The Court of Appeals ruled that this was not the case, and that the judge had carefully applied the logic of the guidelines to the higher amount.

Shrivastava v. Mates [93 Md. App. 320 (1992)] raised the question of the application of guidelines when such application is in conflict with a pre-existing agreement between the parties. The parties in this case were divorced in 1983. The child support was determined as part of a separation agreement, and included specific provisions for alteration of the child support amount. In 1990, the custodial mother requested a change in child support, based on the guidelines, which, when applied to this case, would increase the award by more than 100 percent. In February 1991, the master who heard the case recommended an increase in child support, utilizing the guidelines with adjustments for health care and educational support provided in the original agreement. Both parties appealed, and the circuit court held that the existence of the agreement was "a sufficient reason for deviation from the child support guidelines" (Shrivastava v. Mates [93 Md. App. 320 (1992)], 330). Upon appeal, the court of special appeals ruled that the circuit court in so ruling had improperly "elevated the parties' contractual expectation over the best interests of the children" (ibid.). The court of special appeals also noted that the circuit court had not considered the best interests of the children, nor had it made "the necessary findings accompanying its departure from the guidelines." Therefore, the guidelines were determined to be presumptively binding (as stated in the legislation), and the necessity for written justification for any deviation was affirmed. The decision also discussed the factors to be considered in making any such deviation.

The father also attempted to argue that because the agreement had been entered into prior to the adoption of guidelines, the application of the guidelines in this case would constitute a violation of the contract clause of the U.S. Constitution (Article I, Section 10). The court rejected this argument, noting that the guidelines serve a legitimate state purpose, and that a negotiated amount of child support, even prior to the adoption of the guidelines, was not considered binding on court determinations—a court was always bound to consider the best interest of the child (Shrivastava v. Mates [93 Md. App. 320 (1992)], 332). Here, the Court was following previous federal court decisions that interpreted the guidelines as serving a legitimate state purpose.

Two cases in particular dealt with the transition to the use of guidelines. *Walsh v. Walsh* (1993 Md. App., decided 4/8/93) raised the question of modifications in cases in which support was awarded after the guidelines took effect, but in which the guidelines were not followed in determining the support award. The parties to this case were divorced as of May 24, 1990; joint custody was awarded although the two children were to remain primarily in the physical custody of their mother, who was awarded child support. Maryland's child support guidelines became mandatory effective April 10, 1990, but the guidelines were not followed in this case; rather, the child support amount was arrived at by agreement of the parties.[12] In 1991, the children's mother filed for a change in the child support award based upon a material change in circumstances. She argued that the law specifies that adoption of the guidelines is considered a material change in circumstances if the support award would change by at least 25 percent if the guidelines were applied, and that in this case the award would be nearly doubled. The circuit court ruled, and the court of special appeals affirmed, that in this case, since they were already in effect when the divorce order was entered, the guidelines did not constitute a material change in circumstances. Thus, the guidelines could only be considered a material change in circumstances for cases entered prior to the adoption of the guidelines. The court also specifically set aside the question of whether this ruling applied to orders entered during the year the guidelines were advisory and not mandatory.

In *Gates v. Gates* [83 Md.App. 661 (1990)], a mother filed for increased child support, and the circuit court increased the award from $300 to $600 per month. The reasoning was that $600 was the amount that would be awarded based upon the child support guidelines, which were advisory but not mandatory at the time of the hearing. The father appealed, and here the court of special appeals held that the guidelines could not be the sole basis for an alteration in a child support award. The circuit court judge had stated, in making his decision to increase the award, that the $300 award was reasonable, and that the guidelines were the only reason that the award was altered. This was crucial to the decision by the court of special appeals to overturn the decision. The special appeals court decision noted that the law states that the guidelines are by themselves not the basis for alteration of a child support award.[13] The decision of the circuit court was thus reversed and remanded.

Thus, in terms of the transition to the use of guidelines, Maryland courts have held that the guidelines by themselves do not constitute a basis for modification of a child support award amount.[14] However, guidelines have been held to serve a legitimate state purpose, and to be the presumptive basis for all support awards. Further, guidelines trump private contractual agreements with respect to support award amounts. Courts have clearly upheld the legitimacy of guidelines, and, as noted below, judges in all jurisdictions report that they utilize the guidelines in most cases for determining the support award amount. Here, then, state purposes related to securing adequate financial support for children and recovering state expenditures on AFDC justify the valuing of public purposes over private agreements, and courts have interpreted child support law with respect to guidelines in this way. Thus, as is true nationally, Maryland courts have upheld the legitimacy of guidelines, although their application to cases settled prior to the implementation of guidelines has been somewhat limited (Fader 1990). Maryland courts have accepted guidelines as a legitimate form of public ordering.[15]

Evaluation of the Guidelines

The federal law requires periodic review of the guidelines by the child support agency and legislature. In compliance with this requirement, the Maryland CSEA prepared a report to the General Assembly on child support guidelines in the fall of 1992. The CSEA wanted the review to be as positive and uncontroversial as possible.[16] Therefore, rather than gathering data from case samples, the information collected for this report was obtained by a survey of local administrators conducted by the state office. An administrator from the state office asked respondents—usually the director of each local agency—several questions: whether or not the guidelines were being utilized, the number or percentage of cases in which there were deviations from the guidelines, reasons for deviation, the percentage of cases for each reason, and what issues with respect to the guidelines should be addressed in the report to the legislature. Since administrators do not regularly collect data on whether the guidelines are followed or the reasons for deviation, they were told that they could provide an estimate rather than actual data.

All jurisdictions reported that they were using the guidelines, although the estimated percentage of cases in which jurisdictions deviated from the guidelines ranged from 60–70 percent in Anne Arundel County to 5 percent in Howard County. Based upon these reports, the state administrative office then calculated a statewide average of 17 percent of total cases in which there was a deviation from the guidelines.[17]

In this self-study, the reason most frequently cited by administrators for deviations from the guidelines amount was the non-custodial parent's second family. Other reasons were also cited, such as in-kind contributions or agreement of the parties in non-AFDC cases. Judges and masters also used a rather wide variety of means for taking account of the second intact family.[18] Several counties, in responding to the questionnaire, felt that the second family question should be addressed by the legislature. A number also commented, however, that the guidelines were excellent in terms of reducing conflict between parents and providing greater objectivity and fairness. This experience was confirmed in my interviews with administrators; one termed the guidelines "a godsend," and most indicated that their jobs had been made much easier with the adoption of guidelines.

According to the survey of local courts conducted by the Maryland Child Support Committee of the Judicial Conference, judges' views of the guidelines, though generally favorable, are slightly different than the views of administrators. All twenty-two responding jurisdictions reported using the guidelines and most reported that they did establish orders that deviated from the guidelines, albeit infrequently (Maryland Judicial Conference 1993, Appendix A, 6). Most also agreed that the guidelines generally result in a fair support award (ibid., 8); the two dissenters stated that awards were too high, especially for low-income noncustodial parents. However, most judges agreed that the guidelines needed improvement; the most frequently cited desired improvement was the need for specific guidance on how to handle second families when calculating the support award (ibid., 8).

Application of guidelines in Maryland seems to result in higher awards. Table 3.1 presents information on the average monthly support award in 1989, prior to the existence of mandatory guidelines, as compared to later years.

In general, child support guidelines add predictability and legitimacy

TABLE 3.1
Average Monthly Support Award, Maryland

	FY89	FY92	FY93
AFDC	$101	$150	$157
Non-AFDC	$212	$225	$211
Total	$140	$178	$178

Source: Maryland CSEA, 1994, and data supplied by the Maryland Child Support Enforcement Administration.

to the process of determining child support awards. They also constitute a fixed rule, and are another step toward administrative ordering in child support law. The Maryland child support guidelines took some time to adopt, but they seem to be having the desired effect of providing a uniform, standard amount of child support for persons of similar income in the state of Maryland, and of increasing child support award amounts.

Administrative Structure of Child Support in Texas

In Texas, unlike in Maryland, the adoption of child support guidelines was not marked by controversy. Texas adopted advisory guidelines through a court rule in 1987, based on the percentage-of-income model. In response to the requirement for mandatory guidelines in the Family Support Act of 1988, the Texas Legislature adopted guidelines in 1989, again based on the percentage-of-income model. In 1993, Texas revised its guidelines by adding a multiple family formula to the calculation—if a non-custodial parent has other children that he or she is supporting, the child support obligation is reduced.

When the attorney general's office originally took over child support services, the county-based administrative structure was retained. In 1991, the Child Support Division was reorganized into two separate divisions, one for litigation and one for enforcement (Texas Office of the State Auditor 1992, 2). The goal of this reorganization was to separate the legal aspects of child support from the administrative functions. One of the concerns that motivated this reorganization was that attorneys were often supervised by child support officers who were not attorneys, and, it was felt, did not sufficiently understand the legal aspects of child support. A related goal was "improving the image of the program with the court system" (ibid., 12).

Unfortunately, this reorganization effort did not work very well. First, having separate divisions whose heads reported to different deputy attorneys general created a series of coordination problems. To successfully work any given case, the two divisions would have to coordinate efforts; however, the lines of authority between the divisions were not entirely clear. The management audit conducted in 1992 suggested that more extensive coordination and joint planning on the part of the two divisions was needed (Texas Office of the State Auditor 1992, 12–15). Although the Child Support Division did try to further coordinate the activities of the two divisions, the Child Support Division recognized in 1994 that coordination would not be possible without reorganization. Thus, the division again combined the two functions, creating a single line of authority.

Under the present structure, the regional offices have area managers who need not necessarily be attorneys, and who are assisted by a special counsel on legal matters. The fifty-nine field offices are supervised by a managing attorney who reports to the area managers, and by an office manager who works under the supervision of the managing attorney. Office managers are responsible for most of the administrative management, although this varies among local offices. The managing attorneys carry caseloads, so they do a good deal of field work as well as managing the operations of the office.

Although these reorganization efforts created personnel and morale problems in the state office, most of the administrators interviewed indicated that the field offices were less affected. Since the field offices are where the actual work takes place, many administrators felt that the harm caused by the 1991 split was minimized. However, everyone interviewed who had been with the Child Support Division since 1991 indicated that the 1994 reorganization had greatly improved the agency's functioning. One of the field office administrators indicated that what happened in the central offices in Austin had little effect on local offices; despite the reorganizations, the actual work of processing cases had continued uninterrupted.

Another unique feature of Texas' child support program is the fact that the Child Support Division is part of the office of an elected official. In interviews with administrators, I asked about the advantages and disadvantages of being part of the Office of the Attorney General (OAG).

As noted above, most administrators indicated that being part of the attorney general's office was much more desirable than being part of the Department of Human Resources. Reasons cited for this were both that child support was more visible and had more clout in the OAG, and that the mission of the child support program was not in keeping with the social services functions of the Department of Human Resources.

However, many administrators also noted some disadvantages to their position in the attorney general's office. First, sometimes visibility can be a problem, especially if the public has a negative perception of the attorney general.[19] Also, it is possible for the program itself to become politicized or be used for political reasons. Some administrators noted that the agency is sometimes subject to criticism for what they see as political reasons that have nothing to do with child support. One aspect of this problem that administrators cited is that by definition, because of the type of services provided, someone is always going to be unhappy with the division's performance. When citizens complain to their legislators, the Child Support Division gets a lot of political pressure, especially during the legislative session. While this would be true even if the attorney general were not elected, some administrators expressed concern that the politicization of the Child Support Division was not likely to improve child support services.

Administrators' ideas about what, if anything, could or should be done regarding these disadvantages varied widely. Most administrators felt that the visibility of being in the OAG outweighed the disadvantages. One administrator described the politicization of child support as simply part of Texas politics, stating that it would be the case (even if less so) whether or not child support was under the authority of an elected official. In other words, this administrator felt that public policy implementation in Texas is generally subject to a great deal of political controversy, regardless of the administrative structure of the implementing agency. Another felt that child support should be moved and become a free-standing agency. This administrator thought that the period in the attorney general's office had been useful in terms of raising the stature and visibility of child support, but that the program was now at a point where it would function better as a separate entity. Others were relatively comfortable with the current organizational structure noting, again, that the administrative structure and location of the central office may not directly affect day-to-day field operations.

In Texas, implementation difficulties have included such organizational factors as the administrative location of the child support agency and the organization of functions within the agency. An ongoing difficulty is the role of the child support program within the Office of the Attorney General and in relation to other elected officials.

Both Texas and Maryland have experienced administrative and political difficulties in implementing their respective child support programs. In part this reflects unique political factors within each state. It also may reflect some of the conflicting goals of child support, as the next section discusses.

Cost Savings versus Social Welfare

It was noted in chapter 2 that most social policies have multiple goals, and that child support is no exception. Although having multiple and conflicting goals is not in itself an indictment of a social policy (Marmor, Mashaw, and Harvey 1990), the way that these conflicting goals are resolved, or coexist, as a policy is implemented reveals a great deal about the policy itself. Two goals of child support, in particular, may conflict:

the goal of saving state funds may conflict with the goal of child well-being (depending upon the definition of child well-being). The way that this conflict works out in practice is illustrated through two examples: attempts in Maryland to limit access to child support services, and what child support administrators in both Maryland and Texas say about their work and the goal(s) of their agency.

Maryland: Limiting Access to Child Support Services

The conflicting goals of child support policy are reflected in many aspects of program implementation. In the early 1980s, the Maryland legislature attempted to limit access to the program to low-income recipients, and to charge fees for services to non-AFDC custodial parents. Thus, they were limiting the program to cost savings measures and restricting the social services aspects of child support policy and the goals of child well-being and parental responsibility.

In general, Maryland has repeatedly been slow to implement federal mandates. This is especially true with respect to the adoption of child support guidelines, as discussed above. It has also been true with respect to other aspects of child support law.

Beginning with the Social Services Amendments of 1974, states were required to provide services to all custodial parents who applied, regardless of their status with respect to AFDC. However, this requirement—to provide services to custodians not on AFDC—was a temporary provision, not made permanent by Congress until 1980. The federal mandate was thus not entirely clear, and many states did not comply. To remedy this situation, the Child Support Enforcement Amendments of 1984 specifically stipulated that services were to be provided to all custodians who were eligible, applied, and paid the application fee where required (OCSE 1993b). According to federal law, these services were to be provided regardless of the custodian's income.

The Maryland legislature attempted to limit the number of persons eligible for child support services. In 1981, Chapter 402 provided, among other things, that support enforcement services would be provided to all custodial parents who could not afford a private attorney and whose income was below 50 percent of the median family income in Maryland. Thus, the Maryland legislature attempted to add a means test to a program that federal law specified as a non-means tested service. The legislature's goal was to prevent expansion of the program, thereby limiting state administrative and legal costs.

In response to the clear illegality of this requirement, legislation was passed during the 1983 Maryland legislative session that removed the means test for child support services. Implementation of this change was scheduled for July of 1984. Parents Without Partners, represented by the National Women's Law Center, filed a complaint against the Child Support Enforcement Administration in December of 1983 challenging the 1981 law, which was still in effect. The case was settled by consent decree; the court ruled that the original Maryland statute that provided for a means test was in violation of federal law and ordered that services be provided to all applicants, without regard to income, and required immediate implementation.[20]

The legislature also tried to provide localities with a means to recover administrative costs for collecting child support through fee collection. Chapter 402 of 1981 authorized the collection of fees for services provided to non-AFDC custodial parents. Any fees were to be collected by county child support agencies from the non-custodial parent, and could be retained by the local jurisdiction. Federal law allows the collection of fees either from the custodial parent or the non-custodial parent, but also requires that each state have a statewide plan and provide uniform services throughout the state. Despite the stipulations of state statutes, Maryland's administrative child support plan at the time (required by federal law) specified that there was no application fee, and no fee for services. However, some local jurisdictions charged a fee for services. In most cases the fee was a percentage of the child support payment (3 or 5 percent), and in many cases this fee was deducted from the child support payment itself, effectively making it a fee to the custodial parent. In December of 1983, a class action suit was filed against the state, claiming that the varied practices of local agencies violated both federal and state law. The court found that the state had indeed violated federal law by failing to provide uniform administration of child support services throughout the state, and enjoined the local jurisdictions involved from further fee collection (see *Jenkins vs Massinga*, 592 F.Supp. 480 [1984]).

Thus, it was not until 1984 that Maryland came into compliance with the federal requirement to provide services to all eligible persons, including custodial parents not on AFDC. Maryland was certainly not the only state that was slow to comply with this requirement. Maryland's experience illustrates the implementation difficulties of federal mandates that depend on states to put them into practice, as well as some of the problems faced by state administrative agencies when the state legislature, or some of its members, disagrees with the substance of its mission.

More importantly, however, this process illustrates the conflict between the cost savings functions of child support policy and its social services features. In one sense, if the goals of child support policy were limited to cost savings in the AFDC program, the Maryland legislature was correct: to accomplish this end services should be limited to custodial parents currently receiving AFDC and to low-income custodians likely to require AFDC without an enforced child support order. The discriminatory effects of such a policy, however, are also clear. Limiting services to low-income custodians would make only the non-custodial parents of low-income children subject to the federal-state child support program. Low-income non-custodial parents would therefore be subject to more stringent laws and regulations regarding the support of their children, a practice which would likely be a violation of the equal protection clause of the Fourteenth Amendment. Further, if cost savings were the only goal, then charging what amounts to a user fee for child support services also seems reasonable. The main problem in Maryland was lack of co-ordination among counties, the state child support agency, and the state legislature.

As chapter 2 indicates, however, this policy also serves other public purposes, including promoting child well-being and parental responsibility. Providing services to only one group of custodial parents would not only be discriminatory, it would also contradict state interests in child well-being and parental responsibility, as well as the notion that *all* children need and deserve the economic support of their parents. Further, some non-AFDC custodial parents and their children need the support enforcement services that only child support agencies can effectively provide, especially for locating absent parents. Even though child support agencies were initially intended to recover AFDC expenditures and thus provide cost savings, they also provide social services. Given Maryland's one-time application fee of $20 for non-AFDC custodial parents, these services are a bargain for applicants who would otherwise need to hire their own attorneys. The administrative costs involved in providing these services are absorbed primarily by the federal government, as noted in chapter 2; Maryland, like all states, realizes an annual revenue benefit due to federal incentive payments.

The conflict between cost savings and the provision of social services is evident in many aspects of the child support program. The views of child support administrators in both states also reflect this conflict.

Administrative Philosophies of Child Support Administrators

Although the impetus for the child support program comes from social welfare policy, it is enforced through courts and public bureaucracies, and primarily involves the reallocation of private—-not public—funds. Indeed, the primary goal is to collect and redistribute monies, not to provide specific social services to families subject to child support services. Through interviews with child support administrators in both Maryland and Texas, we learn how practitioners see the mission of child support agencies, and the values and norms promoted by the child support system. Administrators were asked a variety of questions about their work and their agency's mission, as well as questions about the kinds of messages that the child support system sends (or should be sending) to custodial and non-custodial parents.

When asked to state the main purpose of the support enforcement system, all administrators mentioned the establishment and enforcement of child support orders. Beyond this, there were marked differences in the philosophy of administrators, falling into two general categories. Some administrators described their mission in terms of the enforcement of rights and responsibilities and the goal of collecting support; others focused more on providing services.

Several Maryland administrators, and all of the Texas administrators interviewed, fell into the first group, and focused primarily on the establishment and enforcement of child support. Other related duties, such as establishing paternity, were also mentioned. These administrators described the purpose of child support law as a matter of obtaining for children the support to which they are legally entitled. As one administrator put it,

> The main purpose is to provide the services that are available by law to as many people as possible as effectively as possible ... Guaranteeing the rights of children, except with respect to child support, is not part of this purpose. We do not have the legal tools to do this.

Another noted that, whether the goal was to save money for taxpayers or collect support for children, the goal was to collect and distribute funds to the appropriate party. And yet another simply said, "The bottom line is to get the support order."

The Maryland administrators who shared this focus, in various ways, also expressed concern that the system was becoming too involved in social welfare functions. One administrator was quite critical of the federal and state child support system because she felt it was "run by social workers." This administrator felt that local administration through the courts was the best way to run a child support system. This administrator stated that there was a "dichotomy of interest" between what she described as police functions and social service functions. Since she saw child support as primarily a police function, she saw any social service function as detracting from the real mission of the agency. Federal initiatives that have moved the system toward the use of administrative processes and greater uniformity were, according to this administrator, both wrongheaded and a recipe for decreased efficiency and increased waste.

Another administrator stated that the system was changing from being oriented towards cost savings and, instead, becoming more focused on social services. This administrator cited the federal requirements of the addition of services such as medical insurance as part of support orders, and the inclusion of foster care cases in the child support caseload, as evidence that the system was becoming more service oriented. She clearly stated that there was a conflict between "cost-effectiveness" and "social work." She noted that the actual costs of providing support enforcement services were quite high, and that support agencies would never be able to collect the total cost of these services, even if custodial parents were charged fees for services.

A third Maryland administrator stated that the purpose of child support agencies is to secure child support, and thereby to maintain some stability and integrity for children. He stated that children are the real clients of child support agencies, and expressed concern that agencies sometimes end up serving the custodial parent, which he saw as undesirable. Within this description, children are the clients and the only service that the agency provides to children is child support collection. He also criticized the increasing role of federal mandates for taking away the primary goal of increasing the amount of child support collected. He described the federal mandates as being "process-oriented," when what was really needed was an orientation toward results—that is, collections. He also described the state program as taking a "social work approach" to child support, when what was required was to look at the work of child support agencies in business terms.

One Texas administrator specifically noted that "we're not social workers." Several administrators expressed concern about federal mandates and state policies that focused on functions that they saw as social services or social welfare oriented, and dismay that such functions seemed to increasingly be the focus of federal child support policy. All of the Texas administrators focused on fulfilling two functions: doing the legal work necessary to establish a support order (which in many cases includes paternity establishment), and enforcing that order through the collections process. As one stated, "Our goal is to establish and enforce child support orders for children in Texas."

Thus, these administrators clearly differentiated between public policies that focused on the enforcement of the absent parent's legal obligation to support his or her child(ren)—and the recovery of government AFDC expenditures through the enforcement of this obligation—on the one hand, and public policies focused on providing services to help children and their custodial parents on the other. The clear mission of child support, for these administrators, was related to the former set of goals: enforcement of legal obligations and cost recovery.

The other group of administrators described child support in terms of providing for the well-being of children and their custodial parents. They utilized language that focused more on the needs of custodial parents and their dependent children when describing their mission. As one of these administrators described the mission of her agency

> [Aside from] establishing a child support order, and establishing paternity, . . . I also see a service as it relates to the overall process. We try to train our staff to treat each person, each child, and to stay focused on the child's best interest . . . we try to train ourselves to be equipped to go just a little bit further. If there are health care issues, we try to work with them on that, if there are custody issues, we try to work with them on that.

This administrator also noted that clients were referred for other services if this was deemed appropriate. Clearly, this reflects a more service-oriented approach to the work of the agency. In describing the accomplishments of her agency, this administrator attributed improved collections to this approach, which she termed more holistic than focusing simply on enforcement.

Other Maryland administrators interviewed also seemed to focus on the consumers of their services. One described the mission as a way: ". . . to help single parents become or remain financially independent." Another administrator described the mission in terms of encouraging parental responsibility, and helping families with only one parent in the home.

These administrators' view of their agency's mission was thus more focused on the needs of children and their custodial parents. Further, they did not see a divergence of interest between the custodial parent and the child(ren). While they each, in one way or another, acknowledged the centrality of the mission of collecting child support, they emphasized their efforts to go beyond this task by providing other services.

Summary

These differences among administrators' views of their mission seem to illustrate the argument presented earlier regarding the conflict between state interests in cost savings and in the economic independence of family units versus state interests in other aspects of child well-being such as minimum standards of care for children. They also reflect the multiple purposes of child support policy discussed in chapter 2. This sample is a small group of administrators; nevertheless the differences in approach and perception are striking. This conflict seems to reflect the dual goals of cost savings and providing social services that child support policy entails.

Yet in the end, despite these differing administrative *philosophies*, it is clear that the primary *function* of child support agencies—recognized by all administrators interviewed—is to collect and distribute support payments. The "tools" available to child support agencies have to do with this function, and not with providing other sorts of services to separated families—regardless of how worthy that mission is, how much those sorts of services are needed by these families, or of the additional services that support agencies might try to provide when possible. Nevertheless, the goals of child well-being and parental responsibility, and the needs of families affected by child support policy, have pulled some child support agencies in the direction of providing services regardless of the administrative costs.

Performance

We now turn to an examination of program performance—how well has each state accomplished the goals of increased collections, efficiency, and compliance with federal requirements? The formal measures that exist consist of federal and state program audits and actual data on program performance. The audits focus primarily on two aspects of child support administration: results, both in terms of number of cases handled and amount of collections, and case processing, namely the timeliness and effectiveness with which child support agencies handle each case. Federal audits, state audits, and program collections data will each be examined in turn.

Federal Audits

The federal Office of Child Support Enforcement conducts regular audits, generally every two to three years, of each state to monitor state compliance with federal law and guidelines. The audits consist of federal administrators selecting a sample of cases and measuring program performance on a variety of measures, including the timeliness of case processing and the use of all available establishment and enforcement tools. Auditors also conduct interviews with state administrators and examine documents, financial data, and state reports. Programs are measured on their performance in thirteen different service areas. For a successful rating in each service area, the state must have taken action on the required service in at least 75 percent of the cases sampled.

If states are found to be deficient in any of these areas, they can be penalized through a reduction ranging from 1 to 5 percent of their federal AFDC payments. States are given a period after the audit to take corrective action, during which time penalties are held in abeyance. If state corrective action is found to be sufficient in the follow-up audit, penalties are not assessed. According to the most recent OCSE report, the most frequent deficiencies found are in six areas: medical support enforcement, services to non-AFDC families, wage or income withholding, maintenance of records and reports, providing services in interstate cases, and distributing collected support payments (OCSE 1995a, 54).

Maryland

The most recent completed audit by the federal OCSE of Maryland's program that was available at the time of this study found a number of deficiencies in state operations. This audit covered the period from October 1, 1987 to September 30, 1988, and found some deficiencies similar to those that had been found in the previous audit (OCSE 1992d). Case sampling to assess the success of case processing indicated deficiencies in two areas of program services: wage and income withholding and medical support enforcement. The state was also found to be in marginal compliance in the provision of all available services to non-AFDC individuals. The state was found to be deficient in reports and records maintenance because six of the eighteen required reports were inaccurate, and the state could not provide a statewide universe of Title IV-D cases. State-written procedures for posting security to obtain payment of overdue support and state guidelines for setting child support awards also did not meet federal standards. The latter failure was a result of guidelines not being in place by October 1987, and not being mandatory by October 1989, as required by federal law. Since, as noted above, this was altered by the legislature before the final audit was issued, the OCSE auditors made no recommendations.

OCSE auditors recommended specific improvements in the wage withholding and medical support enforcement deficiencies, as well as in posting bond, maintenance of reports and records, and in ensuring provision of all services to non-AFDC clients. In other areas (those defined as noted, but not affecting the assessment of substantial compliance), OCSE recommended improvements in the parent locator service, in reporting mechanisms prior to implementation of the automated system, in proper distribution of collections, in recording of the proper date of collection (this affects distributions for AFDC clients), and in the use of wage liens.

As a result of this audit, Maryland was found not to be in substantial compliance with federal requirements, and therefore was subject to a 1 percent reduction in its Title IV-A (AFDC) payments. Because Maryland undertook a corrective action plan that was approved by OCSE, the penalties were not implemented.

Texas

The most recent federal audit of Texas covered the period of the calendar year 1992 and was conducted from May 1993 through February 1994 (OCSE 1995b). In this report, the only deficiencies found were in the area of written procedures and of expedited processes. At the time of the audit, Texas did not have written procedures in the areas of medical support enforcement and withholding of unemployment compensation. Further, Texas' procedures did not meet the criteria in effect at the time of the audit for expedited processes. However, as part of the Omnibus Reconciliation Act of 1993, the criteria for expedited processes had been changed. Therefore, Texas was not cited for this deficiency in the final audit. Federal auditors also noted Texas' need to improve in several areas not officially cited in the audit: the accuracy of the collections and accounts receivable data as kept in Child Support Division records and reported to OCSE, provision of services in interstate cases, and the development of procedures to comply with new standards for program operations.

In all other areas, Texas performed quite well based on the case sample, with appropriate action taken by child support workers in 85 percent or more of cases in the sample (OCSE 1995b, 21). This was a significant improvement over performance in the previous audit, which covered federal fiscal year 1987, and in which Texas was originally found to be noncompliant in establishing paternity, providing for wage withholding, taking action in interstate cases, and developing parent locator services. Texas was able to meet performance standards, though in some cases marginally, in the follow-up audit conducted in 1991 (OCSE 1992c). Thus, Texas has improved significantly in their compliance with federal case processing requirements during the past decade.

States have complained a great deal about the federal audit process: that the audit process itself takes too long, meaning that states are judged on actions taken as much as five years previously; that the federal regulations are often slow in coming, so that states do not receive adequate notice of how to properly carry out federal mandates; and that federal audits have little to do with program outcomes, but dwell on procedures and records maintenance. Some of the frustrations that states experience are expressed in Maryland's response to the most recently completed audit (see OCSE 1992d). The federal office has begun to review its audit procedures with the goal of focusing more on program outcomes than on case processing (OCSE 1995a). A legislative proposal to make this change was included in the Child Support Responsibility Act of 1995 (H.R. 785) (Subcommittee on Human Resources 1995, 24).

State Audits

Both child support programs are also audited by state agencies. The child support program in Maryland is audited by the Maryland State Department of Fiscal Services, Division of Audits, which audits all state programs. The Texas child support program is audited by the Office of the State Auditor.

Maryland

In Maryland, these audits look primarily at internal operations and management, especially of fiscal operations. This is done by looking at practices at two or three local agencies as well as the state office. Audits of CSEA are done every three years. Findings of the most recent audits included some serious problems with accounting procedures at local agencies. Problems were found in following proper procedures for the control of cash receipts and disbursements, including failure to utilize and/or account for pre-numbered receipt forms, failure to maintain control over unidentified collections, inadequate control over checks, failure to reconcile bank accounts and service charges, and failure of the state administration to properly monitor local accounting records and practices.

Fiscal Services found problems with the distribution of collections and incentive payments in Maryland, stating that the state distributed too much of the federal payments to local governments. The audit found that one local department underreported AFDC collections, so payments were due to federal and state governments. Moreover, the audit also found inadequate procedures with respect to both overpayments in AFDC cases and the handling of excess collections of child support.

With respect to case processing, in some cases the automated files often did not have Social Security numbers recorded, even when they were available. In some instances, local departments also failed to establish wage liens even when information was available to do so, and also failed to obtain new withholding orders when the absent parent changed employment.

These audits point up a series of problems with case processing and local and state practices in Maryland. This may in part be a reflection of limited resources: in large counties, case workers generally have more than one thousand cases at any given time. Some of the difficulties noted here are also the result of differences among local systems in program practices, and the continuing lack of a statewide automated system.[21] Some of these problems reflect more general problems in program implementation for any program of this size and type. Federal requirements have also changed continuously, especially during the past decade, demanding that state and local agencies continually change their practices to meet the new requirements.

Texas

The Texas Office of the State Auditor conducted a management audit of the Child Support Division in 1992. The objective of this audit was "to review the existing management control system" of the program (Texas Office of the State Auditor 1992, 44). The intent was a comprehensive overview of the management of the program, which involved examining organizational structure, procedures, use of resources, reports and evaluations, and compliance with state and federal law.

The audit report made a number of suggestions for improving the management of the child support enforcement program. First, the report noted that a large proportion of the caseload consisted of unobligated cases, most of which required paternity establishment. It criticized the Child Support Division for reporting results only in terms of obligated cases (cases with a support order) rather than in terms of the overall need. The report also noted that Texas' performance goals were stated primarily in terms of collections, whereas federal standards focus more on paternity establishment and the timely processing of cases. The audit clearly stated that both could be accomplished simultaneously, but focusing on collections may not necessarily meet federal requirements.

The report also commented on the (then) recent reorganization of the

Child Support Division into two separate departments, enforcement and litigation. Auditors expressed concern that there was insufficient coordination of goals and division of responsibilities between the two divisions. The report also noted that no single administrator had authority over the child support division, since the head of each division reported to a different deputy attorney general. Given the administrative structure of the program, with fifty-nine field offices and eight regions, the auditors expressed concern that management goals could not be clearly communicated with this new organizational structure.

As already discussed, this reorganization proved to be problematic, and the division has since eliminated the separate departments. In the management response to the 1992 audit, the division acknowledged that there had been communication problems in relation to the reorganization, and noted that they were acting on many of the audit recommendations.

At the request of the state legislature, another audit was conducted in 1995 which looked at the entire Child Support Division and studied the functioning of two field offices, one in the Houston area and one in the Dallas area.[22] Auditors collected information on case processing and disposition as well as the treatment of clients in the two field offices.

To study the case management and processing system, auditors examined approximately fifty case files in each office. Auditors found no problems with treatment of clients or with inappropriate information being retained in case files. They did find problems with the timeliness of case processing in both field offices. Some delays in case processing were beyond the control of child support workers, such as delays in court scheduling. However, others were due to the failure of child support workers to follow up on necessary actions, document what was happening in a case, or coordinate in a timely way with another field office. Communication with parents regarding their cases was another problem. The main criticism here was that there was no regular communication with parents regarding their case, only communication for specific kinds of actions.

Overall, this most recent audit suggests several arenas for improvement. Among these recommendations were to standardize legal functions and provide better training to legal support staff, and to enhance communications among the state office and area and field offices. The audit also recommended several ways in which resources could be used more effectively, and noted some of the external factors—such as court master procedures that were not uniform, or the lack of sufficient access to other state data bases for non-custodial parent information—that negatively affected child support services. The report also noted that the administrative processes passed by the legislature would streamline some procedures. The OAG, in its responses, agreed with many of the recommendations, noted its many resource constraints, and remarked that the automated system, when implemented, would greatly assist in speeding up case processing.

Collections Data

Despite some of the difficulties described above, some of which are simply inherent in any policy implementation process, collections in both states have gradually increased, as is true nationwide. Table 3.2 presents collections data for selected years for Maryland; table 3.3 presents similar data for Texas. Maryland has a higher overall collections rate than the national average; in fiscal year 1993 the percent of cases with collections was 34 percent statewide (Maryland CSEA 1994, 37). This figure is distorted somewhat, since the statewide average would be much higher if Baltimore City were not included. Baltimore City's rate of collections is 16 percent; without Baltimore the statewide average rate is 54 percent (ibid.). Although the state reports do not indicate the collections rate by type of case, it is possible to calculate this for both states from the federal report for FY 93. Table 3.4 presents this information.

TABLE 3.2
Maryland Child Support Collections

	FY82	FY86	FY90	FY92	FY93
AFDC	$15.9	$28.4	$39.4	$52.1	$54.0
Non-AFDC	$39.9	$69.4	$122.9	$153.7	$174.9
Total	$55.8	$97.8	$162.3	$205.8	$228.9

Source: OCSE Annual Reports to Congress, various years. Collections are in millions of dollars.

TABLE 3.3
Texas Child Support Collections

	FY82	FY86	FY90	FY92	FY93
AFDC	$6.8	$17.8	$39.7	$59.2	$66.2
Non-AFDC	$6.97	$25.8	$92.7	$192	$243.3
Total	$13.77	$43.6	$132.4	$251.2	$309.5

Source: OCSE Annual Reports to Congress, various years. Collections are in millions of dollars.

TABLE 3.4
Paying Cases and Cases with Orders

	Maryland:	Texas:	National:
Paying cases as a percent of total cases with child support orders for Fiscal Year 1993:			
AFDC	23.9%	33.3%	31.3%
Non-AFDC	46.7%	44.4%	43.0%
AFDC Arrears only	6.3%	18.3%	13.5%
Total	31.7%	39.4%	32.9%
Cases with Support Orders as a Percent of Total Caseload:			
	77%	35.7%	55.4%
Paying Cases as a Percent of Total Caseload:			
	24.4%	14.1%	18.2%

Source: OCSE 1995a, Tables 33 and 34, State Box Scores, and pp. 63–64.

Clearly, despite both states' administrative difficulties and lack of compliance in some areas of federal requirements, overall collections have risen markedly in the past ten years, as have rates of collection. This is partly a reflection of the tools now available to support agencies, especially the use of wage garnishment, which now accounts for nearly half of all collections nationwide. It also reflects the increased emphasis on paternity establishment subsequent to the Family Support Act of 1988, encouraging states to pursue support orders in these cases by providing federal funds for the establishment of paternity.

Some proposed reforms of the child support system center around possibilities of further federalizing support services (Subcommittee on Human Resources 1993). On this question, the strengths and weaknesses of the current system of coordination among federal, state, and local governments are likely most evident in a state such as Maryland that utilizes a mix of state and local administration. As noted, Maryland has been slow to comply with some aspects of federal child support law, such as the requirement to serve all custodial parents and the requirement for mandatory guidelines in the establishment of child support award amounts.[23] Maryland has also had difficulties in complying with the federal data collection requirements, in part due to the lack of a statewide automated system or even a statewide data bank of cases. And, in some arenas such as compliance with use of guidelines as a rebuttable presumption, there is variation among the counties (Maryland CSEA 1992). Yet, as table 3.4 shows, Maryland has also been more successful in some areas, such as establishing support orders and actually making collections, than many states.

Texas' performance difficulties resulted in part from poor performance in the initial years of the child support program, prior to its transfer to the Office of the Attorney General, as evidenced in the tripling of collections during the four-year period from fiscal year 1982 to fiscal year 1986 (see table 3.3). Other difficulties include the high rate of out-of-wedlock births in the state; as a result the majority of cases in the sample discussed in chapter 4 required paternity establishment services in addition to the establishment of a support order. Texas also has a lower percentage of cases in which a payment is actually made compared both to the national average and to Maryland (see table 3.4). Nevertheless, collections have continued to increase markedly in Texas as elsewhere.

In comparing the administrative organization of Texas to that of Maryland, it seems that centralization, within states and perhaps nationally, is a more feasible administrative approach to the implementation of child support policy. However, despite its drawbacks, local administration in some Maryland counties has also allowed for local innovation, such as a mediation program conducted in Prince George's County, or the administrative consolidation of child support and court processes in Montgomery County. In this respect, some degree of local autonomy may be desirable.

Any federal program the size and scope of the child support program takes both time and resources to implement. One of the problems cited frequently by the administrators interviewed (most of whom had worked in child support agencies for more than ten years) was the rapid evolution of federal law, especially since 1984. These changes had increasingly added requirements in the scope of child support agencies' mandated services. At the same time, case loads had risen rapidly, and support agencies had not, in these administrators' view, been given enough resources to implement these increasing requirements. The size of each caseworker's case load—often 1000 cases or more in both states—made it impossible to meet all of the demands being made on child support agencies.

Like most federally-mandated, state-implemented programs, child support policy has taken time to implement, and some states have much better programs than others. Texas, while still nineteenth in overall performance, was the most improved child support program when the Subcommittee on Human Resources of the House Ways and Means Committee evaluated programs in 1991 (Subcommittee on Human Resources 1991). Although Maryland ranked forty-ninth in this study (partly due to failure to provide data), in most comparisons with other states, Maryland usually falls somewhere in the middle—neither the worst program nor the best. Texas and Maryland ranked fairly closely in a 1994 Children's Defense Fund study, and were toward the middle of most rankings (Ebb 1994). Despite their differences, these two states likely provide an accurate picture of typical state practices in child support program implementation.

Conclusions

Child support policy in both Maryland and Texas has reflected the conflicting goals described in general terms in chapter 2, particularly the conflict between cost savings and the other goals of the child support program. Child support policy in both states has also been the subject of a variety of political and administrative conflicts. The detail presented by this study of child support policy in practice thus supports the more general description of the features of this relatively recent form of federal law: that it reflects conflicting goals, as do most social policies.

What is not yet clear is the impact of this policy on those who are its subjects. The next chapter will discuss the consequences of child support policy for the men, women, and children whose lives are affected.

Notes

1. A list of interviewees and dates the interviews were conducted is included in appendix B.

2. The U.S. territories of Puerto Rico, Guam, and the Virgin Islands, as well the District of Columbia, participate in the AFDC program, and therefore also in the child support program. For ease of reference, all will be referred to as states.

3. As of 1993, forty-six states or territories had child support programs located in a social welfare agency, four in the attorney general's office or justice department, and three in the revenue or taxation department (OCSE 1993b).

4. Maryland does not have a separate family or domestic relations court, although legislation passed in 1993 permits counties to form such courts.

5. Of course, the higher collections per case may or may not be attributable to the existence of administrative processes.

6. The authority for this requirement came from P.L. 90–248, which required the assignment of child support to the state agency providing AFDC services.

7. Both attorneys general have also featured their child support efforts prominently in their reelection campaigns.

8. The Child Support Enforcement Amendments of 1984 required the adoption of advisory guidelines; the Family Support Act of 1988 required the adoption of mandatory guidelines.

9. For other discussions of guidelines, see Erickson 1992; Garfinkel 1992; Roberts 1991; Wetchler 1992. There is a great deal of controversy over whether the economic studies on which these estimates of the cost of caring for children really measure such costs accurately. The various methods for calculating the costs of children, and for establishing guidelines, are each the subject of a great many studies.

10. For an extensive discussion of the economics of the Maryland guidelines, see Wetchler 1992.

11. The Maryland guidelines legislation originally contained a table by which the support award is determined, but the table only included monthly incomes in the range of $500 to $10,000. Federal audits noted that this does not comply with the federal requirements (OCSE 1992d).

12. In practice, agreement of the parties is considered sufficient written justification for a deviation from the guidelines.

13. However, the court also notes in footnote 2 that the law states this is the case unless the alteration is 25 percent or more—which is the case here.

14. It seems likely that holding otherwise would subject courts to increased litigation over modification of child support awards.

15. One other factor made clear in the above cases is the significant difference between the amounts of support awarded before and after guidelines came into use. Clearly in most of these cases, the use of guidelines significantly altered the way that support amounts were decided and the resulting support awards.

16. The information in this section is based on an interview with and documents supplied by the administrator who conducted the study.

17. Obviously, the accuracy of this figure, based on self-reported estimates by administrators, is speculative at best. Therefore, one of the questions addressed in the analysis of cases from Prince George's County was the proportion of cases in which the guidelines were followed and the reasons for deviation (see chapter 4).

18. There were at least five different methods reported, ranging from calculating the total support award for all children and then dividing by the number of children, to negotiation between the parties, to the discretion of the court.

19. It should be noted here that the current attorney general has a fairly positive public image.

20. See *Parents Without Partners vs. Massinga*, Civil Action No. JH-83–4314.

21. The story of the difficulties Maryland, and many other states, have had in designing and implementing a usable automated system for case processing would itself take a chapter. The Family Support Act of 1988 required that automated systems be in place by October of 1995, with 90 percent federal funding. At the time of this study, neither Maryland nor Texas had a system that complied with

federal operation requirements, although several local jurisdictions in each state were the sites of pilots for the new system. Whether these systems will actually provide the needed functions is still an open question. And Texas and Maryland were not alone—according to the administrators interviewed, only one state met the October 1995 deadline. Thus, Congress extended the deadline to October 1997 (H.R. 2288, passed September 1995, and signed on October 12, 1995 as P.L. 104–35).

22. This audit came about partly as the result of complaints made to legislators by dissatisfied parents.

23. As noted, to some extent this reflects the philosophical objections of some state legislators to federal involvement in family law.

4

Child Support Policy in Practice

Much research on child support looks at the aggregate effects of child support policy on various aspects of the lives of those affected by it. This is partly because of the availability of large data sets of information which make such statistical studies possible. Certainly, a great deal can and has been learned in this way. There are few studies, however, that actually ask the people affected by child support policy what it means or has meant in their lives, and how it has affected them.

Child support is not only a public policy that has implications for family law and social welfare policy, or that is the ground for disputes among administrative agencies or federal, state, and local government bodies; it is certainly not a public policy that has effects only in the aggregate. Rather, child support is a public policy that deeply and personally affects the lives of many people, children and adults alike. In any analysis of this public policy, then, it is important to understand the impact of child support law on the real people whose lives are its subject. It is at this level that the actual meaning of the families-state relation in child support policy is most clearly evident.

This chapter reports findings from three sources of data on the people who have used, or been subject to, the services of the child support agency in Prince George's County, Maryland and in Lubbock County, Texas. In Maryland, data was collected from court records on a sample of cases in which a support order was entered in 1993. In Texas, data was collected on cases filed during the first three months of 1995 for which a final order was entered at the time of the study. The first part of this chapter discusses these cases in both states, providing some basic descriptive information about the families in the sample. The next section of the chapter discusses the results of a survey of custodial and non-custodial parents drawn from this sample. Finally, a small sample of survey respondents in both states were interviewed. These sources provide a picture of how custodial and non-custodial parents view the child support process, and how it has affected their lives.

Court Case Samples: Description and Analysis

Maryland Case Sample

To analyze the effects of child support law in practice in Maryland, data on a sample of child support cases from Prince George's County was collected from court records. From a list of child support cases in which a support order, temporary or permanent, was entered during an eight month period in 1993, a random sample of 315 cases was selected. In this sample, a total of 267 cases were complete at the time of the study, 103 of which were AFDC cases, and 164 which were non-AFDC cases. The discussion that follows summarizes some of the data gathered on these 267 cases.[1]

As reported in table 4.1, the majority of these cases involved only one child (79 percent). The average number of children per case was 1.24. And, as is true nationwide, the majority of the custodial parents in this sample were women. Usually the woman was the mother (92.5 percent), although in a few cases there was a custodial relative—an aunt or grandmother (see table 4.2). There were four foster care cases among the AFDC cases. In seven non-AFDC cases (2.6 percent) the father was the custodian.

Most non-AFDC case files contained data on the custodial parent's income; the average annual income for the 156 cases in which this information was available was $20,285. Fewer files contained information on the non-custodial parent's income.[2] In the ninety-two non-AFDC cases

TABLE 4.1
Number of Children by Type of Case, Prince George's County

	One:	Two:	Three:
AFDC	88	14	1
Non-AFDC	123	35	6
Total	211	49	7
Percent of Total Cases	79%	18.4%	2.6%

TABLE 4.2
Custodian or Guardian by Type of Case, Prince George's County

	Mother:	Father:	Relative:	Foster Care:
AFDC	91	0	8	4
Non-AFDC	156	7	1	0
Total	247	7	9	4
Percent of Total Cases	92.5%	2.6%	3.4%	1.5%

in which this information was available, the average annual income of non-custodial parents was $20,333. Thus, custodial parents and non-custodial parents in non-AFDC cases in this sample had nearly identical incomes; a t-test comparing the means found no statistically significant difference.

AFDC cases generally included information regarding the amount of the monthly AFDC benefit as well as the non-custodial parent's income. The average AFDC benefit for the ninety-one cases in which this information was available was $338; the median benefit was $294. The average non-custodial parent income in the seventy-eight AFDC cases for which this data was available was $14,786. As anticipated, the income of non-custodial parents in non-AFDC cases was significantly higher than the income of non-custodial parents in AFDC cases. A t-test comparing the two sets of data showed that these differences were statistically significant (see table 4.3).

To summarize the characteristics of the typical parties in this sample, the majority of custodial parents are women, and most cases involve one child. When the custodial parent is not receiving AFDC benefits, she and the non-custodial parent are likely to have relatively similar incomes.

TABLE 4.3
Absent Parent Income of AFDC and Non-AFDC Cases,
Prince George's County

	Number of Cases:	Monthly Income:	Two-tailed probability results:		
			t	DF	p value
AFDC	82	$1232	-4.4	169	0.0000
Non-AFDC	92	$1698			

Notes: In this test, the p value indicates the probability that there is no difference between the mean incomes of the population represented by these two samples.

However, a non-custodial parent whose child is receiving AFDC benefits is likely to have an income that is on average $6000 per year less than the income of those non-custodial parents whose children are not on AFDC.

Guidelines in Prince George's County

Data was also collected regarding the amount of child support ordered and whether the child support guidelines were followed in each case. Table 4.4 summarizes the average monthly support awards in AFDC and non-AFDC cases, as well as the overall average amount of support awarded. The average annual support awards for all cases was $3216; for AFDC cases the average was $2532, and for non-AFDC cases it was $3636. These awards are somewhat higher than the national averages in FY 93 of $2000 in AFDC cases and $3300 in non-AFDC cases (OCSE 1994b).

Table 4.5 reports the number and percent of cases in which the child support guidelines were followed. As noted, not all case files contained information about the non-custodial parent's income. When this information was available, it was usually contained on the guidelines worksheet. It was therefore possible in these cases to determine both whether the guidelines were followed and the reason for any deviation from the guidelines. When this information was not in the file, it was not possible to determine any reason for deviation from the guidelines. However, it was possible to substitute a proxy variable based on the dollar amount of the support award. Since in most cases the use of the Maryland guidelines results in an exact (not rounded) dollar amount, awards that came to a dollar amount such as $227 or $342 were likely to be guidelines-based; awards such as $100 or $200 were less likely to be the result of a calculation based on the guidelines. Table 4.5, therefore, reports actual data as well as proxy data.

Overall, guidelines were followed in 70 percent of all cases; deviations from guidelines were less likely in AFDC cases than in non-AFDC cases.

TABLE 4.4
Monthly Child Support Award Amounts by Type of Case,
Prince George's County

	Mean	Median	Lowest	Highest
AFDC	$211	$198	$25	$728
Non-AFDC	$303	$293	$100	$763
Total	$268	$239	$25	$763

TABLE 4.5
Use of Guidelines by Type of Case, Prince George's County

	Followed:	Not Followed:	Percent of Cases Using Guidelines:
Actual Data:			
AFDC	64	14	82%
Non-AFDC	59	39	60.2%
Total	123	53	69.9%
Proxy Data:			
AFDC	82	21	79.6%
Non-AFDC	103	61	62.8%
Total	185	82	69.3%

This is slightly lower than the estimate of 82 percent guidelines adherence made by the state office in its report to the legislature in 1992.[3] Deviations were almost always reductions from the guidelines amount. The average downward deviation in AFDC cases was $80, and in non-AFDC cases, $99.

In those cases where actual data was available and the guidelines were not followed, the reasons for deviation were noted as well as the amount of the deviation. This information is summarized in table 4.6. Finally, a comparison between the mean child support awarded in cases in which guidelines were followed and the mean amount awarded in cases in which the guidelines were not followed showed no statistically significant differences in the whole sample nor in the sub-samples of AFDC and non-AFDC cases.

In terms of the actual support award, average awards are slightly higher than the national average, but incomes in Prince George's County are also higher than national averages. Guidelines were followed in the majority

TABLE 4.6
Guidelines Deviation Reason by Type of Case, Prince George's County

	Other Children	Agreement of Parties	None Given	Other Reasons
AFDC	5	3	4	2
Non-AFDC	3	17	14	5

of cases, although they were more likely to be followed if the child involved was receiving AFDC. This fact, combined with the higher proportionate percentage of income paid at lower income levels when Maryland guidelines are applied (Wetchler 1992), means that lower income men are likely to pay a higher percentage of their income in child support. When guidelines are not followed, written justifications are usually—but not always—given, and deviations are almost always downward.

Texas Case Sample

Because Lubbock County has a slightly different method of court record maintenance than Prince George's County, the cases were selected by the date the case was originally filed with the court.[4] Cases that were filed during a three-month period in 1995 were selected. The sample included a total of 220 cases. In about half of the cases (108), ongoing support had been ordered at the time of the study. In order for the Maryland and Texas data to be comparable, the data reported and analyzed below is on the 108 cases with orders for ongoing support at the time of the study.

Texas cases had slightly different types of information available than Maryland cases. For example, Texas court files do not routinely report whether the custodial parent is receiving AFDC benefits. This information is occasionally available in cases where income amounts are recorded, but it was not possible to distinguish all cases in this way. Further, income information for custodial parents and non-custodial parents is not routinely recorded unless there is a deviation from the standard Texas guidelines. Even here, often the non-custodial parent's income is the only one reported, since Texas uses the percentage-of-income model for establishing support.

Similar to Maryland, the Texas sample consisted overwhelmingly of cases involving one child. However, there were cases with up to six children in Texas, and thus the average number of children per case in the Texas sample was somewhat higher, about 1.5 children per case. As in Maryland, the mother was the custodian in the vast majority of cases: 104 out of 108 cases. In two cases the father was the custodian, and in two cases another relative—an aunt or grandmother—was the custodian.

It was also possible in most cases to collect data on whether the Texas child support guidelines were followed. The Texas guidelines were adopted by the courts in 1987 and by legislation in 1989. They were altered in 1993 to provide multi-family guidelines, with lower support awards in cases where a non-custodial parent has other children to support. Courts are also permitted to presume earnings of at least minimum wage when no wage information is available. Thus, data was collected on whether the guidelines were followed, whether multi-family guidelines were applied, and whether the minimum wage presumption was utilized (see table 4.7).

Guidelines were followed in almost all cases in the sample—only three cases involved a deviation from the guidelines. One of these was due to agreement of the parties, one because the obligor was paying for health insurance, and the third was because the obligor's only income was from Supplemental Security Income (SSI). The minimum wage presumption was utilized in 57 percent of cases, and 36 percent of cases involved the use of multi-family guidelines.

Average support awards in Texas were lower than in Maryland—$177 compared to $268—perhaps in part due to the extensive use of the minimum wage presumption, but also because average earnings in Lubbock County are lower than in Prince George's County. Retroactive support, or arrears payments, are treated somewhat differently in Texas than in Maryland, resulting in higher arrears awards in Texas. In Maryland, retroactive support is only ordered to the time that paternity is established, whereas in Texas retroactive support is ordered back to the date of the child's birth. This results in high arrears amounts, especially in cases with older children in which the parents have been separated for a number of years. Average award and arrears amounts are reported in table 4.8.

TABLE 4.7
Use of Guidelines, Lubbock County

	Number of Cases	Percent of known Cases
Followed:	13	14%
Not followed:	3	3%
Multi-family guidelines:	24	26%
Minimum wage presumption:	44	47%
Multi-family with minimum wage presumption:	9	10%
Unknown:	15	NA

TABLE 4.8
Award and Arrears Amounts, Lubbock County

Average Award: (monthly)	Lowest Award:	Highest Award:	Average Total Arrears:	Highest Total Arrears:
$177	$65	$630	$5065	$22680

Survey Results

To ascertain what child support means in the lives of custodial and non-custodial parents, a survey was conducted in each county studied of those parents in each sample for whom complete addresses were available and in which there was a temporary or permanent child support order. In Maryland, the sample size and response rate were such that the data collected could be analyzed with some degree of confidence. In Texas, due both to sample size and the lower response rate, not enough surveys were returned to run valid statistical analysis. Thus, the data reported here is from the study conducted in Maryland.

It should be noted that in the interviews conducted with child support administrators in both states, they were asked whether their agency had ever surveyed the families on their caseload regarding support services. Only one agency had conducted such a survey—Prince George's County—and this was not a self-study but part of a county-wide quality management study. Two reasons were given by administrators for not conducting such a study: first, it would raise expectations that changes would be made when in fact the agencies did not have the resources to change. Second, many administrators said they already knew what people would say because they received complaints all the time from custodial and non-custodial parents alike. One survey of recently divorced individuals was conducted as part of the Maryland Governor's Task Force on Family Law's study; although the study was about Maryland family law, the survey instrument did include some questions regarding child support. Other than this survey, there does not seem to be any other study in Maryland that asks people about their experiences with the child support system. Thus, although the sample is relatively small, this study appears to be unique.

Design and Methodology

From the set of court records in Prince George's County discussed above, a survey was mailed to custodial mothers and non-custodial fathers. The survey was designed primarily to solicit opinions and experiences with respect to the child support process. The survey questions were identical on both surveys, with the exception of one question that asked about payment and receipt of child support payments. Respondents were asked a series of questions about their experiences with child support, including specific questions about their own case as well as general questions about their perceptions of the fairness of the child support process. Respondents were also asked their opinions with respect to possible changes in the child support system, as well as basic demographic information.[5]

Overall, the respondents to the survey were overwhelmingly African American: fifty-eight respondents or seventy-seven percent of the total sample, thirty-eight women (81 percent of women) and twenty men (71 percent of men). Most of the women respondents were single parents: thirty-five women, or 74.5 percent, lived in a household with children and no other adults present. However, thirteen of the men, or 46.5 percent, lived in households with children present; the remainder lived by themselves or with other adults. The average age of all respondents was 30.5 years and was virtually identical for women and men. Most of the cases involved one child: fifty-nine, or 81 percent of valid cases.[6]

Findings

All questions which asked for respondents' opinions utilized a five-point Likert scale, from "strongly disagree" to "strongly agree". To analyze this data, responses were coded from 1 to 5, with 1 representing the response "strongly disagree" and 5 representing the response "strongly agree". To compare the responses of male non-custodial parents to those of female custodial parents, a statistical test was run for each question which compared the mean responses of each group. Here, data is reported only for those questions on which the difference between the mean responses of the two groups were statistically significant (see table 4.9).

As might be expected, perceptions regarding the fairness of the child support process by female custodial parents and male non-custodial parents were quite different. Only 17 percent of the women respondents disagreed or strongly disagreed with the statement, "I felt the outcome of my child support hearing was fair to me"; 65 percent of male respondents disagreed or strongly disagreed with this statement. Most (68 percent) of the female respondents agreed that the child support award amount was fair; sixteen of the male respondents (55 percent) disagreed with this statement. Twenty-one, or 72 percent, of male respondents disagreed with the more general statement, "I feel the child support system is fair to people in my situation"; only fourteen female respondents, or 29.7 percent, disagreed with this statement. Eighteen male respondents agreed with the statement "I thought the judge/master was unfair to people in my situation," whereas only nine female respondents agreed with this statement. As table 4.9 shows, the differences between these responses were statistically significant.

Responses to this last question may also reveal some response bias between male and female respondents to the survey. In Prince George's County, child support cases may be settled by consent without going to a hearing. If the parties do not agree, the case then goes before the Master for Domestic Relations. It may be settled before the master, with review and final approval by a judge. Fourteen female respondents, or 30 percent, responded that this question was "not applicable" to their case, meaning that they never appeared before a judge or master, but settled their cases by consent. Only three male respondents, or 10 percent, reported that the question was not applicable. This would seem to indicate that male respondents to the survey were more likely than the female respondents to have gone before a judge or master.

Nevertheless, it is clear that custodial parents are more likely than non-custodial parents to feel that they have been treated fairly by the child

TABLE 4.9
Custodial and Non-Custodial Parents' Experiences with Child Support

Question:	Valid Cases:		Mean:		Separate Variance Estimate with Two-tailed Probability		
	Men	Women	Men	Women	t value	DF	p
Fairness of hearing	28	44	2.07	3.34	4.15	54.09	0.000
Fairness of award	27	43	2.19	3.16	3.24	51.3	0.002
Fairness of system	28	45	1.75	3.07	5.32	70.62	0.000
Unfairness of judge	26	27	3.58	2.41	-3.11	49.71	0.003
Helpfulness of support agency	27	43	2.30	3.28	3.31	56.02	0.002

Notes: Questions are found on the survey in Appendix C, questions 7, 8, 11, 9, and 12, respectively. Mean is the mean score of valid responses coded on a Likert scale from 1 to 5, with 1 corresponding to "strongly disagree" and 5 corresponding to "strongly agree". In this test, "p" represents the probability that there is no difference between the means of men's and women's responses in the population represented by this sample, and thus no difference in their opinions.

support process. This held true for perceptions of the child support agency as well: thirty-one, or 66 percent, of the women agreed that the child support agency had been helpful, while sixteen, or 55 percent, of men disagreed with this statement (see table 4.9).

Respondents were also asked a series of questions about possible changes in the child support system. With these questions, there was greater agreement. Both custodians and non-custodians overwhelmingly agreed that job training should be offered to both custodial and non-custodial parents. Sixty-seven respondents, or 92 percent of valid responses, agreed that custodial parents should be offered job training; the same number of respondents, and 89 percent of valid responses, agreed that job training should be offered to non-custodial parents. A majority (62 respondents, or 85 percent) also agreed that counseling should be provided for parents who live separately. Similarly, seventy-one respondents, or 95 percent, thought that the state should assist parents with visitation problems. There were no significant differences between custodians and non-custodians on these questions.

A narrower majority of respondents agreed with a question about child support assurance. Obviously, one cannot explain in a survey all the details of child support assurance proposals, so the question simply stated, "The state should pay custodial parents a minimum child support payment whether or not the non-custodial parent pays child support." Forty-six respondents, or 63 percent, agreed with this statement; twenty-one disagreed. There were slight gender differences here: thirty-two custodians (70 percent) agreed, and eleven disagreed; fourteen non-custodians (50 percent) agreed and ten disagreed. This difference was statistically significant (see table 4.10).

Respondents were also asked who should handle child support cases. The question was intended to ascertain respondents' views regarding administrative versus judicial processes for handling child support. The responses to this were more evenly distributed: forty-one agreed (55 percent) and twenty-six disagreed (35 percent) (10 percent offered no opinion). However, women had a less favorable view of case workers than men: twenty-one men, or 75 percent, agreed that case workers should handle child support; only twenty women, or 43 percent, agreed with this statement. These differences were also statistically significant (see table 4.9). This may be related to perceptions of the fairness of judges or masters; since most non-custodians felt that the judge or master in their case was unfair to them, they might expect to be treated with greater fairness by case workers. And some may simply want the system to work better than it now does: one respondent did not answer the question but wrote instead, "I don't care who handles it, but something should be done."

TABLE 4.10
Custodial and Non-Custodial Parents' Opinions of Changes to Child Support

| Question: | Valid Cases | | Mean | | Separate Variance Estimate with Two-tailed Probability | | |
	Men	Women	Men	Women	t value	DF	p
Child support assurance	24	43	2.67	3.70	3.21	52.61	0.002
Administrative process	26	41	3.53	2.61	-2.87	52.13	0.006
Change Maryland guidelines	28	45	4.60	3.53	-3.80	53.64	0.000

Notes: Questions are found on the survey in Appendix C, questions 19, 23, and 24, respectively. Mean is the mean score of valid responses coded on a Likert scale from 1 to 5, with 1 corresponding to "strongly disagree" and 5 corresponding to "strongly agree". In this test, "p" represents the probability that there is no difference between the means of men's and women's responses in the population represented by this sample, and thus no difference in their opinions.

Finally, respondents were asked questions about the Maryland child support guidelines. In the section of the survey that asked questions about respondents' own cases, they were asked whether the guidelines had been followed in their case. Twenty-seven respondents stated that they did not know. Another eleven stated that this did not apply to their case; however, since by definition the sample included only cases in which an order had been established, and the guidelines are required by law, it is likely that the child support guidelines were not explained to these respondents, or that they did not understand that the guidelines applied to their case. If this is correct, then thirty-eight respondents—fully half of all sample members—did not know about the guidelines or how they were utilized. The numbers were approximately the same among custodians and non-custodians; 48 percent of women and 52 percent of men knew whether or not the guidelines had been used.

Of the thirty-seven respondents who knew whether or not the guidelines had been followed in their case, thirty-one reported that the guidelines had been followed, and six reported that they had not been followed. This is a slightly higher number (84 percent) than the numbers for the overall sample reported above.

In the section of the survey that asked about possible changes to the child support guidelines, respondents were asked whether the guidelines should be changed, and if so, how they should be changed. Of those offering an opinion, fifty-one respondents, or 67 percent of the entire sample, agreed that the guidelines should be changed. Here, however, differences between custodial and non-custodial parents were clear. *All* twenty-five non-custodial parents who offered an opinion agreed that the guidelines should be changed. On the other hand, twenty-six custodial parents agreed that the guidelines should be changed, and ten disagreed. Table 4.10 shows that the differences were statistically significant.

These differences were also clear in the way that each group thought that guidelines should be changed. Since respondents could check multiple answers to the question of how guidelines should be changed, responses were summarized in two different ways. First, single responses were coded as such and multiple responses were coded together. Then, the types of responses were coded according to categories: raising support award amounts, lowering them, consideration of new family arrangements, using after tax income to calculate support, and other responses (this included respondents' written comments). I wanted to know first whether respondents thought guidelines should be higher or lower; if multiple responses included one of these categories, they were coded as "higher" or "lower," regardless of the other responses. Sorting the coded responses by gender revealed, somewhat predictably, that all respondents who thought guidelines should be higher were custodial parents; all respondents who thought guidelines should be lower were non-custodial parents. The numbers, however, were lower than one might expect: fifteen custodians of the twenty-six who responded to this question said the guidelines award amounts should be higher, and eleven of the twenty-six non-custodians believed the guidelines should be lower.

Summary

Although there is agreement on some general public policy questions, the experiences with the child support system of women who are custodial parents are decidedly different from the experiences of men who are non-custodial parents—a result that one certainly would expect. In general custodial parents expressed a higher level of satisfaction with the child support system than some might expect. But, as the administrators interviewed had indicated, both custodial and non-custodial parents have complaints about how the child support system operates.

A number of respondents to the survey expressed appreciation for being asked their opinion. Several respondents called me to inquire about the survey, most wanting to know whether their answers would make any difference—whether there was any possibility that the support system might be changed. Of course, responses to the survey seem to indicate that custodial parents and non-custodial parents would recommend different kinds of changes to the system with respect to guidelines and case processing. However, the amount of concurrence on some types of changes to the system is also interesting. Particularly so is the extent to which respondents wanted more assistance from the state in terms of job training for parents who needed it, and assistance with visitation problems. For the most part the parents in this survey did not want the state to leave them alone. However, they did want state services to work better for them. For some, this meant more timely enforcement of a support order; for others, it meant more consideration of their individual circumstances. This desire for improvement in the services of child support agencies (whatever improvement meant to the individual parent) was also borne out in the individual and focus group interviews discussed in the following section.

Individual Interview Results

Included with each survey was an invitation to parents to participate in more individualized interviews. These interviews were conducted in person and by telephone. A total of four male non-custodial parents were interviewed in Maryland and Texas. Eleven female custodial parents were interviewed, four at the focus group meeting in Maryland and seven interviewed individually in Texas. The results of these interviews are summarized below. Some biographical details of individual cases have been changed to protect the confidentiality of respondents.

Custodial Parents

The experiences of the women interviewed were quite diverse, as were their views of the system. Six participants had sought child support for their own children as non-AFDC applicants; one was currently receiving AFDC benefits for her own children; two had obtained child support because they were former recipients of AFDC; one was receiving food stamps and was referred to child support services; and one participant had temporary custody of a relative's child and had applied for child support services through her application for Medicaid as a means to obtain health care for the child while she was her guardian. A total of five African American women, three white women, and three Hispanic women were interviewed.

Direct Applicants for Child Support Services

The experiences of women who were not receiving AFDC or other benefits generally fell into two categories. Some were fairly satisfied with the way their child support case had been handled and with the results. Generally, these women had cooperative relationships with their former partners, who were willing to pay support. These women were receiving their support payments—two even expressed concern for the financial situation of their former partners, or for the way that child support had affected the non-custodial parent.

Other women interviewed were quite dissatisfied with the child support system, mostly because it had not worked well in their cases. All of the women in this group had legally established support orders, but none had actually received regular support payments.

Finally, women who applied for child support through the AFDC or another social services program had a variety of experiences with the child support system. Each of these groups will be discussed in turn.

Two of the women interviewed expressed satisfaction with the system. A third woman was satisfied with the outcome of the process, though not with the process itself. Each of these women had relatively cooperative relationships with the non-custodial parent, and each had begun receiving support payments at the time of the interview.

One custodial parent was particularly pleased with the way her case had been handled. She noted that the process worked much more quickly than she had anticipated. Within a month of her completing the paperwork to apply for child support services, the father had been located; within another two months they had gone to court to establish paternity and child support. Throughout the process, she said, the child support office had handled her case very professionally and efficiently, and she was "impressed" with what they had done. She noted that the child's father had cooperated in the process, and that she had also made some concessions by waiving all retroactive support as well as settling for a support amount below the guidelines amount. She indicated that it was important to her to have a cooperative relationship with her child's other parent and that she was willing to make concessions in order for this to happen. This parent felt that most problems with enforcing child support stem from lack of cooperation on the part of non-custodial parents and their employers, rather than from child support agencies.

A second custodial parent also expressed general satisfaction with the process of establishing and enforcing child support. She applied for services, received notice of a hearing date within a few months, and was able to establish paternity and ongoing support for her child through consent in an administrative hearing. Shortly thereafter, her former husband's wages were garnished and she began receiving support payments.

In fact, this custodial parent's main concern was her estranged husband's financial situation. He also owed support for two other children, and she was concerned that once his wages had been garnished for the two support orders, he was left with very little take-home pay.

> I don't think they took into account the fact that he has to live off his job. He doesn't have anywhere to stay and he doesn't have any money to really eat. . . . It's like they just want the money and that's it. I don't think they understand that he has to have something to live off of too. . . . I think it was unfair to him in that they didn't consider the amount that he'd be paying for the other two kids. . . . He comes over and stays on the weekends and really helps out with the baby. I think it's, the reason I'm so concerned is that he's talking about quitting his job, that's why, and when he quits, then I won't get anything at all. And I'd rather get a little bit than none at all.[7]

This custodial parent was satisfied with the child support system in general, with the exception of her concern for her former husband's financial situation.

A third custodial parent was satisfied with the outcome of her child support case, but not with the process by which it was handled. She noted that since she was given very little information about the process itself when she applied for services, she did not know whether her case had been handled properly. Hearings were scheduled in her case and then canceled without her being informed. When the hearing was finally held, the child support officer did not inform her of what the proceedings would be like, what the guidelines were, or how the support amount was to be established. Thus, she felt completely left out of the process and did not understand what was going on.

Further, she noted that her child's father had tried to set up a payment plan in advance of the hearing, but was not able to do so. In addition, although he had no doubt as to whether the child was his, his private attorney advised him to have a paternity test.[8] As a result, he had to pay for the paternity test. He was found to owe back support, so he also had to pay court costs. Thus, she noted, he ended up paying much more than if they had been able to settle the case by consent, which he had been willing to do. This custodial parent was supportive of the child support process, and was glad that child support services were available to her and to other custodial parents. She thought that some of the measures used in her case were probably necessary in cases where the non-custodial parent was not willing to pay. However, in her case, she stated that it would have been better if they could have handled it without going to court. Her child's father was willing to cooperate and to pay support, but she felt that the system itself has been set up to assume that the non-custodial parent will be uncooperative.

On the other hand, three women interviewed were quite dissatisfied with the child support system. These women expressed a great deal of frustration with the system and their stories are typical of the problems often cited with child support enforcement.

One woman had two children with her first husband, and had been trying for several years, unsuccessfully, to receive support for them from her ex-husband. She had also remarried, and had a young daughter who was less than one-year old at the time of the interview.

This custodial parent was in regular contact with her ex-husband, but he owed over $14,000 in back child support. He had only made two payments—one of them partial—since the transfer of her case to the current local child support agency several years before the interview. She indicated that he regularly changed jobs in order to avoid child support payments. Recently, after being detained for non-payment, he had given the court false information about his employer, and had been released on the basis of that false information.

She had been very diligent in following up on the progress of her case. Although she had not received a payment in more than two years, she wrote letters every month to the child support agency when she did not receive a payment on its due date. She had even followed up on the issuing of a warrant for her ex-husband when he failed to appear for a court proceeding: she called the sheriff's office, found out who the officer was that was supposed to serve the warrant, and asked him why, in more than two months, only one effort had been made to serve the warrant. She told the officer that she had just spoken on the phone with her ex-husband, that he was home, and that the officer should go serve the warrant. While describing some of the events in her case, she expressed frustration that she had to go to such great lengths to get the system to work properly, especially when she was working so hard (she had been working two jobs) just to provide basic necessities for her children.

> They put a continuation on it [the case]. . . . So he went back to jail for another case . . . and they released him, and then he had to go back to court, but he didn't show. So they had issued out a warrant on him. They should have never let him go. Period. . . . Because he's job-hopping, and I'll never get my money. . . . He keeps telling me, I just got a job, and I've got all this money, but you have to give me a chance to pay and not make me go into court or else I'll lose this job, and then you're not going to get anything because I won't have a job. And you can tell it really frustrates me because when I talk about it I get so hyper and upset about it, I'm just fed up.

This custodial parent had clearly made many efforts to obtain support for her children, and had remained in steady contact with the child support agency, without success.

A second custodial parent also had had no success in enforcing her support award, despite the fact that she knew exactly where her estranged husband was working and had given the child support agency all of the information required to establish and enforce a support order. Her two children were both preschoolers. She was in regular contact with her former husband, but he had not paid any child support since they had separated.

She had gone through the application process, gotten a hearing within a few months of applying, been awarded more than she expected for her two children, and her former husband had signed the support order. After this initial success, however, nothing happened. He did not make any payments. Wage garnishment had been ordered, but because her husband was considered a contractual employee, his employer would not deduct support payments. She describes what happened after she received a letter stating that the wages could not be deducted.

> So then in April of '92 I got a letter from them [the child support agency] saying they couldn't take it out of his paycheck . . . because he is, well he's considered self-employed, he's a contractor. He works right around the corner, and his company will not take it out because they don't take out anything—they don't take out Social Security, he has to pay his own Social Security, he has to buy his own health insurance—so they don't take out child support either. So in essence, my letter stated that they could not, due to the fact that he was not an actual employee but a contractor with this company, they could not enforce the withholding agreement. So I got that letter in April of '92 stating that, and they said that he had ninety days to tell why he wasn't paying, and I guess that ninety days isn't over yet.

She had tried to call the child support office several times, but had not been able to get through to a caseworker by telephone.

To make the situation even more frustrating, her former husband taunted her about the fact that the child support agency had not succeeded in enforcing her support order. She described how he had recently received a letter from the agency, and had brought it over to her home and laughed at her, saying that she had wasted her money in applying for child support services, and that the reason he did not pay support was because she would waste money on things. She reported

> he thinks it's a big joke, because, you know, he lives in the same place, and they send him little letters. And he laughed at me, and he told me, because

when we went down there, it was mostly blacks down there, right? He said, "Look at y'all foolish black sisters down here making fools of y'all selves." So it's a joke to him. And the system allows these men to think it's a joke. And him and another guy were sitting there laughing because the guy had dodged the system for almost ten years and he was telling him how he had like four or five babies and what he does to dodge the system. And I think that the enforcement process [needs improvement], especially when the women provide the information to them. . . . Because he works at that job with no fear of quitting. . . . He works. . . . He has a nice apartment. . . . He has two cars. . . . And there's nothing, I feel that there's nothing I can do, there's nothing I can do.

In addition to trying to call the agency, she had also tried talking with her former husband's employer, because they knew her and knew about the children. She described being hurt by the fact that his employers knew her and knew her children, but still felt no obligation to help her collect the child support award. She described the frustration of knowing that he had regular income, and yet was unwilling to pay his child support, despite the expenses she incurred with child care and her children's needs.

And it's like, he's doing this to me, but it's our children who [suffer], because I don't need his money, I have a job, I say to him, I don't need your money. . . . so it's just stuff like that.

She said that she wanted to ask for her application fee back because of the child support agency's failure to enforce her order.

A third woman also indicated that she was dissatisfied because there had been no results in her case. She noted that hers was an interstate case since her two children's father lived in another state. However, she had given the child support agency complete information on her former partner, including his relatives' addresses as well as his place of employment. The child support agency had located him once, but he then changed employers. As a result, although she had first applied for support services about two years prior to the interview, she had never received any payments.

This parent noted that the child support agency was overwhelmed with cases. She said she always had to call them to find out what was happening with her case. She noted that she did not know what steps they were taking on her case at the time of the interview, but knew that it would be up to her to contact them to find out what steps were being taken. She related an instance when she had gone in for a hearing and had waited for three hours before the child support staff person even asked her why she was there. She commented that she gets copies of letters sent to the non-custodial parent, and they often have conflicting due dates and amounts owed, so that she wonders about the child support agency's level of coordination and the accuracy of the letters. In describing how well her case was handled, she stated that the child support agencies are "overloaded" and have too many cases to handle all of them well. Her main complaint then was with the child support agency's lack of communication with its clients.

This parent made an interesting point in answer to the question of whether the child support system was fair to children. She noted that, at no point during the entire process, had anyone ever asked her anything about her children. "The whole thing has been financial. And we need the money, but I think the kids need more than that."

This parent described herself as "disappointed" that there had been no results in terms of support collection in her case. She cited an instance of an acquaintance who was in his twenties, whose non-custodial parent was finally paying the retroactive child support owed from when the acquaintance was a child. Since she has a legally established support order, and her former partner owed more than $20,000 in back support, she stated that she believes he will be found eventually and his wages will be garnished. She said, "My kids might be grown up, but they will find him eventually."

Social Services Applicants for Child Support Services

Five of the women interviewed had received child support services in conjunction with applying for AFDC, Food Stamps, or Medicaid benefits. Three of these women were no longer receiving benefits at the time of the interview.

The first woman had heard about the child support system from friends, and thought that the system worked like a child support assurance system: that she would be guaranteed child support whether or not the non-custodial parent paid. She had two separate support cases for her three children, and in both cases paternity and support orders were established within a period of six to seven months. She had never received any support payments, however, from either father.

She said she had contacted the child support agency many times but had gotten no results, so she had finally stopped calling. She did not know the present location of one father (although he had been located at the time support was established), but she knew where the other father was and that he was not employed. She noted that when she had contacted the child support agency, they told her that they could not do anything as long as the non-custodial parents were not employed. This parent was not satisfied with the outcome of her case, and felt that parents who do not pay support should be threatened with contempt and jailed if they continue to fail to pay.

Overall, she felt the child support system was not fair to anyone involved: it was not fair to custodial parents because they have all of the responsibility of caring for the children and get little or nothing for it. Even if she were to receive the $50 per month to which she was entitled, this would not be enough to make up for the amount of responsibility she has in relation to the non-custodial parents. Further, she felt the system was not fair to non-custodial parents, since they are often not informed about what is happening with their children. Most of all, this parent felt the child support system was unfair to children, since "they are the ones who are suffering if the father doesn't want to pay support or be part of their life." She felt she had not been kept informed by the child support agency and that her case had not been pursued as it should have been.

The second woman's experience with the AFDC support system was somewhat different; she had applied for child support when she applied to receive Medicaid for a relative's child, for whom she had temporary custody. She was married and had children of her own. She also had a job with medical benefits, but her health insurance provider would not permit her to place the child on her insurance policy because she was only a temporary guardian. She went to apply for Medicaid only, but was told she had to apply for child support as well, and could not only file for Medicaid. There was some confusion as to who needed to file; she went in to apply, and was told that the child's biological parent needed to file the application. When the relative went in, she was told that the respondent, being the current guardian, should be the applicant. This parent then described how she was treated during the application process.

> I mean, that part was just humiliating. Because you go in there, and it's like you're doing something wrong. You know like in my case it wasn't my child, but she was still entitled—there were two people who made this baby, and someone should be financially responsible for it. It shouldn't be if they're still out partying, well that's too bad. My thing was that, I just don't think that they, you know you go in there, the whole point of it is, this is supposedly for these children. And you go walking in, and it's like you're the bad one for trying to get this money for this child.

Although she had not intended to obtain child support from her relative, she was told that she had to file for this as well in order to obtain Medicaid. She filed and eventually the child's biological parent did have her wages garnished for a small monthly payment.

Overall, this parent clearly stated that she wished she had never gone through that process, and had only done so because she wanted to be sure that the child had health benefits while living with her. Asked what the best part of the child support process was, she hesitated, then said, "The best part of the whole thing is not having to go back there."

It should be noted here that this parent was talking about the application process not for child support services with the child support agency, but about the process of applying for Medicaid benefits. Thus, her negative experience was with the social services agency, not with child support services. By contrast, most non-AFDC custodians had described the initial process of applying for child support services as working fairly well for them. None of them described feeling humiliated by the process. The contrast between the way that the child support system works for custodians receiving AFDC and how it works for non-AFDC custodians will be discussed further in chapter 5.[9]

Another woman received child support services when she applied for food stamps. A friend had told her that when she received food stamps she would receive child support services as well. She was unable to work due to a disability, and her husband had left her with two children to support. She applied for food stamps, and subsequently received a letter regarding child support.

This respondent was extremely disturbed about how the child support system had worked in her case. She went to the hearing with a notarized statement from her former husband stating the child support amount he was willing to pay. However, at the hearing, the support award amount was determined according to the guidelines, and was less than this amount. In addition, because one of her children was over eighteen, no support was ordered for this child. The respondent felt this was particularly unfair because her former husband had not supported the child when he was younger, yet no retroactive support was ordered.

In general, this woman felt that the child support worker in her case was on her former husband's side, and she felt betrayed by this. Although she had received a few support payments, they had recently stopped. She had tried to contact the child support agency about her situation, but had gotten a recorded message. She stated that she wanted to work, and had tried to go back to work, but had become sick. Thus, the lack of child support for her child left her with very little income. She had only a small disability payment and food stamps, and occasionally, although it embarrassed her, she received assistance from local churches.

This respondent felt that her situation had adversely affected her children. She said that her former husband was never really there for her children, and that although her children didn't complain, she knew they also resented the fact that their father did not provide for them and was not around.

A fourth respondent had obtained child support when she applied for AFDC benefits at the time of the birth of her first child. Although she was not familiar with the child support system, she stated that her caseworker told her about it and said that it would be beneficial for her child. She stated that she had only had contact with the child support agency at the time of the hearing. Although it only took a few months from the time she applied for support and the time she obtained a support order, she had been told it would take some time before she received any support payments because her former partner did not have a job. She indicated that she had never received any payments for either of her children, even though support orders had been established for both of them.

This parent did not state any complaints about the child support system even though it had not worked very well for her. She noted that she spends a lot of time and all of her income on taking care of her children, so that it was only fair to expect some assistance from the other parent. In her case, one of the fathers did spend time with his child, even though he didn't pay support; the other father neither saw the child nor paid support. She noted that the father who did care for his child was trying to be a good parent, in part by getting more education so he could better support the child. Thus, it was less important to her to receive support payments from him at present, since she anticipated that in the future he would be better able to support the child. At the time of the interview, she had recently obtained a job and so was no longer receiving AFDC benefits, but was concerned about what she would do when her Medicaid benefits were no longer available, because her job did not offer health benefits. She stated that she was working hard, and trying to do what was right for her children, but that it was difficult. She lived with several family members, but was the only person in the household with a job.

The final respondent had also received child support services as a result of receiving AFDC benefits. In her case, however, it had taken almost five years from the time she initially applied for benefits to the time that she obtained a support order. She had also had little contact with the child support agency, because her caseworker had handled everything except the hearing. She had never received any payments. Since the time her case was initiated, she had obtained a job and was no longer receiving AFDC.

Her case was an interstate case, and her former partner had taken a number of measures to delay the case. At first he did not respond, and then he initiated a case in his own state, in part, she thought, to delay enforcement. He requested a paternity test, and then never showed up to take it—again, she felt that this was an effort to avoid enforcement. At the time of the interview, there was a dispute going on as to which state support order amount should be enforced, because the orders were for different amounts.

This parent was very knowledgeable about the child support system, although she said she hadn't known anything about it before she tried to utilize support enforcement services. Of her own case, she said, "It took a long time and it was really frustrating." She thought that the child support system could be greatly improved in regards to interstate cases through greater nationalization. She felt that there should be a national law so that only one state would handle each case, and that the law should apply equally to all states. In cases like hers in particular, she felt that, because both she and her former partner lived in her present state of residence when the child was born, the case should have been handled entirely by her home state.

In more general terms, however, this parent expressed some ambivalence about child support and child custody policy. During the interview she cited numerous examples of cases where the application of child support law seemed unjust to her, such as when a custodial parent has remarried and has, along with his or her new partner, a much higher income than the non-custodial parent. However, she did state clearly that the principle of support was more important, in her case and in general, than the actual money provided. The principle that someone who "makes a child is obligated to do something [for that child], they can't just walk away" was important. Thus, she could see circumstances where it would be fair that, instead of providing monetary support, a non-custodial parent might spend time caring for the child.

The women who received child support services because they had applied for social services thus had a variety of experiences with the child support system. In general, they had had less success in receiving child support payments than the women who were not receiving social services benefits, which is in keeping with national enforcement data. Four of the five custodial parents in this group expressed frustration with some aspect of the child support system, although some were more frustrated than others. All noted that they had been given very little information about the process. For one woman, applying for assistance through applying for Medicaid was a humiliating process. Nonetheless, she clearly articulated the child's right to receive services, noting that in volunteering to be the child's temporary guardian she was trying to act in the child's best interest. Another woman felt that the child support system favored her former husband and did not adequately consider the needs of her children. And they all noted, in one way or another, that they were trying to do what was best for their children, regardless of whether the other parent paid support or not.

Child Support as Public Policy

The custodial parents were asked how they thought the child support system worked overall for custodial parents, for non-custodial parents, and for children. Several custodial parents noted that it seemed that guidelines worked in their favor. Because of the many cases where support payments are not made, however, many custodial parents felt that the enforcement process favors non-custodial parents. When asked about child support and children, one woman began to talk about the ways in which the lack of child support harmed her children

> I can't do things that I want for my kids; they can't get into any extracurricular affairs, I can't put them into ballet. . . . My daughter, she wants this stuff, and I can't afford it. There are not a lot of programs out here that are free. You have to pay twenty bucks. Well, $20 is a lot of money. . . . And the kids are hurting. My kids will look at me and say, "Mom, can we go to the movies this weekend?" And I'll say, "I'm sorry, we can't". I'll try to rent a movie if I can afford $2.50 or $3.00 at Blockbuster or something. But I sometimes can't. And they're sitting in the house or playing on the playground not going anywhere. "Mommy, what are we gonna do this weekend?". . . . It's horrible.

With respect to visitation, two of the three women who were satisfied with their child support cases indicated that their former partners were actively involved and very helpful with their children. The other women interviewed, however, said that their former partners did not see as much of their children as the women would have liked. Several described instances where they had urged their former partner to visit the children and he had indicated little interest. One woman indicated that she had to overcome some of her feelings of anger toward her partner to do this, but that she felt this was best for her children. She also noted that, if her partner saw his children regularly, perhaps he would see their needs and then be more motivated to pay child support. Most respondents stated very strongly that people should be required to pay child support whether or not they visit their children. Although they may have hoped for a link between visitation and support on the part of their former partner, they clearly felt that visitation and support should not be linked in public policy.

In general, these custodial parents expressed varying degrees of satisfaction (or frustration) with the child support system depending upon their circumstances. For some, the system worked relatively well, and they were satisfied with the support process. These respondents tended to have more cooperative relationships with their former partners. For others, the system—at least with respect to enforcement—had not worked well, although they had responded to it differently: some by becoming very active advocates for their case, others by becoming frustrated and having no further dealings with the child support agency.[10] For these women, the lack of child support was a source of continuing frustration, and in some cases, a source of serious financial hardship. They were frustrated both with the system and with their former partners. This was evidenced when, toward the end of the focus group meeting, custodial parents were asked to state one thing that would make their lives better. One woman immediately replied, "Responsible men." The other women concurred.

Non-custodial Parents

A total of four non-custodial parents were interviewed, two African American, one Hispanic, and one white. As might be expected of non-custodial parents who would volunteer for such an interview, each of the non-custodial parents interviewed was currently making his support payments. Each also had a somewhat clearly articulated view of the child support system. One expressed relative satisfaction with the child support system; the other three expressed varying degrees of dissatisfaction.

The first respondent indicated that he had no complaints about the existence of the child support system or the available enforcement mechanisms as long as they were used fairly. He felt that the child support guidelines were fair and did not mind making his regular support payments, which were paid through wage garnishment. His main complaint about the system was that it seemed to be geared, in his view, toward processing cases quickly. In his case, he felt that everything was rushed through, and that he did not have enough notice or information to really play a role in the process. He had hired an attorney, and his attorney handled everything for him—including appearing at the hearings, as the respondent lived several hundred miles away. He was not really aware of the procedures to be followed, and when he called the child support agency with his questions (including whether he would be able to get custody), they informed him that he would need to contact an attorney for those sorts of concerns.

Although this parent had no complaints about the amount of current support he was paying, he felt that the back support he was ordered to pay was too much. He said that the court did not really consider the fact that his child had lived with him for a year, and that he had also contributed to her support directly. He was ordered to pay retroactive support even for the period that he had had custody of the child.

This respondent noted that he felt the child support system was fair in cases like his, where he knew the child was getting the support that she needed. However, he cited the case of a custodial parent he knew who was only receiving $50 per month for two children; he stated that this was not enough support and was therefore not fair in her case. He supported enforcement mechanisms such as wage liens and license suspension, "as long as they consider the job status" of the non-custodial parent, taking into account periods of unemployment. Although he would have liked more information about his case and more time to consider issues such as custody, this non-custodial parent was basically satisfied with the child support system.

A second respondent was supportive of the child support system in principle but felt that his case had not been handled well. He stated that he had always paid child support "because I think it is morally right to support my child." The child support laws, he said, were good, but in his case he felt they were used by his former partner because she was angry with him. He had wanted to avoid going to court, and had been willing to negotiate with his former partner, but she had not wanted to do this.

This father indicated that he did not know much about the child support system before he was affected by it. He felt that he was not provided enough information, and was confused by the information that he was provided. When he received the court order, he was not sure what it meant, because he was already providing support. He did not feel that there was an intent on the part of the child support agency to fail to inform him, but he was frustrated by the fact that he would receive conflicting letters, and letters would arrive only a few days before a scheduled court date. He would then call the agency and find that the court date had been canceled.

Once a support order was established in his case, a further problem occurred. A new wage garnishment order was issued, but the old order was not canceled. As a result, his employer applied both the old and the new wage garnishment orders, leaving him with very little income. He had gotten that problem straightened out by the time of the interview, but it had taken several months.

Overall, this parent felt that the child support system favored his former partner. He said that this was, in a sense, right, since the purpose was to advocate for the child in her custody. However, he felt the system could be much more fair to people like himself, who wanted to cooperate and pay support, in terms of establishing the support amount and coming to an agreement without going to court.

The third interviewee talked about how different the support system was now than it had been for his parents, who had separated when he was a child. His father had supported them by paying the mortgage on their house, sending his mother $200 per month, and providing extra things when he or his siblings asked for them. His parents had not gone to court to determine a child support award; rather, they had made their own arrangements. By contrast, he described his own experiences

> The system is like, you know, I'm paying $300 a month for one kid so. . . . I'm not trying to say I should be paying more or less, I just feel that the system that they use and the procedures, I just don't understand how they, I know they got a lot of deadbeat parents out there, but the people who are not deadbeat—the people who want to do the right thing—seem like they're not looking with any consideration of that.

This parent made it clear that he wanted to support his child, but found the child support system somewhat alienating. Asked about whether he had any direct contact with the child support agency, he stated

> I don't even know where the [child support] office is at, and they were always on the side of my wife. She had taken me in to court for $150 that she said she didn't get, and the child support people were there with her. And we're there in the court, and I hear people they owe $1000, $5000; and I'm there from 1 p.m. to 7 p.m. for $150 . . . that's a long time for $150.

Asked for his opinion of the child support agency, he said

> I just think it's misinformed. And I know they have a lot of problems, and their concern is the child—and I think that's right, because there's no one to defend the child, and the child needs defending—but because of that, I think they assume that the person [the non-custodial parent] is not willing to work with them. And I come in, and I'm willing to work, I'm going to pay it. You know, I'm honest; if I say I'm going to pay it, I'm going to pay it.

He also resented having his wages garnished. He described how, because the agency had mistakenly sent out the garnishment order for the wrong case to his employer, it took more than four months for the wage garnishment to take effect. During that time, he paid his former wife directly. He was then called to court again because the support agency thought he was not paying at all because the payments had not gone through the agency. Given his experiences with the child support system, this parent felt that child support had become much too centralized, and should return to being a matter settled between private parties.

The fourth respondent interviewed was deeply dissatisfied with the child support system. He felt that he had been "duped" by a woman who planned to take him to court for child support and live off of his payments. He also felt that the child support agency did not care about the particular circumstances of his case, but simply wanted his money. He thought that the custodial parent had planned to have several children out of wedlock in order to collect AFDC, and that he had to pay the consequences while she lived off of the AFDC payments and child support income.[11]

This non-custodial parent had hired an attorney to handle his case. Because he owed retroactive support and had requested a paternity test, he had to pay court costs, attorney's fees, and the cost of the paternity test in addition to his child support. He stated, "You have no rights whatsoever. They can take you to court, you have to take time off of work, and you have to pay for everything." He felt that the guidelines support amounts were too high, and that the credit given for the other children he supported was inadequate. He was resigned to making his payments, but was very resentful of the system and of the custodial parent. Although he had visitation rights, he had had no contact and had no plans to have any contact with the child.

The alienation that this parent expressed was echoed in some of the comments added to the Maryland survey by non-custodial parents, especially in relation to the determination of a child support award amount. While there were a few complaints about visitation, most of the written comments addressed the question of the amount of support, how it was determined, and the fact that it is not tax-deductible for non-custodial parents. One man noted that he had been voluntarily paying more in child support prior to the child support hearing, and that the application of child support guidelines actually reduced his obligation. Another noted a similar frustration with the way the child support guidelines worked in his case, and the fact that his financial circumstances were not considered.

My wife walked out on me . . . then requested child support. She left bills that I had to pay. I told the Master this and he said HE DID NOT CARE

ABOUT ANY BILLS THAT I HAD. He didn't not (sic) say one word
about visitation. I HAVE NO RIGHT (sic)!!" (emphasis in original).

Another man noted that his job was seasonal, but this was not considered
in determining how much he owed. Yet another respondent noted

> In my case I'm still in high school trying to better myself and make some-
> thing better for my son. I do all I possible (sic) can for my son. But the state
> doesn't want to hear all that. They just want their money.

To some extent this kind of alienation is inevitable when citizens become
subject to the coercive power of the state. Clearly, in a policy such as child
support, the issues touched upon are highly personal. To some extent this
alienation may reflect the fact that the reach of state power in child support is much more extensive than it was two or three decades ago, as
the story cited above regarding the respondent's parents' child support
arrangement indicates. And to some extent it reflects the fact that state
power is now being used on behalf of children, and therefore to some
extent on behalf of custodial parents.[12] Nevertheless, some of the interviewees and many of the survey respondents were clearly alienated and
frustrated by their experiences with the child support system.

Conclusions

This sample of cases from two counties in Texas and Maryland provides
some information on what child support policy means in the lives of people affected by it. In Maryland, custodians and non-custodians in the
sample had relatively equal incomes; non-custodians whose children received AFDC benefits had significantly lower incomes than non-custodians whose children did not receive AFDC. Guidelines were generally followed, but deviations were usually downward, and in Maryland
guidelines were more likely to be followed in AFDC cases.

As anticipated, the survey indicated that experiences and opinions of
the child support system are different for women who are custodial parents than for men who are non-custodial parents, although there are some
areas of agreement. In part, this may reflect the differences between problems experienced by the subset of male non-custodial parents who responded to the survey, versus the kinds of problems experienced by the
subset of female custodial parents who responded. Non-custodial parents
who were not making their support payments, for example, were unlikely
to respond to the survey or agree to be interviewed. On the other hand,

custodial parents who had denied visitation to the other parent, for example, were probably less likely to respond to the survey, as some of the first questions asked were about visitation. Of course, differences also reflect differences among the experiences and attitudes of custodial and non-custodial parents.

The individual interviews provided further insights into the different experiences and frustrations of parents in their interaction with the child support system. When the child support system had worked fairly well for them, both custodial and non-custodial parents expressed general satisfaction with the process. For others, the support enforcement process did not work, and caused them a great deal of frustration.

In a sense this bears out what administrators said when asked whether they solicited input from custodial and non-custodial parents: that everyone affected by it dislikes the child support system, as evidenced by the regular letters of complaint that these agencies receive. Both custodial parents and non-custodial parents have complaints about the process and the way that child support agencies operate. Such complaints reflect not only the differences between custodians and non-custodians, but the differences among different families and different individual circumstances. They may also reflect the fact that child support is, for many people, a painful symbol of a change in familial relationships; contact with child support agencies comes at a time when individuals as family members may need multiple kinds of support services, most of which child support agencies are not intended or equipped to provide.

This chapter began by noting that few studies actually examine what child support means in the lives of individuals and families. Although the custodial parents in my survey were more satisfied with the child support system than many observers might have anticipated, it is clear that for many custodial parents going through the process of obtaining child support for their children is frustrating. Even with the tenacity shown by some custodial parents, actually achieving results in terms of paid child support may be difficult. For custodians who obtain services through an application for social services, the chances of success seem to be smaller. And for non-custodial parents, becoming subject to child support law is alienating, since it is primarily concerned with obtaining support dollars, regardless of their particular circumstances.

For both non-custodial parents and custodial parents, dealing with the child support system can be frustrating and alienating, and has a substantial impact on their individual and family life. The experiences reported here provide a great deal of information about what child support means in the lives of the individuals surveyed and interviewed. In turn, this data provides insight into the meaning of the child support system as it affects families. The next chapter addresses this question more specifically by analyzing the impact of child support on gender relations in families, and on families of differing economic status.

Notes

1. For more detailed information on data collection, see appendix C.

2. According to the supervisor of child support court case records in Prince George's County, the child support agency is required to have this information in their files, but it is not required to be filed as part of the court records.

3. See the discussion of this study in chapter 3.

4. For more information on data collection methods, see appendix C.

5. For more detailed information on the survey, as well as a copy of the survey form itself, see appendix C.

6. A valid case or a valid response refers to the number of surveys in which the respondent answered the question, providing a measurable response. On the opinion questions, this refers to responses that actually offer an opinion (as opposed to responding "not applicable," or failing to answer the question).

7. It should be noted that if this description is accurate, then the child support guidelines were not properly used. Both Maryland and Texas guidelines have provisions for support being paid for other children. Texas has multi-family guidelines, as noted above. In Maryland, if a non-custodial parent owes child support for other children and is actually making payments, that amount is deducted from his or her gross monthly income. Further, federal law imposes limitations on the amount of a person's income that can be garnished. Nevertheless, paying child support for three children in three different families would certainly require a significant portion of one's income.

8. This appears to be common practice; in both states, for most of the paternity cases in my sample, the majority of alleged fathers did not hire an attorney. But for those who did, a paternity test was requested in most cases.

9. It should be noted here that there is a difference between how applicants for services are treated by service providers and the institutional structure of child support policy in terms of who benefits and who does not. All of the administrators interviewed indicated that their efforts were to provide the same services to all child support clients, regardless of their status with respect to AFDC.

10. At one point during the focus group meeting, one of the women began encouraging another woman to become more of an advocate, pointing out that as her children became older they would have more needs.

11. Court documents indicated that the custodial parent in this case was not receiving AFDC benefits at the time of the study.

12. I will take up the question of the implications the child support system has for gender relations in families in chapter 5.

5

Feminism, Women, and Child Support

The discussion to this point has focused on child support policy without considering the role that gender plays in the construction and implementation of this policy. Clearly, however, one reason for the economic problems of single-parent families, especially female-headed families, is the tenacity of traditional gender roles in families, as well as the persistence of gender inequality in the marketplace and society. This chapter considers the role of gender in child support policy, utilizing feminist scholarship as it relates to families, to social welfare policy, and to family law, as well as examples from the survey and interview results reported in chapter 4.

Feminism and Families

Feminism and Family Policy

The history of feminism in the United States is in part a history of advocacy for changes in the legal system and in public policy. Many of these reforms have been in the arenas of social welfare policy and family law. What are the consequences of such institutional reforms? In particular, what are the consequences of reforms that are intended, in part, to improve the circumstances of women's lives?

Scholarship on a variety of social welfare and legal reforms suggests that reforms are limited by existing institutions and policies, as well as by social reality. Feminist scholarship on the welfare state suggests that these reforms tend to reinforce existing gender roles as well as racial and class divisions (Abramovitz 1988; Chunn 1992; Gordon 1990a). Feminist scholarship in the field of family law suggests that legal reforms are often implemented in ways that perpetuate gender inequality and disadvantage women (Fineman 1991; Singer 1992; Weitzman 1985).

Contemporary child support law provides fruitful ground for feminist analysis of legal and social welfare reform. As outlined in the preceding chapters, the current child support regime in the United States is intended both to provide cost savings in the AFDC program and to provide greater economic security for children with absent parents. The law is focused on children whose parents live separately, regardless of whether the child's mother, father, or another party is the custodian. Despite the growing number of men who are custodial parents, it remains true that the over-whelming majority of custodial parents are women. Further, because of lower household income in female-headed households, child support con-stitutes a larger proportion of household income for women who are cus-todial parents and receive child support (17 percent) than for men (7 per-cent) (U.S. Bureau of the Census 1995, 9). Providing greater economic security for children with absent parents necessarily means improving the economic security of the household of which they are a part. Thus, though child support law provides economic support for children with absent parents, custodial parents also benefit from the economic security of regular and reliable support.[1] Indeed, child support policy is in part a response to a social problem created by traditional divisions of paid and unpaid labor, which feminist scholarship has shown to be a major cause of women's economic vulnerability (Abramovitz 1988; Barrett 1988; Okin 1989). Since female-headed households constitute the majority of single-parent families, and because their economic problems are usually more severe than those of most male-headed single-parent families, the analysis here focuses on the consequences of child support policy for female-headed single parent families.

Support law as currently constituted in the United States is a public policy with multiple, sometimes conflicting, purposes. This in itself is not surprising; most public policies are in fact multifaceted—developed through compromises between contested political positions and imple-mented through public bureaucracies which are themselves complex and contradictory. In child support policy, these conflicting purposes may work to advantage some women and disadvantage others. In addition, policies such as child support may simultaneously offer women access to resources while reinscribing traditional gender roles.

Questions that might be asked with respect to gender and child support policy include: Does the current child support law benefit some women more than others? Are there ways in which improved enforcement disad-vantages women, or some women? What kind of gender regime is the current child support regime? What does it say about contemporary family life, and about the state's role in supporting families with children? As has been previously discussed, child support policy is shaped institutionally by both social welfare policy and family law. The discussion below addresses the intersection between child support as social welfare policy and child support as family law. Each section begins with a discussion of feminist literature on the subject, and then turns specifically to a discussion of child support policy, using examples from the empirical studies discussed in previous chapters.

The Dual Systems of Welfare and Child Support

We can summarize the separate and unequal character of the two-tiered, gender-linked, race- and culture-biased U.S. social welfare system in the following formulas: Participants in the "masculine" subsystem are positioned as *rights-bearing beneficiaries* and *purchasing consumers of services*, thus as *possessive individuals*. Participants in the "feminine" subsystem, on the other hand, are positioned as *dependent clients*, or *the negatives of possessive individuals*. (Fraser 1989, 153)

Feminist Scholarship on Social Welfare Policy

Feminists have criticized the contemporary U.S. welfare state on a variety of fronts. Feminist scholars have noted that the welfare state as created in the New Deal era consisted of two separate tracks of entitlement programs: one track based on social insurance, and the other consisting of means-tested programs (Fraser and Gordon 1994; Gordon 1990b). This dual-track system had roots in state-based social welfare policies (Nelson 1990; Skocpol 1992). Women who are single parents who receive social services are served primarily through means-tested programs, generally referred to by the public as "welfare"; social insurance programs, such as unemployment insurance and old age insurance, are generally seen as legitimate entitlements for deserving citizens. Much of social welfare policy as created during the New Deal was specifically designed to exclude African Americans or to maintain racial hierarchies (Amott 1990; Quadango 1988). Thus, racial, gender, and class hierarchies have historically been reinforced by the U.S. welfare state.

Some of these feminist arguments draw upon the institutionalist literature on the formation of the U.S. welfare state, which has emphasized state capacity as the source of American exceptionalism with respect to welfare policy.[2] These scholars argue that for a number of reasons—

including federalism, the late development of a sizable national bureaucracy, and widespread patronage-based political corruption—conditions for welfare state formation were not ripe in the United States until the 1930s, in contrast to European states which formed welfare states in the nineteenth century or early twentieth century (Skocpol, Weir, and Orloff 1988; Skocpol 1992; Skowronek 1982). This kind of analysis is useful in understanding the historical development of the welfare state, and most especially in understanding the distinctive nature of the division between social insurance programs and income transfer programs.

Yet, as Barbara Nelson points out, this literature focuses analysis on state characteristics, not on the characteristics of populations served by particular welfare policies (1990, 129). Thus, the state formation literature may overlook the specific groups of persons for whom the U.S. welfare state was designed.[3] Nelson's analysis of state-level Workmen's Compensation and Mother's Aid programs prior to the New Deal focuses on the categories of persons these policies were intended to include and exclude. This helps to highlight the ways that these policies were differentiated by, and intended to reinforce, traditional gender roles. Recipients of social insurance programs were treated as public, independent citizens, while recipients of Mother's Aid programs were treated as private, dependent subjects.[4]

Nelson, and other feminist scholars, argue that these gendered social welfare policies that predate the New Deal shaped the formation of the New Deal welfare state—including the creation of social insurance programs for workers on the one hand, and assistance programs such as ADC[5] for women on the other (Abramovitz 1988; Gordon 1990b; Mink 1995; Skocpol 1992). Thus, the public/domestic split (Okin 1991) that had been reproduced and reinforced through social welfare policy throughout U.S. history (Abramovitz 1988; Pateman 1988a) was also present in the social welfare policies that emerged during the New Deal.[6] Despite changes since 1935, and the addition of programs such as Medicare and Medicaid, the basic institutional structure of the New Deal welfare state persists to the present. Thus, the dual-track welfare state described by feminist scholars is still with us.

Despite this gendered nature of social welfare policy, programs such as AFDC *do* provide some resources, however inadequate, to women who need assistance. Given present political and economic institutions, feminists cannot therefore reject a welfare system out of hand, despite the fact that there is much to criticize in the present welfare system in the United States (Fraser 1989, ch. 7). As Fraser argues, the combination of the fiscal crisis of the state and the feminization of poverty means that struggles over social welfare policy will be increasingly important for women; thus, they deserve close attention from feminist scholars (1989, 144-45). The welfare state has a mixed effect for women: it both empowers poor women by providing access to resources and restricts poor women through the social control aspects of the welfare system. Clearly the welfare state presents a double-edged sword for poor women, and for feminist scholarship.

The double-edged nature of the welfare system is evident not only in its institutional features, but in political discourse with respect to the welfare state as well. Fraser and Gordon show the history of "dependency", and argue that the United States developed a specific use of welfare dependency in the early twentieth century that constructed dependency as negative and as a character flaw (Fraser and Gordon 1994). Thus, in the twentieth century, "economic dependency" becomes intertwined with "moral and psychological dependency"—terms that are closely associated in political discourse with race, class, and gender. It is in this way that the (statistically unrepresentative) poor black teenage welfare mother becomes the symbol of dependency as a negative character trait.[7]

As Fraser and Gordon point out, much of the current liberal and conservative discussion of welfare ignores the way that dependence and independence are related to gender inequalities, and does not question the association of independence with wage labor (1994, 328–29). Nor does it raise any questions about the relationship between the structure of the family system and the structure of the economy, despite the fact that families and economy are deeply intertwined. In short, when economic dependency is perceived to be caused by psychological dependency (and not the converse), the economic and political institutions that are at the root of poverty become invisible and irrelevant. The "solution" to the "problem" of "dependency" thus becomes separated from economic and political institutions that cause and construct dependency; what emerges are policies that discipline the poor—especially poor women—by linking benefits to specific behaviors.

The ideological nature of these definitions of "dependence" and "independence" also become clear when examining child support policy. In child support policy, dependency is defined in a particular way. Custodial parents who request access to state monies by applying for AFDC are seen as dependent; custodial parents who receive child support payments are defined for the purpose of this policy as independent. These differences were evident in chapter 4 in the treatment of the custodial parents in the support application process who were not using AFDC services, versus the treatment of some of those who applied through social services programs. Nonetheless, to the extent that custodial parents need child support payments to supplement their economic resources from wage work, family support, and/or AFDC, custodians and their children are "dependent"—for the duration of the child(ren)'s minority—on the income and willingness to pay of the non-custodial parent. Child support policy thus reinforces the economic dependence of custodians on their former partners. However, since such dependence is in accord with traditional gender roles, and because it does not involve direct transfer payments from the state to the custodian, it is not seen by policy makers as undesirable or stigmatizing.[8] "Dependence" on the state is undesirable; "dependence" on the absent parent's income and willingness to pay is not. Further, "independence" is defined as reliance on child support payments and on wage labor—despite the fact that low wages and the lack of benefits such as health insurance and adequate, affordable child care make it nearly impossible for many custodial parents to be "independent" in this sense.

Thus, feminist critiques of the welfare state have pointed out that welfare policy is dualistic and structured along gender lines. Further, such constructions and institutions are related to traditional gender roles in families, and to the association of women with dependency and of men with independence. Conversely, non-feminist discussions of the welfare state seldom address underlying assumptions regarding the gendered nature of wage labor and of families, or the links among poverty and gender and racial discrimination in both economy and society. These gendered and racialized constructions of the welfare state have also shaped policies that are linked to welfare programs, such as the child support program. Discussions of child support often fail to give attention to the fact that for a certain class of custodial parents—those on AFDC—the child support system is designed not to provide resources to the custodial parent and his or her dependent child(ren), but is intended to recover government AFDC expenditures. Thus, the purpose of the policy has very little to do with the well-being of poor children or their custodians. In child support policy, AFDC recipients are set apart as different from custodians not on AFDC; AFDC recipients are subject to more extensive state control than other custodial parents, with very little benefit to themselves and their children.

State Interests and Child Support

The child support program, established by the Social Services Amendments of 1974, was "directed at the goal of achieving or maintaining economic self-support to prevent, reduce, or eliminate dependency" (Social

Services Amendments, Part A, Sec. 2001). Without the linkage to the AFDC program, it is unlikely that federal involvement would have emerged when it did. Given this founding link between child support and AFDC, it is not surprising that contemporary child support policy is subject to the same sort of gender, racial, and class divisions that are seen in welfare policy in general.

The child support establishment and enforcement mechanisms are available to custodial parents through two different means. Some custodians establish and enforce child support directly through the court system using private attorneys, most often as part of the divorce process. Since there is no mechanism for directly collecting information on all cases processed in this way, it is hard to tell whether custodians who do not use child support bureaucracies are more or less successful than those who do in collecting support.[9] One advantage of such arrangements is that the custodian's attorney represents his or her legal interests; by contrast, child support bureaucracies consider the child to be their client, not either parent. As for attorneys who work with or for child support agencies, they represent the legal interests of the agencies, considering the child support agency itself to be their client (OCSE 1992a, ch. 4).[10] This leaves the custodial parent with no direct legal representation. Thus, custodians who can afford to utilize private attorneys at least have a better chance of having their own interests represented in the support establishment and enforcement process.[11]

The other means by which a custodial parent can establish and enforce child support payments by the non-custodial parent is through using the child support agencies discussed in previous chapters. These services are available to all custodial parents regardless of income, though some states require the payment of a nominal application fee.[12] Because of the large caseloads that child support workers handle, as well as the legal status of the child, and not the parent, as the client of the child support agency, custodians who utilize child support bureaucracies must, to a large extent, become their own legal advocates.[13]

Custodians who use child support bureaucracies are also subject to different treatment depending upon whether they are AFDC recipients. First, custodians who are not on AFDC can *choose* whether or not to pursue child support services, and thus can decide whether obtaining and enforcing a support order is in their child's, and their own, best interest. This is not true for custodians on AFDC. Second, for custodians not on AFDC, any child support collected is paid to the custodian for the care of the child. This is also not true for custodians on AFDC: most of the child support collected on their behalf goes to federal, state, and local governments as a reimbursement for AFDC expenditures. Third, child support awards are linked to the income of the non-custodial parent. Since, as was shown in the previous chapter, the non-custodial parents of children on AFDC usually have lower incomes than other non-custodial parents, custodians who leave AFDC and continue to receive child support payments are likely to have a much lower child support award than custodians who have not received AFDC. This is borne out in the 1993 OCSE collection data: in cases where child support was collected the average amount collected for AFDC cases was about $2000 per year; for non-AFDC cases, it was about $3300 (OCSE 1994b, 5-6). Further, the rate of collections in non-AFDC cases is significantly higher than the rate of collection in AFDC cases: in FY 93, the rate was 26.1 percent in non-AFDC cases compared to 11.7 percent in current (non-arrears) AFDC cases (OCSE 1994b, 6).

Custodial parents who apply for AFDC must cooperate in the establishment and enforcement of child support in order to receive AFDC. They must assign their child support benefits to the state, and are required to cooperate in the location of the absent parent and the establishment of paternity and a support order. As Deborah Harris has persuasively argued, the entire process of child support—from application through distribution—generally works in a way that removes control from these women, and works more to the advantage of the state than of the individual custodians and their children (Harris 1988).

Cooperation includes not only identifying the other parent, but also providing any information that the applicant has regarding the location and current employment of the absent parent. Exemptions to this mandatory cooperation are permitted in cases where the custodian has good cause, including fear of physical or emotional harm to the child—or to the custodian if such harm would impair his or her ability to care for the child (Mannix, Freedman, and Best 1987). However, few exemptions are granted. Out of a nationwide total of 2.9 million AFDC child support cases opened in FY 92, there were a total of 9,403 good cause requests; good cause was found in 5,885 (or 0.2 percent of all AFDC cases) (OCSE 1994a). Further, even if good cause is found this does not mean that the state will not pursue child support; it only means that the custodial parent does not have to cooperate in this pursuit in order to keep her AFDC grant.

When the applicant is the child's mother and paternity has not been established, she must answer a series of questions regarding her sexual activities at the time of conception, a description of the "alleged father,"[14] his behaviors toward the child in question, and any physical similarities between the child and father. This is done in all cases, regardless of the fact that most fathers admit paternity without contest.[15] If the "alleged father" contests paternity, all parties are given a blood test to determine paternity.

Some custodial parents also feel humiliated by the process of applying for social welfare benefits. One custodial parent, a respondent in the survey of custodial and non-custodial parents discussed in chapter 4, included a letter with her survey expressing a series of frustrations with the child support process as it is linked with AFDC. She described the effects of the experience of applying for AFDC and cooperating in the establishment of paternity and child support in this way:

> Women pay the price in the first place, when they apply for aid. They are treated badly 70 percent of the time by case workers who pass judgment on them—they are asked personal questions, they make you feel like a whore, they make you feel ashamed, they make you feel ignorant, they make remarks about your situation that are unprofessional. . . . I don't think I'll ever be able to leave this experience behind. If I were to ever need assistance again, I would never, ever again turn to the state . . . for help.

As reported in chapter 4, one woman's experiences were similar. She was trying to obtain Medicaid for her relative's child, but was humiliated by the treatment she received, and felt she was treated by the local social services office as though she had done something wrong in applying for these benefits.[16] She felt this way even though it was not her biological child for whom she sought services; therefore she was not even subject to the kind of personal questioning that the above survey respondent reported.

After the custodial parent has cooperated in this entire procedure, and assuming that child support is actually established and collected—which, as already indicated, occurs in less than 12 percent of AFDC cases nationwide—very little of the money actually goes toward the custodial parent and his or her dependent children. In fact, until 1984 in most states, *none* of the child support collected in AFDC cases went to the custodian unless the support award exceeded the monthly AFDC grant.[17] The Deficit Reduction Act of 1984 provided for a $50 pass through or bonus payment to the custodian per month. However, the Deficit Reduction Act also put in place the practice of income deeming: this is when income of all household members (even siblings who may have a regular child support award outside of the welfare system) is attributed to welfare recipients for purposes of determining their AFDC grant amount. In addition, the Deficit

Reduction Act required that all siblings be included in an AFDC grant. Thus, custodial parents on welfare became subject to further impoverishment and reduction of their ability to make decisions that would benefit their families (Hirsch 1988). This practice was challenged, but was upheld by the Supreme Court in *Bowen v. Gilliard* (107 S. Ct. 3008, [1987]). In his dissent, Justice Brennan suggested that in addition to its other negative effects, this practice would be destructive to the relationship between children and their non-custodial parents (ibid., 3026–29).

The $50 bonus payment from child support collected is not counted as income for purposes of determining the amount of AFDC, and is only paid to the custodian when the non-custodial parent makes a timely payment in a particular month. Although the bonus does not reduce the AFDC grant, this payment is counted as income if the recipient is on food stamps—reducing the value on average by $17 per month (Roberts 1991). Of 2.4 billion dollars collected nationally in FY 93 for AFDC child support cases, approximately 19 percent was paid to custodial parents; the remainder went to federal and state governments to reimburse the costs of AFDC (OCSE 1994b). In FY 93, about 12 percent of all federal, state, and local AFDC expenditures were reimbursed from child support payments (OCSE 1994b).

Child support thus provides few advantages in terms of access to more economic resources for custodial parents who are AFDC recipients. Most of the revenue from child support collections for AFDC recipients goes to state and federal coffers. For this class of child support obligees, the foremost governmental interest seems to be in cost savings. Despite Congress's stated effort to make child support services available and provide them equally to all custodial parents, in practice the system does little to serve the needs of AFDC custodians; in these cases, state interests take precedent over either the child(ren)'s or the custodian's interests. Thus, the system as currently structured seems to be in keeping with feminist critiques of the welfare state in the United States: the support enforcement system divides families along class lines, providing resources and services to custodial parents who are not on AFDC, while providing greater social control of custodians who are on AFDC, with little in the way of additional resources.[18]

Treating families differently according to class status has a long history in the U.S. (Abramovitz 1988). Jacobus tenBroek documented the "dual system" of family law in California almost three decades ago: the family law of the poor and civil family law (tenBroek, 1964/5). As discussed in chapter 2, tenBroek traced the evolution of the Elizabethan Poor Law and family civil law as it was adapted in U.S. law, and demonstrated the differences that remain between the institutions and principles of the two systems. This dual system of family law still operates in the federal child support enforcement program. In practice the child support services offered through child support bureaucracies constitute two systems; one system operates for custodians who apply for AFDC, the other operates for non-AFDC custodians who obtain child support through child support bureaucracies.

For the child support system to really serve the needs and interests of the poorest custodial parents and their children, major changes in the goals and structure of the program would be required. Recent years have seen multiple proposals for administrative reforms. For example, the Commission on Interstate Child Support recommended a series of changes to improve the interstate enforcement system (U.S. Commission on Interstate Child Support 1992). Since the late 1970s, Irwin Garfinkel and colleagues have been advocating a child support assurance system. This is a non-means tested benefit that would provide a guaranteed minimum child support payment to custodians regardless of whether child support was collected in their case (Garfinkel, 1992; Garfinkel, McLanahan, and Robins, 1992). Such a system was proposed in the 102nd Congress by the Downey-Hyde Child Support Assurance Act (testimony on the bill can be found in Subcommittee on Human Resources, 1993a). The Clinton administration had proposed some reforms of child support along with their welfare reform proposal. A number of child support provisions were also included in welfare reform measures considered by the 104th Congress.

With the exception of child support assurance, most aspects of these proposals focus on ways to improve the administrative functioning of the child support system, either by further federalization, by altering current practices so that there is more uniformity among the states, or by adopting administrative practices in lieu of court-centered procedures. If such changes are adopted and bring about higher collections rates, they could certainly benefit custodians not on AFDC by increasing child support collections. For custodians on AFDC, however, many of these proposals for improving administrative efficiency will provide little benefit.[19]

Coercion, AFDC, and Child Support

Drawing on social control theories of the purposes and functions of the welfare state, many feminists have argued that, in addition to reinforcing traditional gender role divisions, the welfare state functions to control the lives of poor people, especially poor women (Gordon 1990b). AFDC, in particular, has been criticized as a form of "public patriarchy" (Abramovitz 1988, ch.1; Brown 1981) that is aimed more at social control than at assistance (Barrett 1988). Yet Fraser also notes that in some ways all recipients of public benefits—at least those benefits identified as "welfare"—are treated as subjects of the "juridical-administrative-therapeutic state apparatus" (1989, 153-156).

In one sense, the institutions of the state, which have historically been used to discipline women—especially women with children and insufficient resources to support them—are now being used to discipline men through the child support system. This is partly why some non-custodial parents feel alienated by the process. Women are required to cooperate in this coercion, and are themselves coerced, through the paternity establishment system and the mandatory requirements of the AFDC program. The mechanisms of legal coercion—from paternity establishment to incarceration for contempt—discipline the behavior of men, especially poor men. Thus, both women and men become subject to state coercion through this system. This coercion is far from benign, as the experiences of some of the respondents to this study indicate.

This does not mean that child support does not help some women and their children. Nor do I mean to suggest that the state should have no role in child support; in general terms, the enforcement of child support is a legitimate and appropriate use of state resources. The power of the state is not always deployed in ways that disadvantage women and the poor. However, the way that state power is deployed is exactly the matter under consideration here, and the results are mixed and cut in contradictory directions. As the results of the current structure of the child support system are assessed, it is crucial to understand how this power is deployed, the kind of gender regime that is created, and the extent to which it both disciplines and assists women and their dependent children.

Women and Family Law

At present it seems as if feminist "legal theory" is immobilized in the face of the failure of feminism to affect law and the failure of law to transform the quality of women's lives. (Smart 1989, 5)

Feminist Scholarship on Family Law:
Formal, Not Substantive, Change

Since the early 1980s, feminist legal theorists have been engaged in a series of disagreements about the most effective strategies for affecting legal reforms, through courts as well as through legislation, which will benefit women. Some feminists argue for an equality-based approach in which women are treated the same as men (Littleton 1987; Williams 1982); some argue for a difference-based approach that takes account of biological and socially-constructed differences between men and women (West 1987). Others argue that for a legal strategy to actually help women in practical terms in the real world, it must take account of domination and the power differential between men and women (MacKinnon 1989). Underlying these disputes are very different philosophical positions regarding the nature of gender differences and similarities.

This philosophical and strategic debate among feminist scholars has emerged in part because, while a good deal of progress has been made, formal legal reforms have failed to bring as much change in gender relations as many feminist scholars and advocates had hoped. Thus, as Carol Smart puts it in the above quotation, legal reform has not transformed "the quality of women's lives."

There are multiple reasons that this is so. First, any legal reform has limited effects on social reality. To cite the example most closely related to child support law, no-fault divorce laws that require equal treatment of divorcing partners do not make those partners equal in terms of access to resources, or in terms of present and future earning capacity. Feminist scholarship on the results of no-fault divorce laws shows that legal reforms can have perverse and unexpected effects, and that much depends upon how the law is implemented (Fineman 1991; Singer 1992; Weitzman 1985, 1987).[20] In child support, no matter how effective the establishment and enforcement mechanisms become, there will be those non-custodial parents who are unable to pay, as well as those willing to go to great lengths to avoid paying. Thus, there will be custodial parents and children who will not benefit. In addition, as discussed above, unless the way that the institutional link between AFDC and child support functions is changed, custodians and children on AFDC will receive very little benefit.

Thus, any legal reform has limitations in terms of what will actually happen in practice. As Smart argues, this is especially so in the relationship between feminism, women, and law. Drawing on postmodern theory, Carol Smart argues that though law is in fact "a plurality of principles, knowledges, and events," law presents itself as a singular, unified entity, and is thereby empowered (1989, 4). In a liberal legal order, law has the power to "impose its definition of events on everyday life," and in doing so it disempowers other modes of inquiry and forms of knowledge. In practice, legal reforms not only have limited effects, but may disadvantage parties who do not fit into the assumptions upon which the law is based.

In a liberal republic, law characteristically strives for uniformity of treatment of all persons classified in a particular way. Yet, because the law may be blind to differences among those classified as members of a particular group, the effects of law in practice may be different for less powerful groups of people. The law may work well for some and not for others, be desired by some and not by others, although they are all classified together by the legal system. In the case of child support, there are many differences among women who are custodial parents; these differences are based on race, class, work history, AFDC/non-AFDC status, and educational attainment, as well as in their desire for assistance from the state in their pursuit of child support. Support enforcement may thus have differential effects on different groups of women: it may work very well for middle-class women, but may bring about more harm and/or social control for poor women.

Law is not, then, so much a tool of liberation or oppression as it is a site of struggle (Smart 1989). Changing the form of law—as in the case of child support, changing from case-by-case, judge-made law to statutory and administratively-centered law—changes the nature of those power struggles, but by itself does not necessarily liberate, for example, children and their custodial parents. As the results reported in chapter 4 indicate, experiences with the child support system vary widely, but for some parents are frustrating and alienating. Clearly, as indicated above, the law of child support enforcement, while it may assist custodial parents in some senses, can also be used as a means of regulating the lives of poor women (Abramovitz 1988; Harris 1988; Hirsch 1988). Thus, it is important, especially from a feminist perspective, to look at the practice of this transformed and extended system of law. So, if one goal of feminist scholarship is to point toward the possibilities for—as Kathleen Jones has put it—a more woman-friendly polity (Jones 1990), legal reforms are the beginning, not the end, of feminist inquiry.

One possible conclusion from this skeptical view of legal reform is that the subjects of legal reform do not benefit from it. Perhaps legal reform, given its limits, is not the route to pursue in seeking a woman-friendly polity. Should we be this pessimistic with respect to child support law?

A Feminist Perspective on Child Support: Power Relations in Separated Families

As indicated in chapter 2, reforms to the child support system that originated twenty years ago did not emerge out of direct concern for improving the conditions of the lives of women who are custodial parents so much as to recover some of the costs of AFDC. Nevertheless, feminist legal advocacy groups as well as organizations of custodial parents have been involved in lobbying (as well as litigation) for reform and improvement of the child support system. One question that arises is whether a legal reform that is not specifically intended to improve women's lives may yet have that unintended effect. In cases that do not involve AFDC, improving the economic circumstances of custodial parents is a somewhat necessary side effect of redistributing the income of non-custodial parents to their children. How has child support law affected women not on AFDC? To some extent this depends upon their particular circumstances, and on whether the non-custodial parent is inclined to be cooperative.

Given the feminist literature on family law, especially on divorce reform, one is led to ask whether the current child support system alters gender-based power relations in non-AFDC separated families. It seems that current child support law does indeed alter the balance of power between custodian and non-custodian, both in terms of the mandatory mechanisms of child support guidelines for determining support award amounts, and enforcement mechanisms such as wage liens.

As discussed previously, guidelines establish a presumptive formula for calculating the child support award. For women who actually receive the child support payments awarded, the existence of guidelines alters the power relationship between the custodial and non-custodial parents.

Especially in divorce decisions, child support awards prior to the implementation of guidelines were seen as claims by the custodial parent on the non-custodial parent. A common complaint prior to the establishment of guidelines was that the support award was determined according to what the non-custodial parent had left over after meeting his expenses. Thus, all of the non-custodial parent's expenses (including car payments and entertainment) were deducted, and child support was awarded from whatever was left. On the other hand, to justify increases in the support award, custodial parents had to painstakingly document every expenditure on the child and justify such expenses as legitimate.

Child support awards under guidelines are not so much a claim by the custodial parent on behalf of the child; they constitute a claim by the state, on behalf of the child, to the resources of the non-custodial parent. The fixed rules that guidelines represent place the custodial parent and the non-custodial parent in different relation to each other and to the state. Under guidelines, the burden of proof rests on the non-custodial parent to show why the guidelines amount should not be followed. Mandatory guidelines thus tend to empower the historically disadvantaged party—the custodial parent and the child(ren). Rather than placing the burden of proof on the custodial parent to justify expenditures on the child (the practice prior to the adoption of guidelines), the award is based on each parent's income, and calculated according to a state-established formula. The fact that it is the state, not the custodial parent, imposing the support award amount, is in itself an important step in altering the balance of power between parents who live separately. In this sense, then, mandatory guidelines for support awards alter power relations in separated families.

Fixed rules, and their accompanying enforcement mechanisms, provide equal treatment for persons equally situated (in economic terms), reduce litigation, remove the child support amount as a bargaining chip in divorce proceedings, and provide higher and more realistic amounts of child support awards. Moreover, fixed rules and related enforcement mechanisms are an important form of public moral ordering. While it is true that deviations from the guidelines are typically downward (Erickson 1992), guidelines have generally increased support award amounts (Dodson 1994).

Although the fixed rules of guidelines apply across income categories, support guidelines may be less beneficial to poor women for a number of reasons. First, since the awards are based on income, the amount of support is lower (whatever a particular state's formula)—both because these women's earnings are lower than middle-class women, and because their partners or former partners tend to have lower earnings. Second, if the non-custodial parent does not have steady work (which is more likely for lower income men), it will be more difficult to collect the award. Any in-kind support offered by the non-custodial parent (however much it does or does not assist the custodian) is not considered in the child support order. And for women on AFDC, very little of the child support money collected actually finds its way to their children. Finally, it is the rare AFDC case in which the child support award is more than the AFDC benefit.

The mechanisms available to the state in its effort to recover AFDC expenditures are also available to custodial parents not on AFDC, whether they utilize the child support agencies or private attorneys. These mechanisms are fairly powerful: mandatory wage liens,[21] liens on property, credit reporting, and federal and state tax intercepts, to name a few. Such mechanisms are most effective in cases where the non-custodial parent has steady employment and does not change jobs frequently, is easily locatable, and has assets. Given the obvious, that middle- and upper-middle-class men are more likely to have these characteristics, these laws seem more likely to benefit middle-class custodians.

Thus, in child support, and probably in alimony (Bell 1988; Singer 1989) fixed rules seem to provide more predictable results; therefore, they provide at least some families affected by child support law more reliable economic support. For non-AFDC recipients, the support enforcement system does place the resources of the state behind the claims of the child and the custodial parent, altering power relations in separated or separating families. The custodial parents interviewed in this study seemed to agree in this respect, that the guidelines especially seemed to work in their favor. In those cases where wage liens could be established, the enforcement aspect of child support generally worked well. However, for some custodial parents, the enforcement mechanisms did not work well at all despite their best efforts.

Certainly, most public policies are contradictory and multifaceted in both intent and effect, and child support is no exception. Further, many public policies benefit some groups at the expense of others. While fixed rules seem to help at least some women, they may be less beneficial to more vulnerable custodians. Thus, at least for the present, the fixed rules of child support guidelines and enforcement may provide better outcomes than judicial discretion did for middle-class women, while providing fewer benefits to poor women, and little or no beneficial effect for women on AFDC—at least with respect to the provision of income.[22]

Conclusion

Thus, changes in the very concepts of citizenship, childrearing and paid work are necessary, as are changes in the relationships among the domestic, official economic, state, and political public spheres. (Fraser 1989, 129)

Does the child support system alter, subvert, or maintain the conservative aspects of law and of the social welfare system? It seems to have cross-cutting effects. For some custodians, the guidelines and mandatory enforcement mechanisms place state power behind the claims of the children in their care, as opposed to the claims of the non-custodial parent. Child support law thus indirectly alters gender relations in separated families, since most custodians are women. Mostly, however, child support policy in intent and in many cases in effect places state power behind the claims of children to their absent parent's economic support.

Yet there are limits to the benefits derived from child support enforcement. Despite the gender neutrality of support laws, and their application to persons of all income classes as well as to both male and female absent parents, the current child support regime is still based upon gendered ideas of family life. To the extent that child support is seen as *the* solution to economic problems of separated families, it is still based on the notion of the "family wage"—despite the fact that few families were ever able to attain this ideal (Gordon 1990b). To the extent that the AFDC program is left intact by child support policy, reforms fail to attend to what poor women would actually need in order to support their children (Bergman and Renwick 1993). The system as a whole emphasizes the responsibility of individuals for the support of their legal children; thus, it fails to adequately attend to questions of collective responsibility for children's well-being, despite the multiple ways that certain kinds of families have received substantial government aid throughout U.S. history (Coontz 1992). To the extent that child support falls more harshly on the poor, both male and female, it raises questions about the actual purpose of this policy. The next chapter returns to the question of the place of child support in families-state relations in the United States, addressing both the benefits and the limitations of child support policy.

Notes

1. Of course, this is a source of contention on the part of many non-custodial parents, who object to what they perceive as redistribution of their resources to the custodial parent (not the child). The analysis here assumes that the interests of custodial parents and of their children are quite similar with respect to economic security: economic security for the custodial parent means economic security for the child(ren).

2. "American exceptionalism" refers to the fact that in terms of the time of its formation and the structure of its programs, the U.S. welfare state is quite different from its counterparts in other industrialized democracies. See the discussion of social welfare policy in chapter 2.

3. Skocpol's more recent work, *Protecting Soldiers and Mothers*, seems to recognize this, as she develops a complex analysis of what she terms "maternalist" and "paternalist" social welfare policies that developed prior to the New Deal.

4. The mapping of gender roles onto the formation of the two-track social welfare system does not mean that all men who are recipients of social welfare programs are treated as independent and all women as dependent. Rather, contemporary recipients of social insurance programs, male and female, are seen as "deserving," while recipients of public assistance programs are seen as "undeserving" (Katz 1989).

5. AFDC, or Aid to Families with Dependent Children, began as part of the New Deal social welfare programs as ADC, or Aid to Dependent Children; the custodian was not included in the grant.

6. This is not to say that the public/domestic split always takes the same form; there are historical differences in the way the public/domestic split is perceived and implemented (Abramovitz 1988; Skocpol 1992).

7. This is also how the term *underclass* comes to mark not the lack of economic opportunities of a set of people, but the behaviors and characteristics of the people themselves.

8. The view of custodial parents with respect to child support may vary quite widely, depending upon their relationship with the absent parent. Some custodians may wish no involvement at all on the part of the absent parent, and this may include child support.

9. Because of differences in the way data is collected and reported, it is difficult to compare Census data to OCSE data (Committee on Ways and Means 1993, 741–43).

10. Depending upon the administrative structure of the state or local agency, the attorney may be an employee of the agency or a state's attorney in a contractual agreement with the agency.

11. This is certainly not unique to child support, but is generally true of legal representation.

12. Initially, the services of child support bureaucracies were made available to non-AFDC families on a temporary basis; this aspect of the program was made permanent in 1980. As chapter 3 indicates, in practice, many states did not comply with this aspect of the law until well into the 1980s, especially until 1984 when the Child Support Enforcement Amendments made it clear that the program was to serve all custodians that applied and paid the application fee.

13. Advocacy groups for custodial parents, such as ACES (The Association for Children for Enforcement of Support) and OECS (Organization for the Enforcement of Child Support), have also become advocates for the legal interests of custodians, as well as a means for custodians to learn their rights in the process and how to become their own advocates with child support agencies. Some parents become very good at advocating for themselves, as evidenced by some of the interviewees in chapter 4.

14. This is the term used before paternity is established. Contrary to common perception, the father's name on the birth certificate does not establish paternity. This is a separate legal process. The only time that paternity is automatically established is if the parties are married at the time of birth—and in this case in most states the child is considered the child of the mother's husband whether or not he is actually the biological father.

15. In Prince George's County, Maryland, these questionnaires are placed in the court record, which is a public record; the names of all parties are included. This information was not included in the Texas court records studied.

16. It was not the child support agency about which she complained, but the social services office.

17. This was rare, both because this was prior to federally mandated guidelines—meaning that awards in general were low—and because most absent parents

of children on AFDC have low incomes. A few states used what is called a "fill-the-gap" approach, permitting AFDC custodians to keep their child support payments to fill the gap between the state AFDC payment and the state standard of need.

18. It should be noted that I am speaking here of the institutional structure of the child support system, and not of the treatment given to individual custodial parents by child support workers. As noted earlier, all administrators reported their efforts to treat recipients of child support services equally, regardless of their status with respect to AFDC. One respondent, who had worked in poverty law before becoming a child support administrator, noted that "poor people generally are treated badly" by society, but that the effort of his agency was to provide all children the same level of service.

19. Reforms of the child support system will be discussed further in chapter 6.

20. Singer (1989) and Sorenson (1992) have shown respectively that the disadvantages to divorcing women reported by Weitzman may not be due to no-fault divorce laws themselves, and may vary a great deal depending upon how economies of scale are measured in separated families. Thus, the problem may not be the legal reform itself so much as how judges interpreted the meaning of the laws, and the pre-existing power inequalities between men and women in divorcing families (Okin 1989, ch. 7).

21. Wage liens for collection of support awards were made mandatory for cases at least thirty days in arrears by the Child Support Enforcement Amendments of 1984, and are mandatory in all cases as of January 1, 1994.

22. Whether fixed rules are desirable in other arenas of law that affect women remains an open question. Karen Czapanskiy, for example, has questioned whether child support guidelines will really benefit women, since set rules in family law have generally operated to women's detriment (Czapanskiy 1990).

6

Child Support and the Families-State Relation

This book began with a discussion of the role of families and family life in a liberal republican regime such as the United States. At the outset, I argued that families have both public and private dimensions, and that thinking of families as simply private entities is both inaccurate and misleading. This chapter takes up these questions again, first by analyzing child support policy in light of state purposes, and then by exploring ways in which the families-state relation needs to be rethought.

Child Support, Families, and State Purposes

Chapter 1 outlined the principles that should guide the families-state relation in a liberal republic. These include, from liberalism, the need to clearly identify state purposes with respect to families, and to limit state action regarding families to those aspects of family life clearly related to state purposes. From republicanism, there is a clear concern for the care and moral education of children. Given a liberal republic with a market economy, there is a clear state interest in limiting the state's economic obligations in the support of families. However, it is important to note that there are multiple facets to state economic policy as it relates to families. Finally, equality is central to both liberal and republican understandings of political life; given the extent to which equality in families affects equality in other arenas, equality is an important aspect of family life in a liberal republic.

Chapter 1 also outlined some of the interests in government policy toward families that individuals have as family members. Given liberalism's commitment to privacy, adults have substantial liberty interests in the choices and decisions they make about their familial life. Yet these choices are limited when they make other family members vulnerable; in these circumstances, state policy that seeks to limit the vulnerability of less powerful family members becomes justifiable. Families also look to the state to provide basic economic conditions that make family life possible. Keeping in mind these principles and interests on both sides of the families-state relation, as well as the analysis of child support policy in the preceding chapters, we are better able to assess child support policy.

The Strengths of Contemporary Child Support Policy

Contemporary child support policy reflects several of the state interests identified above. First, it reflects state interests in children's basic well-being. In any kind of regime that wishes to sustain itself, the state has legitimate interests in whether children receive some minimum level of care and economic support. The republican tradition indicates that this interest is fairly significant, since children are also citizens, and will become active participants in the republic. In a liberal regime, given its commitment to limiting state power and maintaining some arena of private life, the state will not be the primary direct provider of children's care. Therefore, a liberal republican state does have an appropriate interest in ensuring that people who choose to become parents assume, to the extent that they are able, sufficient responsibility for their children.

Child support policy thus reflects these legitimate state interests. The use of public resources to establish and enforce child support is a supportable public policy, in light of the state's interests in child well-being, cost savings, and parental responsibility.

Some of the measures utilized to enforce child support may seem fairly invasive. However, the extent of state coercion usually reflects the extent to which the obligor has attempted to avoid a legally established support obligation. Despite the intense press coverage that occurs in the occasional case of an obligor apprehended and charged with a felony for crossing state lines in order to avoid paying child support, much of the work of child support agencies is relatively ordinary. Felony citations are used much less frequently than the more routine mechanisms of wage garnishment, tax intercepts, or the threat of being jailed for contempt of court. Given the state interest in child well-being, and the extent of the problem of nonsupport, contemporary child support policy, and its use of state resources, is an appropriate state policy in this arena of family law.

Nonetheless, since contemporary child support policy emerged out of concerns regarding the expense of social welfare programs, the primary goal of the program in practice is fiscal savings for the state. The program intends to reinforce private provision for children, and utilizes public resources to ensure that parents do provide economic support to their children. In an era of cutbacks in other arenas of social policy, the child support program seems destined to remain, and possibly to expand.[1] Recent expansions in the effort to establish paternity in all cases seem to point to a program that will include all custodial and non-custodial parents, regardless of their circumstances or desire to participate. Policies such as early and/or mandatory paternity acknowledgment are primarily seen as a way to prevent future state expenditures on locating absent parents and establishing paternity—and thus serve state interests in cost savings. Given this focus on cost savings, contemporary child support policy also has a number of limitations.

Limitations of Contemporary Child Support Policy

Child support policy reflects the conflicting goals and interests that liberal republican regimes have in families: interests in fiscal savings for the state—that is, in families that are economically self-supporting—as well as interests in the education and well-being of children, in equality, and in limiting state action with respect to families. These interests often come into conflict with each other, especially in public policy. In child support policy, the primary state purpose driving the system is the goal of fiscal savings for the state; other state interests in families, such as in an expansive understanding of child well-being or in equality, are not the purpose or goal of this policy.

Child support policy reinforces state interests in promoting private families that are economically self-reliant. Certainly it is desirable that families, whatever their structure, have sufficient resources to provide some minimum standard of living, especially when there are children present. It is also desirable that people who choose to become parents provide resources for their children insofar as they are able. The current structure of child support policy, and the public discussion related to child support, however, may be misleading in at least three ways.

First, in implying that families can and should be wholly economically self-sufficient, child support policy turns our attention away from the fact that state resources are utilized in multiple ways to support ostensibly economically independent families. Such support may occur not only through direct transfer payments, but also through other policy arenas such as housing, transportation, inheritance law, and taxation. Second, it turns the focus of public policy away from collective responsibilities for the support and well-being of children. Third, it ignores the fact that, even with a fully enforced child support order, many single-parent families—especially female-headed families—will still be poor. A discussion of each of these dynamics follows.

First, as noted in chapter 1 in the discussion of families and markets, government economic policy in a variety of arenas provides supports and assistance to families. Much of the expansion of suburban areas during the 1940s through the 1960s was supported by government programs in housing, veteran's assistance, education, and transportation. Tax deductions for dependent care expenses provide some assistance to families with children; the Earned Income Tax Credit provides assistance to lower income families who file tax returns. Tax deductions for homeowners and educational loan programs subsidize the resources of eligible families. The social security program redistributes funds from the currently employed to the formerly employed and/or their dependents. In multiple ways, then, government policy redistributes resources among differently situated families and individuals. The resources spent on AFDC and on the collection of child support pale in comparison to the total resources redistributed through these other public policies.

Second, as public policy the child support program emphasizes private provision of resources, and uses public means to enforce the economic obligations of children's legal parents. As noted in chapter 2, this is a means of promoting parental responsibility, and is one of the stated goals of child support agencies. The clear norm, then, is that it is a child's legal parents who are primarily responsible for providing financial resources for the child's care. The state's role is first of all to enforce this obligation, and to provide state funds through AFDC only when the resources of the child's legal parents are completely inadequate. Parental responsibility is a laudable and supportable goal, as discussed above, but the clear message of the system as currently structured is that individual parents are the primary contributors to the economic needs of children. Collective responsibility for the economic needs of children begins only when the economic resources of parents cannot meet the most basic needs of food and shelter. Private provision for children is the goal of the support enforcement system.

Aside from emphasizing only one of the many collective *interests* a liberal republic has in the well-being of children—interests in limiting state expenditures through private provision—this emphasis contradicts the many collective *responsibilities* any society interested in its own survival has towards its children. In particular, it offers a very narrow understanding of child well-being—an understanding that limits collective responsibilities to the public enforcement of private provision. This is especially true if child support alone is viewed as a solution to the problem of child poverty and poverty in separated families.

The federal Office of Child Support Enforcement recognizes the narrowness of an economic understanding of child well-being to some extent when it argues, as noted in chapter 2, that child support can help with other aspects of child well-being: it can help provide a sense of identity, improved self-esteem, and so on. In the end, however, this is not what child support programs are mandated or equipped to do. This is not to say that child support agencies should necessarily perform social welfare functions; but if child support agencies remain primarily collection agencies, it would serve us well to place this policy in context, and recognize its limitations in terms of the overall needs and well-being of children in separated families.

Third, many families with an enforced support order will still be poor. According to Census Bureau data, 24 percent of custodial parents had incomes below the poverty line in 1991. If the full amount of child support had been paid in these cases, 21 percent would still have been below the poverty line; those raised above the poverty line would still be among the near poor (U.S. Bureau of the Census 1995, 9). It is true that child support is more important to the household income of poor families; it constituted 34 percent of the household income of poor women who were custodial parents in 1991, compared to 15 percent of the household income of non-poor custodial mothers (ibid.). Nevertheless, the average amount of child support due and paid to poor custodial mothers was $1922 for 1991—58 percent of the $3331 due to non-poor custodial mothers. And the child support paid to custodial mothers did not bring their mean household income of $18,144 even close to the $25,184 mean household income of custodial fathers due support who *did not* receive payments. Custodial fathers due support who *did* receive payments had a mean household income of $33,579 (ibid.). Clearly, women's earnings need to be much closer to men's earnings before children in female-headed single-parent families will come close to the earnings of male-headed single-parent families.

Also somewhat troubling is the tendency of the child support program to expand its mandate to encompass all custodial parents, regardless of whether they wish to receive child support services. This policy began with custodians on AFDC, but developments such as the paternity requirements of the Omnibus Budget Reconciliation Act of 1993, and mandatory paternity establishment provisions in some states (Monson 1994), seem to be aimed at universalizing child support by making it a requirement whether or not the custodial parent wishes to receive such services. As one administrator put it,

> I think [there has been] an unacknowledged expansion of the concept of child support, moving toward a kind of universal entitlement. . . . More and more, I'm seeing things that indicate to me that we're moving toward a system where you don't have an option to be independent of the system; that the system will become all-encompassing, and everyone will be forced into it whether they particularly want to or not, and that we will—if not us as a state administration, there will be a government agency that will be more involved than we even are now—because everyone will have to be participating. . . . Philosophically [the purpose] in 1975–76 was to recover AFDC payments. I mean, that was pretty simple in terms of what they were after. And then we added the non-AFDC, and then you've just added and added and added; it's really grown a lot in concept since the beginning.

Most people agree that a child's legal parents should be responsible for providing economic support for that child, to the degree possible.[2] But how far should the state go in making this happen? In those instances where a parent has participated in a child's life and later abandons their relationship and/or economic support of the child, there seems to be a relatively clear basis for state action. However, there are many instances that do not fit this category. Is it desirable to require all families, regardless of circumstances, or their desire to participate, to become subject to the child support system?

Again, the limitations of child support policy do not mean it is not a legitimate public policy; to the contrary, I have argued that child support does indeed serve supportable state interests. The limits of child support policy simply mean that it is only one means of providing assistance to separated families, and that we should not expect this policy to accomplish too much by itself. Child support policy, when placed in the context of the range of available policy options for the support of families and family life, serves tenable state purposes.

Despite these limitations inherent in child support policy as currently structured, there are indeed multiple ways in which the current system of child support could be improved. Such improvements would help some of the custodial parents interviewed for this study to have more resources for their children. Thus, it is important to discuss some of the ways that the child support system could be structured more effectively.

Improving Child Support

Improving Support Services

Clearly, there are aspects of the support enforcement system that do not work well for those custodians who seek the services of child support agencies. The large caseloads of child support workers, the relatively rapid changes in federal requirements, the administrative and legal difficulties with the interstate support enforcement system, the cumbersome nature of court-based proceedings, and the relatively recent advent of enforcement mechanisms such as mandatory wage garnishment are all contributing factors. The mobility of many non-custodial parents also contributes to the difficulties inherent in enforcing support. Improvements in the administrative functioning of many aspects of the support enforcement system are therefore desirable. Such improvements would provide a more reliable system for those custodial parents who wish to receive child support services. A variety of mechanisms, some in the proposal stage and some in the process of implementation, are all likely to improve the efficiency of the support enforcement system.

Among the most important areas that needs improvement is interstate support establishment and enforcement. About one third of all child support cases are interstate cases. While there have certainly been improvements in the process of interstate coordination, these cases still take longer to process and are more difficult to enforce (U.S. Commission on Interstate Child Support 1992). A number of solutions have been proposed to this problem, ranging from complete federal centralization of the child support system with enforcement handled by the IRS to greater state coordination and reciprocity.[3] Given that the current state-based system has taken twenty years to develop its current level of success, and that courts and bureaucracies would likely still need to handle the paternity and support establishment functions of child support policy, the administrative upheaval that would come with federalization does not seem a viable solution to support enforcement in the near term. Other solutions, however, might help. First, a truly functional Federal Parent Locator Service or data base through which states could exchange information on obligor parents—both within states as well as nationwide—would especially assist in the enforcement of interstate cases. If all states recognized each other's court orders, either through state law or federal mandates, interstate enforcement would be a simpler process: new hearings would not have to be held in the obligor's state of residence to establish the support order. New employees could be required, when filling out their W-4 form, to report any child support obligations to their new employer. If employers were in turn required to report new employees with support obligations to their state child support agency, and this information was made available in a national data bank, interstate parent locations could occur much more quickly.

Another problem is investment in child support services. This is reflected both in the size of caseloads, and in the amount of overall investment in child support enforcement per case. According to a study by the Children's Defense Fund, states were investing little more per case in 1992 (an average of $132) than they had in 1983 (an average of $130) (Ebb 1994, 8). Further, the caseloads of child support workers had actually increased during that same period (ibid.). Both Maryland and Texas—the states in this study—had more than one thousand cases per child support worker, which is not uncommon nationwide. In a time of tight budgets at all levels of government, increases in funding are not likely to be forthcoming. However, a policy of reinvestment used by some states might provide more funding for support services. Several Texas administrators mentioned in interviews their ability to reinvest the cost savings generated by the child support program back into the program itself, as stipulated in 1989 legislation. This provides more resources for child support services, as well as a built-in incentive for the agency to work as efficiently as possible.[4] States could designate all child support incentive payments specifically for child support services, providing more resources for child support programs.

The automated systems required by the Family Support Act of 1988 also should help child support agencies to utilize their resources more effectively. Unfortunately, however, the process of implementing this requirement has been marked with setbacks, and only one state met the October 1995 deadline for having an automated system in place. As a result, Congress has extended the deadline to October 1997 via P.L. 104–35. Most states contracted with private software developers to design their systems, and did not necessarily get what they paid for—partly because consultants did not always understand what was needed. Both Texas and Maryland were still working on their systems at the time of this study. Texas had a statewide system that had been in use for some time, and both states had pilot systems in place to meet the new requirements, but did not yet have statewide systems that met these requirements. Automation has improved the more routine aspects of child support enforcement, and further automation should bring greater efficiencies.[5]

Improving Support Services for Poor Women and Children

> Whether or not a feminist stance is taken, analyses and policies which do not explicitly consider gender division are neglecting not only a crucial dimension of inequality, but also a set of social processes which affect most areas of life . . . a lack of explicit consideration of gender is in itself likely to contribute to a perpetuation of women's oppression, both at an ideological level (denying it) and through the concrete policies developed and implemented. (Murgatroyd 1985, 51).

In many ways, the child support system provides few benefits to the most vulnerable families: poor families and families receiving AFDC benefits. If public policy were focused, as Nancy Fraser suggests, on the needs of children who live with one parent, how would the policy be different (Fraser 1989)? If we were to change the orientation of child support policy by placing the interests of custodial parents and their children at the center of consideration, what would happen? We would have to ask, what do custodial parents need in order to provide and care for their children?

When this policy is viewed from the perspective of the needs and interests of custodial parents and their children—as opposed to state interests in recovering AFDC expenditures—the first reality to emerge is how inadequate the AFDC grant amount is. In real dollars, benefit levels have declined in all states during the period of 1970 to 1993; the median decline is 45 percent (Committee on Ways and Means 1993, 661–68).

The second reality to be recognized is that child support awards are also generally small (even with the adoption of child support guidelines), and do not provide sufficient income to meet children's needs. The average annual support collected in those cases for which a payment was made during fiscal year 1993 was $2856 (OCSE 1995, 64), with non-AFDC cases averaging around $3300 and AFDC cases averaging around $2000 per year (OCSE 1994b, 32). Clearly, this is not enough to provide sole support for even a two-person family, nor is it intended to do so. Child support supplements the other sources of income required by custodial parents to adequately provide for their children. The effective collection of child support awards will not, by itself, solve the problem of poverty in single-parent households. Rather, it needs to be seen as one component of an effective anti-poverty strategy.

The third factor that must be recognized is the lack of economic opportunities available to many custodial parents, as well as the realities of the low-wage jobs that generally are available. Many women on welfare—more than 40 percent—are in fact working, either while they receive benefits, or when cycling on and off AFDC as temporary work becomes available (Hartmann and Spalther-Roth 1993a). Most of these women remain poor even when they obtain employment, since they work in low-wage jobs in female-dominated occupations; one-quarter of *all* women who work in predominantly female occupations earn wages below the poverty level for a three-person family (Figart and Lapidus 1994, 2). Many of these jobs provide no benefits, not even the health benefits that are especially crucial to custodians with young children.

For many of these women, then, even child support and wage labor combined could not provide sufficient resources for their families. Given that the fathers of their children are likely to be low-income men, many women's circumstances would not be substantially improved even if they were living with their children's fathers.

To survive, then, poor women must rely upon income from the state, income from wage labor, support from extended family members, and income from men through marriage or child support; all of these sources of income are necessary components to an effective anti-poverty strategy for women with dependent children (Hartmann and Spalther-Roth 1993a, 1993b). As Hartmann and Spalther-Roth put it, women may "package" this income in a variety of ways, depending upon their particular circumstances. What poor women really need, quite simply, is *more*—more income and more resources from whatever source available. Child support is one small portion of an effective anti-poverty strategy; to really improve the circumstances of poor women and their children, improved wages and assistance from state resources are also required.

Many aspects of AFDC as it is currently structured, and of the AFDC-child support link, also raise serious questions about the infringement of the custodial parents' rights. Courts have interpreted child support law as primarily intended to serve the purposes of state cost savings, at least in relation to AFDC recipients, and have limited rights-based challenges to AFDC and child support law (Stamm 1991; Mason and Roberts 1989; Hirsch 1988). If custodial parents and their children were at the center of AFDC child support policy, the rights of custodians would be of much greater concern.

Moreover, as discussed above, support enforcement is still less effective than it could be, especially for women on AFDC. Improved collections should be another goal of policies intended to assist poor women and their children. However, child support policy needs to be linked to other arenas of public policy. The benefits of the current child support system rest on other aspects of government economic and labor market policy. Separated families are more vulnerable in the present economy than middle-class "intact" families, for a variety of reasons. The first is simply economies of scale: it is cheaper to maintain one household than two. Further, the current wage labor system does not provide enough jobs that pay liveable wages. Thus, some non-custodial parents are unable to pay child support because they are unemployed. An obvious solution here is to provide job training to non-custodial parents to assist them in attaining the skills that they need to support their children.

Other problems are particular to female-headed single-parent families. Although gains have been made by women in the work force, women, on average, still receive lower pay than men, and are channeled into low-wage jobs; further, there is no national policy with respect to long-term dependent care. Most jobs with adequate pay and benefits are structured to assume that workers have no dependents to care for, and there is no system of child allowances to assist parents with young children (whatever their family structure). Because these economic and labor market institutions are still designed in ways that assume traditional gender roles in family units, they make current child support policy seem a reasonable and sufficient solution to child poverty.

The public discussion of poverty in single-parent families seems to begin and end with child support, as if obtaining and enforcing a support award would solve the economic difficulties of these families. However, as already noted, even if the support enforcement system worked perfectly, many of these families would still be poor.

Focusing on the needs of custodial parents and their children, it becomes clear that to actually solve the problem of child poverty requires a great deal more than child support enforcement. The labor market, job training, career opportunities, and child care are all factors that need collective attention if we are serious about child well-being. As the quote at the beginning of this section suggests, this then becomes a discussion about the regime as a whole, and the design of institutions that would make child well-being a reality.

If women and children matter, then, both resources for custodial parents—whether or not they are on AFDC—and the rights of custodial parents and their children should be considered in any reform of the child support system. Improving the child support system for all custodians would certainly require overall improvement in the effectiveness of the child support establishment and enforcement system. This would also require changes in the AFDC-child support link: changes that would both provide more child support funds directly to custodians, as well as expand custodial parent's options with respect to child support.

Unfortunately, most current discussions regarding the welfare state and family breakdown clearly rest responsibility (and blame and punishment) on individual parents; public policies that would punish poor parents seem to have wide support, regardless of their deleterious effects on children. Much of this discussion seems to rest on underlying assumptions about what families ought to be like. Women, especially poor women who are single parents, are seen as violating a series of societal norms as they relate to family life. Thus, the prospects for child support policy reforms that would provide more benefits to women and children on AFDC are quite dim.

Child Support Assurance

A number of advocates and scholars who have studied child support policy have proposed the adoption of a child support assurance system. Proposals vary, but such systems generally involve the provision of a government-assured minimum benefit level to all participating custodial parents, regardless of whether the non-custodial parent makes a payment in a given period. In some proposals, participants are limited to custodians receiving AFDC benefits;[6] in others, all custodial parents with a child support order are eligible (Garfinkel 1992). The latter type of child support assurance program has the advantage of being non-means-tested, therefore reducing the possibility that program participants will be stigmatized (Garfinkel 1992, 50–51).

Such programs would likely prove beneficial to those custodial parents who wish to receive child support. First, the minimum benefit level would provide a more reliable support benefit for many custodians who would otherwise receive irregular payments or no payments at all. If coupled with improved collection mechanisms, such a system would likely provide more support for children in separated families. Programs such as the Child Assistance Program in selected New York counties have provided additional services to custodians who participated, including job training and the continuation of benefits during the transition period to paid employment (Roberts 1992). Another argument in favor of such programs is the extent to which participants in the New York program found these additional services much more useful and supportive in their efforts to find better employment in order to better provide for their families (ibid.).

Perhaps most important, the use of collective resources to support children also recognizes that there are collective responsibilities to children when the resources of the child's legal parents are not adequate or are not paid. Thus, child support assurance recognizes society's interest in and responsibility for the basic well-being of children, and the state's role in providing economic support.

Even more desirable, from the perspective of recognizing, through policy, collective or societal responsibilities to children, would be a non-means-tested child allowance system. In such a system, support would be available to families with children regardless of family structure. The advantage to such a program is that it is universal, and does not set off or stigmatize separated families or single-parent families. It also appears to be an important component of any effective strategy to alleviate child poverty in advanced industrialized societies; European countries with such policies have much lower child poverty rates than the United States (Danziger, Smeeding, and Rainwater 1995). Unfortunately, the political support even for child support assurance, let alone child allowances, is not sufficiently broad to permit its passage except as local- or state-level pilot projects.[7]

Rethinking Family Policy in a Liberal Republic

Child support is a public policy that serves legitimate public purposes, and is thus worthy of both public support and continued public investments to improve the child support establishment and enforcement system. However, as has already been indicated, child support policy needs to be seen in the context of the families-state relation and the range of public policies that mediate that relationship. Child support must thus be seen within the framework of family policy and the families-state nexus. Thus, the remainder of this chapter will address the more general question of balancing the interests of families and state in contemporary family policy.

State Interests and Real Families

Current discussions about family structure seem to suggest that "proper" family structure provides a solution to all social problems related to families, or to which the condition of families is seen as a root cause. But in doing so, these discussions focus attention on factors that are at best secondary to important social and political purposes regarding families.

As discussed in chapter 1, in liberal republics there are collective interests in the well-being of children. But the focus on family structure attends to only one aspect of these collective interests: that of minimizing state expenditures. This interest is, in many senses, in conflict with a rich sense of child well-being.

In liberal republics, then, some minimal conditions for child well-being are required. Children need at least some minimum level of material well-being: in any society, poverty and malnutrition are not good for children. Aside from the children's own claims to justice, it is also undesirable from the standpoint of their education as citizens that they be regularly abused or neglected. Liberal republics also have stakes or interests in whether families in general provide positive conditions for children: a basic education in citizenship, including the value of a liberal polity; responsibility; a basic work ethic; and a basic moral education, religious or otherwise. In liberal regimes, however, these interests in families are limited, meaning that state action with respect to families should not dictate that these conditions exist; rather the state should provide resources and institutions that make these conditions possible for families.

The real question with respect to family structure is whether it is possible for families that are not traditional (a heterosexual couple with their own biological or legally adopted children) to accomplish roughly the same things as traditional families. Do non-traditional families have access to some minimum set of economic resources and to child care—that is, to resources roughly equal to the economic resources available to two-parent families with minimally adequate financial resources whether due to one, two, or more incomes? This question is fundamentally an empirical one, and an empirical question about which the empirical evidence, to the extent that it exists, is decidedly mixed (Furstenberg and Cherlin 1991; McLanahan and Sandefur 1994). Families that differ from the two-parent, white, heterosexual, middle-class family are generally economically disadvantaged by dominant institutional arrangements: the division of paid and unpaid labor, racial and gender divisions of labor in the labor market, child custody, marital property division, and child support enforcement.

With the exception of the state interest in cost savings—based in the maintenance of present economic arrangements regarding wage labor—other state interests do not require a particular family structure. The argument for family structure allows state economic interests in cost savings to trump all other collective interests in families and family life.

Overall, state interests in families depend less on family structure than on what happens in real-world families. This does not necessarily mean that there cannot be any collective aspirations with respect to family life. In fact, this book began with the notion that there *are* collective aspirations regarding family life in liberal republics. However, a desirable ideal has much less to do with a particular family structure than it has to do with what actually happens in families: with equality of treatment, with freedom for individuals to make decisions regarding their family life, and with the substantive well-being of children. Therefore, to the extent that collective resources are to be utilized in ways that are concerned with child well-being, we need to invest those resources in ways that are non-discriminatory with respect to family structure, and that focus on what real-world families actually need.

In any desirable regime, state power with respect to families can and should be limited. But the problem that diverse families pose for liberal republics is more complicated than it might seem. Questioning the role of families in a liberal polity leads to issues concerning who can form families, whether people should have to be licensed to have children, and under what circumstances the state is justified in intervening in decisions made by family members. As indicated in chapter 1, this is exactly where any discussion of the relationship between families and states does and ought to lead. For anyone concerned about actual political practice, this discussion cannot consist only of a discussion of family structure or the division of labor within heterosexual families. The discussion must be about state purposes with respect to families, and what aspects of family formation and functioning should be subject to state scrutiny, as well as the circumstances that limit state power with respect to families. These are not questions of policy or of merely rearranging some incidental features. They have to be thought of in terms of the entire regime.

Thus, to reformulate an understanding of families it is necessary, as feminists have been arguing for some time now, to reformulate an understanding of the relationship between public and domestic life, and to connect this understanding to arguments about the principles of liberal republicanism. Again, as noted in chapter 1, if desirable societies require that citizens be educated and socialized to be—in some sense—good citizens, then someone must provide for their care and education. If this is not to be done by the state, then families are the likely domain for much of this socialization and care.

The Relationship between Families and the State

> In any event, liberalism's conception of privacy, like its state-society distinction, is not a defence of the domestic-public split. For intimacy needs defending outside of the family, and solitude needs to be defended within the family. The line between privacy and non-private, therefore, cuts across the domestic-public distinction. (Kymlicka 1990, 262)

Liberal republics do require constituting choices regarding public and private, but this does not *necessarily* mean that the sphere of the private is a pre-existing, pre-political sphere. I have suggested that this is precisely the wrong way to think about families. Given the multiple problems with the notion that families and the state exist in completely separate spheres, liberal republics must find ways to value families—and individuals' choices with respect to family formation and dissolution—without enforcing a particular family structure.

The boundary between the public and the private with respect to families might instead be seen as a matter of choices—constituting, collective, political choices—about the kind of regime being formulated and maintained. The relationship between families and the state can then be seen as a relationship in which state policy shapes the possible choices and avenues of action for individuals and for families; conversely, choices made by individuals as members of families, and changes in family practices, shape state policy. Given the commitment in this liberal republic to some distinction between matters that are private and matters that are public, theorists and policy makers need to focus on the ends that are served by a particular policy with respect to families. Put most simply, we need to ask what legitimate state purposes are with respect to families, and then turn to current and proposed policies to determine the best means to serve those state purposes. Further, in a liberal regime, state action with respect to families must be limited. Some matters with respect to families are properly subject to state scrutiny; some are matters that the state cannot justify dictating without becoming an authoritarian state. Certainly, there are multiple state purposes, and they may often conflict in both theory and practice. In some cases, difficult choices will need to be made in the setting of family law and social welfare policy, but these choices should be made with careful attention to the purposes served and the actual effects of putting law and policy into practice. Before returning to a discussion of state purposes with respect to families, however, I want to suggest a framework for rethinking the relationship between families and state.

If we conceive of public and private not as separate spheres but as deeply interconnected entities that still have some separable purposes—not as bounded but as interconnected, then the question of relating public and private becomes one of understanding this relationship. In terms of the relationship between families and the state, families have multiple aspects and many meanings and functions in a liberal republican polity. Families have multiple political, social, and cultural meanings. The role of the state should not be in promoting and perpetuating a reified notion of "the family" at the risk of ignoring the multiple and conflicting political and legal aspects of the interface between state and families.

Instead, we should focus on the multiple intersections between families and the choices individuals make in families, and state law and policy. We should focus not only on real-world families as they are, but also on the actual political and legal questions raised by the interface between families and state.

The relationships that people form in families are deeply intimate and personal, and involve matters in which most people value privacy. Yet these relationships also provide great potential for harm to vulnerable members who may require state protection. How can state law and policy honor the privacy that people value, and yet protect vulnerable persons from harm? Further, is it possible to have a family law and social welfare policy that would not only permit, but would even reproduce gender equality in families? Is it possible for such a family law to be limited, i.e. in this sense liberal?

As argued at the beginning of this book, the boundary between families and the state is permeable and malleable: the laws of the state structure the relationships within families; the institutions of market and economy, as enforced by the state, structure the relative power of family members; the state intervenes in families when a legitimate state interest is involved (e.g. child support, or the protection of the physical well-being of children). Changing family practices require a rethinking of the understanding of appropriate state action in the life of families.

The families/state nexus might be more usefully understood as a relationship in which the state pursues its legitimate ends, which under some circumstances involve protecting the immediate or long-term well-being of some members (even when countered by the claims of other family members). The restructuring of this relationship is crucial to the constitution of families and a political regime that will provide, in its regular workings, for relative gender equality. This goal is not incompatible with the well-being of children, as Cohen and Katzenstein (1988) point out.

Jennifer Nedelsky suggests a way to reconceive the public-private nexus in liberal polities. In her article "Reconceiving Autonomy" Nedelsky argues that dichotomies such as "public-private" were always illusory and inaccurate, and therefore misleading (Nedelsky 1989). Nedelsky points out that boundaries are also points of connection. Focusing on boundaries as points of separation places a focus on rules; moreover, it reifies rights in a way that turns attention away from the nature of decision-making in a self-limiting government (1989, 176) and from the ways in which human beings are connected with one another—the ways that the individual and the collective are enmeshed.

Nedelsky is thereby developing a different way of understanding the connections between individual and collective: recognizing both their ongoing tension, yet also their interrelatedness. This understanding is a useful way to look at the relationships among individuals in families, as well as the relationship between families and the state. If we see that individuals in families are interrelated, yet separate, we can see how family members may have legitimate and conflicting claims. If we see that families and the state are separate and yet enmeshed, with both common and conflicting purposes and interests, we can see that there may be legitimate and non-legitimate uses of state power with respect to families.

Martha Minow has utilized what she terms a social relations approach to develop an understanding of "rights in relationship" in several arenas of law. Her discussion of family law notes this about boundaries, families, and the state,

> Tracing the presence of state power in the family sphere, historically described as removed from the state, suggests something powerful about boundaries: both sides of a boundary are regulated, even if the line was supposed to distinguish the regulated from the unregulated. (Minow 1990, 277)

Minow notes that the history of family law in the United States illustrates two problems: the danger of a system of legal enforcement of "hierarchical status relations," and the inequalities perpetuated by a system that assumes individual autonomy and equality when it does not exist (1990, 268). The former applies to family law as it existed prior to divorce reform in the 1960s and 1970s; the latter to the problems generated by no-fault divorce as generally practiced.

It is important to note what is being said here about family law. Minow is arguing that legal rules serve to structure power relationships among individuals (1990, 302). Thus, rules that recognized the claims of male heads of households—but not of their wives and children—served to reinforce male power in the family, and silence the voices of women and children, however legitimate their claims might be. This did not mean that there was actual consensus in such families; only that the claims of more vulnerable family members were not accorded recognition (292). In a similar fashion, practices in contemporary family law that fail to recognize actual disparities between men and women have served to perpetuate gender inequality (272–75). Thus, Minow focuses attention on the realm of family law in order to illuminate the need to understand the relations among individuals in families as well as the relationship between families and state as relationships in which each party affects the other, and in which state power structures the terms of these relationships.

What does it mean to understand family law, social welfare policy, and the families-state nexus, in relational terms? It means that one needs to look at real-world families as they actually are, and at how public policy, law, and the economy shape those families and the options available to them and to individuals within families. It means that proposals for reform of family law and social welfare policy need to be carefully scrutinized in terms of their actual effects on real-world families. It means that individuals may make decisions with respect to family formation and dissolution that the state must respect, while still ensuring that individuals fulfill their legitimate obligations to other family members. It means that state power must be used carefully with respect to family life, and the purposes for which state power is utilized must be clearly articulated. It means, too, that the effects of proposals for public policy reform on different kinds of families must be carefully scrutinized.

The questions that need to be decided with respect to the relationship between families and the state—questions of family policy and law—affect multiple aspects of family life, and cut across different family forms. Battery and child abuse occur in all types of families; vulnerable members of families should be afforded state protection regardless of family structure. Children deserve basic economic security whether they live with one parent, two (opposite sex or same sex) parents, in a blended family, or with grandparents. Adults should generally have the opportunity to choose with whom they will live and form families. Given the variety of families and family practices, modern liberal regimes must find other means than a naturally and biologically given definition of the family for marking the limits of state power.

In short, much contemporary discussion of the families-state relation leads in the wrong direction, and fails to provide sufficient guidance regarding the relationship between families and the state, the limits of state power with respect to families, and the scope of justifiable state ordering with respect to family life. The problem for political practice is that unless we ask these difficult and crucial questions of public policy and law in the context of their place in a liberal republican regime, we will have no principles to guide practice.

These questions include at least the following:

When adults form families, how and in what way should this be recognized and treated by the state? What obligations do adults incur toward other adults with whom they form families, and should the state regulate adult relationships? If so, how? How much freedom do adults have in choosing domestic partners that will be recognized constructively by state law and policy (e.g. will same sex partners, or non-intimate domestic partners, be recognized)?

What are the obligations of adults toward children with whom they have formed a parenting relationship? What is the relationship between parenting adults who are not a child's legal parents and the children that they parent (e.g. stepparents, birth parents, "surrogate" mothers, care-taker relatives, gay and lesbian co-parents, grandparents)? How ought the state enforce those obligations and regulate conflicts among adults with respect to parenting? When family members have conflicting claims, on what set of principles ought decisions with respect to those claims be made? To what extent are individual parents responsible for the well-being of children? To what extent is the society as a whole collectively responsible for the well-being of children, economically and otherwise? What is the basis for these responsibilities, and how should they be reflected in public policy?

In child support, such questions include: Should biological paternity, by itself, establish an obligation to economically support the child in question (whether or not paternity was chosen by the biological father)? If paternity is to be established through affidavits or administrative processes, how will the rights and obligations of the child, the mother, and the father be distinguished, protected and enforced? If paternity is to be established through administrative processes, will a custody determination be issued at the same time? When and under what circumstances does a biological mother have the right to refuse to participate in paternity establishment procedures? In child support procedures?

When an absent parent is indigent, what kinds of processes should be followed? Should that parent be excused from economic obligations, offered job training, required to participate in job training, be required to pay regardless of financial circumstances? When an absent parent did not choose to become a parent, do the financial obligations remain? What constitutes choosing to become a parent?[8] On all of these questions— questions confronted daily by family courts and by public bureaucracies such as child support agencies—the simplistic answer of a particular family structure provides very little useful guidance.

Solving the Problems of Real-World Families

As should now be clear, the features of real-world families must be central to any discussion of the relationship between families and the state. As Stephanie Coontz has clearly documented, real families in American history have been quite different from the idealized family that many theorists, practitioners, and ordinary citizens imagine (Coontz 1992).

In the end, what is required in any discussion of families is attention to actual problems and questions, including the following:

1. The economy and labor market in contemporary societies make it very difficult for middle and lower income families to survive. If, given current market arrangements, two incomes are required to economically support children, then what the state needs to do is either entirely restructure the arrangement of the labor force (an unlikely prospect in the near term), or ensure that families of all types have the economic resources required to provide at least minimally for their children. This would require effective supports for families such as a reduction of the tax burden on families, the encouragement of affordable child care, and an effective system for child support assurance—or, better, a system of child allowances.

    The structure of the economy—including the tax system, wage-labor, retirement and health benefits—must make it possible for real choices to exist for both men and women with respect to having and raising children and working for wages. This requires at least: equal pay, adequate child care, equal division between men and women of paid and unpaid labor, adequate economic support for families, and the availability of jobs with livable wages. In short, the economy and families must be structured so that one does not have to choose between being an ideal worker and a decent parent.

2. Women are "vulnerable by marriage," as Susan Okin puts it: they are disadvantaged in the labor force because they are paid, still, about 70 percent of what men are paid (Okin 1989, ch. 7). African American women must work longer hours to earn their 70 percent; Hispanic women earn less.[9] Women also tend to be in more marginal or lower-paying jobs, i.e. human service, helping professions, and part-time work; this is especially true for women of color. Further, in a polity that provides little assistance to workers who have children, women are vulnerable as parents. When women are custodial parents, and wish to work for wages, they face the nearly impossible task of finding affordable child care. Workplaces still generally assume that each worker—male or female—has a "wife" at home. Analysis of families that does not include consideration of gender inequality, and of women's vulnerabilities as parents, workers, and wives, is inadequate at best. Ignoring gender in the discussion of family structure is at best inadequate, and is likely to perpetuate gender inequalities.

3. Violence occurs in families of all types and in all income brackets.

Family law and social welfare policy must provide for the protection of vulnerable persons. Any family policy that seeks to encourage healthy family life must face this reality, or face the danger of creating more real physical harm to vulnerable persons than anything that it may accomplish towards creating liberal virtues or more stable families. Family policy must also ensure that family law and public policy does not contribute to, or implicitly endorse (by not opposing), family violence.

4. Individual choice must be recognized as a crucial part of family well-being. Although the state also has a specific and legitimate interest in the enforcement of familial obligations, especially the obligations of parents to children, these obligations should not be structured along gendered lines. The ability, especially of more vulnerable members of families, to make choices for their own well-being is crucial. Women (and men) who are abused must have options and resources to leave their spouses. Children who are abused must be protected. Women must be free to choose to be single parents, for whatever reason; they often choose single parenthood not only for their own well-being, but also for their children's well-being. Gay and lesbian persons should have the same opportunities to choose parenthood, and to have legal recognition of their familial relationships as heterosexual persons do. This *does not* mean, as some cultural conservatives claim with respect to this argument, that anything goes: the state still has some particular interests in terms of the conditions of life in families, especially with respect to ensuring the well-being of vulnerable family members; and we all have humanistic as well as political interests in the well-being of children. Individual choice *does* mean that diverse families are not only capable of providing for the care and education of children, but that such diversity should be celebrated as the strength of a pluralistic society. Ignoring the strengths to be found in the diversity of contemporary families adversely reifies family structure as a solution to all social problems.

5. In divorce law, the interests of children and their custodial parent should be served first as in Britain, where efforts are made by the courts to ensure that the stability of children's lives is maintained (Glendon 1989; Weitzman 1987). Such policies would maintain the child(ren)'s home and school situations, divide property with consideration of the needs of the custodial parent and child(ren), and would consider the value to the child(ren), and thus to the family, of the primary child care provider (Weitzmann 1987, 224-29).

6. Child support law and policy must be placed in context. While sup-

port can and does assist those families who receive it, and while legal parents should bear responsibility for supporting their children, child support policy does not, by itself, provide a solution to the problems of low-income families. However the support system is designed, administrative costs, especially for paternity establishment and interstate enforcement, will likely continue to increase. Although most AFDC collections benefit the government and not children or their custodial parents, overall governmental cost savings will likely continue to be impossible to achieve unless non-AFDC families are charged substantial fees for services. Thus, even though the support system may benefit from administrative restructuring, the limits of the support system in terms of overall family policy must be recognized. More desirable would be a system of child support assurance, or of child allowances, that would recognize some of the state's obligations to families.

Conclusion

As liberals, republicans, and feminists discuss families and public policy, it is crucial to remember that the nature of the families-state relation in liberal republics is fundamentally a question of institutional design that not only cuts across policy affecting families, divorce law, family law, educational policies, and welfare policies, but also cuts across the entire institutional structure of the regime.

What this means is that we can talk not only about a property regime, the relationship between private and public in the design and practice of the property regime, and the types of purposes which the property regime serves in the constitution of the whole. We can also talk in terms of a "family regime": the relationship between domestic and public, families and state, in the design and practice of family law and social welfare policy, and the types of purposes that families serve in the constitution of the whole. Then, to be a liberal republic with respect to the relations between families and the state, the question becomes one of institutional design: how ought policy and law respecting families be designed in a way that is in keeping with the aspirations of the regime?

Families and the state are deeply intertwined and interdependent, yet in a desirable regime families and state also have distinguishable purposes. In principle as well as in practice, some balance must be achieved between the material and normative requirements of the regime with respect to families, and the freedom of individuals and families to make their own choices regarding the nature of family life.

It has been argued here that we need to reconceive the nature of the relationship between families and the state. We need to set out the distinctions between matters that are of interest to the state and subject to state ordering, and matters that are better decided by individuals and individuals within families. We need to discuss what the state ought to do to encourage, enforce, and/or permit a variety of family structures and practices.

Thus, in general terms:

1. In liberal polities, understanding this relationship between families and the state requires an understanding of the fundamental features of the liberal regime, and the place of family law and policy in the principles and practices of the regime.

2. Given the importance of limiting state/public power in liberal republics, the state should restrict its realm of action with respect to families to specific concerns or normative goods that are related to the principles and practices of the regime. Further, state action should be focused on creating the conditions that make desirable family life possible, rather than on intervening in specific kinds of families. In a liberal republic, the state cannot dictate specific positive family practices. However, it can put in place institutional structures that reinforce and make possible conditions in families that provide for the well-being of children.

3. State purposes with respect to families are related to the conditions or practices of life in families, and not a particular family structure or the existence of particular members in particular roles.

4. In addition to state interests in families, the state has responsibilities to families: protecting and empowering vulnerable members of families (while not stigmatizing them as victims); creating an economy that makes families possible, i.e. pro-child (but not necessarily pro-natalist) work, economic, and tax policies; providing family law and social welfare policy that protects children, enforces obligations of family members and recognizes contributions of caregivers, deals equitably with inequalities within and between families, and protects the interests of individuals as family members.

These questions are not merely about particular public policies that will affect a few individuals; they are questions about the kind of polity we want to have—about the design of the regime as a whole. As public policy, child support is linked to the entire structure of the families-state relation. Child support policy, important as it is, should thus be seen as but one component, in a desirable regime, of public policy intended to provide families with the minimum resources that they need to adequately provide for the well-being of children.

Notes

1. Although one thing that the 104th Congress and President Clinton agree on is the need for strengthened child support provisions, at the time of this writing, no major revisions of child support have occurred.

2. As this same administrator put it, "Even people who don't pay their child support say people should pay child support!"

3. For discussion of some of these options among policy makers who advocate different solutions, see the testimony in Subcommittee on Human Resources, 1995.

4. This ability to reinvest savings generated by child support agencies is mentioned in the Report Card as an important factor in Texas' ability to improve their support services so significantly between FY 87 and FY 89 (Subcommittee on Human Resources 1991, 27).

5. A number of the improvements briefly suggested here were part of the proposed Child Support Responsibility Act, H.R. 785, proposed by a bipartisan group of lawmakers from the Women's Caucus. Some of these proposals are discussed in Subcommittee on Human Resources, 1995. Some of the provisions of H.R. 785 and other child support reform bills were included in the Personal Responsibility Act of 1995, which passed both houses but was vetoed by President Clinton. Some of these measures were included in subsequent welfare reform legislation passed in 1996 as this book was going to press.

6. The only program to actually be implemented, in a few counties in New York state, involved only AFDC recipients.

7. For some discussion, see the Downey-Hyde Child Support Assurance proposal (Subcommittee on Human Resources 1993a). Some of the criticisms of this bill on the part of states were related more to the nationalization of child support than to the child support assurance proposal itself.

8. The separation between the fact of conception and the act of non-contracepted heterosexual intercourse may vary in degree of remoteness. Nevertheless in many circumstances the separation is significant enough that it is hard to claim a direct connection between intent to conceive and conception.

9. Based on 1990 Census Bureau figures.

Appendix A

Legislative Histories

Legislative History of Federal Child Support Laws

1950—URESA (Uniform Reciprocal Enforcement of Support Act) passed, providing for interstate enforcement of child support (revised in 1952, 1958, 1968).

1965—Public Law (P.L.) 89–97 allowed state or local welfare agencies to obtain address and place of employment of absent parents from the Secretary of Health, Education, and Welfare.

1967—P.L. 90–248 required AFDC recipients to assign their child support benefits to the state.

1975—P.L. 93–647 Social Services Amendments of 1974, signed into law on January 4, 1975, created Title IV-D of the Social Security Act. 42 U.S.C. 651 *et seq.* This law

1. Established the Federal Office of Child Support Enforcement (OCSE), with responsibility for:
   a. establishing a parent locator service;
   b. establishing standards for state programs/offices;
   c. reviewing and approving state plans;
   d. evaluating state efforts through regular audits;
   e. preparing an annual report to Congress;
   f. certifying cases for referral to the IRS for collections;
   g. certifying cases for referral to the federal courts to enforce obligations;
   h. providing technical assistance to the states;
   i. maintaining records of program operations.
2. Gave primary responsibility for operating child support enforcement to the states. Requirements include

173

a. the state must have a separate organizational unit to administer the program;

b. states must undertake the task of establishing paternity and securing support for individuals who apply for AFDC;

c. states must collect the support payments for distribution;

d. states must enter into cooperative agreements with courts and law enforcement officials;

e. states must establish parent locator services that use federal, state, and local information sources;

f. states must cooperate with other states in CSE;

g. states must retain complete records of collections and disbursements.

3. With respect to AFDC:

a. specific procedures were required for distribution of child support collections made for families receiving AFDC;

b. states are paid incentives for AFDC collections;

c. applicants for and recipients of AFDC are required to assign their benefits to the state, must cooperate with the state in establishing paternity, and must furnish their social security number to the state. (Note that P.L. 94–88, enacted in August 1985, eased this requirement when this would not be in the best interests of the child).

1984—P.L. 98–378 The Child Support Enforcement Amendments of 1984 required the following improvements:

1. Mandatory practices: states were required to enact statutes to improve enforcement mechanisms, including:

a. mandatory income withholding procedures;

b. expedited processes for establishing and enforcing support orders;

c. state income tax refund interceptions;

d. liens against real and personal property;

e. reports of support delinquency information may be provided to consumer reporting agencies;

f. paternity actions may be brought any time prior to a child's 18th birthday;

g. all support orders modified or issued after October 1, 1985 must have a provision for wage withholding.

2. Federal Participation and Audit Procedures:

a. made federal matching funds of up to 90 percent available for development of automated systems;

b. gradually reduced federal matching funds (from 70 to 66 percent) in order to "encourage greater reliance on performance-based incentives";

c. state incentives vary from 6 to 10 percent;

d. states are required to pass along incentives to local agencies;

e. states are required to be audited every three years, audit criteria were changed, and penalties may be imposed.

3. Improved Interstate Enforcement:

a. enforcement techniques above must be applied in interstate cases;

b. both states may take credit for purposes of incentives calculations;

c. demonstration grants were authorized for innovative methods for interstate enforcement;

d. federal audits would assess effectiveness of interstate enforcement efforts.

4. Equal services for AFDC and Non-AFDC Families:

a. Congress' intent was to make the same services available to all families;

b. all mandatory practices must be available to non-welfare families;

c. federal income tax intercept was extended to non-welfare cases;

d. incentive payments became available for non-welfare collections;

e. families terminated from AFDC must be provided support enforcement services without an application fee;

f. states must publicize the availability of services.

5. Other: states were required to collect support in certain foster care cases, collect spousal support if this is owed in addition to child support, notify AFDC recipients annually of collections amounts, establish a state commission to study the operation of child support, formulate guidelines for determining support, offset the costs by charging fees to non-welfare recipients and absent parents, allow families terminated from AFDC to remain eligible for Medicaid for four months, seek to establish medical support awards. The Federal Parent Locater Service (FPLS) was made more accessible.

1984—P.L. 98–494 Deficit Reduction Act of 1984 required that the income of all household members be counted in calculating AFDC eligibility, and that all children in a household be included in the application. This practice is termed "income deeming."

Established the $50 monthly pass through payment for AFDC recipients. This is paid when the child support is paid on time (within the month) by the non-custodial parent, and is not counted in calculating

AFDC eligibility. It is included as income in calculations for food stamp benefits.

1988—P.L. 100–485 The Family Support Act of 1988 made the following changes to the child support enforcement system:

1. Immediate wage withholding:
   a. in IV-D cases, immediate wage withholding must be in effect for all orders issued or modified after November 1, 1990;
   b. in non-IV-D cases, immediate wage withholding takes effect for all cases after January 1, 1994;
   c. there are provisions for exceptions if there is a written agreement among both parties or if the court finds that there is good cause not to require it.
2. The child support disregard must be applied to a payment made by a non-custodial parent in the month it was due.
3. Guidelines for Child Support Award Amounts:
   a. guidelines are made mandatory as a rebuttal presumption; rebuttal must be in writing.
   b. beginning in October 1990, states must review and adjust (if appropriate) orders at the request of either parent or the IV-D agency.
   c. beginning in October 1993, awards must be reviewed and adjusted every three years in AFDC cases unless it is not in the best interests of the child and neither parent has requested it. For other IV-D cases, this process must be available every three years upon parent request;
   d. there are provisions for notification to parents of the review process.
4. Notice of support collected: states must inform families on AFDC of support collected on a monthly basis (as of January 1, 1993); if the Health and Human Services Secretary determines that this poses an unreasonable burden, reports may be issued quarterly.
5. Performance Standards for Paternity Establishment:
   a. beginning in FY 92, states must meet federal standards for paternity establishment, such that the paternity establishment percentage must be at least 50 percent, at least equal to the average for all states, or have increased by three percentage points from FY 88 to FY 91 and by three points each year thereafter.
   b. states must require parties in a contested paternity case to take a genetic test, and may charge individuals not receiving AFDC for these tests;

   c. states are encouraged to adopt a simple civil process for voluntary acknowledgement of paternity, and a civil procedure for establishing paternity in contested cases;

   d. the federal matching rate for laboratory testing to establish paternity is 90 percent.

6. Standards for Providing Services and Distributing Collections: the Secretary of Health Human Services must issue regulations establishing the standards that states must meet, including time limits governing distribution of collections under the IV-D state plan.

7. Mandatory Automated Systems: states that do not have automated systems must have a plan in place by October 1, 1991 and must have them in effect by October 1, 1995. Federal matching rate is 90 percent but expires September 30, 1995.

8. the federal Departments of Labor and of Health and Human Servcies must enter into an agreement to make wage and unemployment information available for FPLS.

9. Social Security Numbers must be required by states in the issuing of birth certificates; it is used only for support enforcement and not printed on the birth certificate.

1992—P.L. 102–521 Child Support Recovery Act of 1992 made it a felony to cross state lines for the purpose of avoiding past due child support payments.

1993—P.L. 103–66 The Omnibus Budget Reconciliation Act (OBRA) requires the establishment of a voluntary process for paternity acknowledgement, including hospital-based procedures for acknowledgment of paternity.

1995—P.L. 104–35 extended the deadline for states to have automated systems in compliance with the Family Support Act from October 1, 1995 to October 1, 1997.

Legislative History of Child Support Laws: State of Maryland

1929—Chapter (Ch.) 561 stated that the father and mother are "joint natural guardians" and are equal in their "powers and duties" with respect to children. In **1951**, via Ch. 678 (Senate Bill 363) this law was altered to provide that both parents are responsible for the support of minor children.

1976—H.B. 1478, enacted as Ch. 778, created the Division of Child Support in the Social Services Administration of the Department of Human Resources, provided for the establishment of paternity, location of absent parents, and some enforcement mechanisms. Full services were available to AFDC recipients, but not to non-AFDC recipients.

1978—Via Ch. 885 (H.B. 607, altering Articles 88 and 89) the Division was renamed the Bureau of Support Enforcement and moved to the Income Maintenance Administration within the Department of Human Resources (DHR). Some staff performing support enforcement functions in the Division of Parole and Probation were transferred to the Department of Human Resources, as were the staff of circuit courts that elected to transfer support functions to the state. The cases that were transferred included AFDC cases, non-AFDC cases, and cases not covered by the federal law (93-647).

1980—Chapter 549 (S.B. 641, codified at Article 88A, Section 59e), enacted the Tax Refund Intercept Program (TRIP) which authorized the interception of tax refunds of obligors more than 60 days in arrears if the arrearage had caused the family to go on AFDC, and rights had been assigned to the state. The full refund was to be paid to the Bureau of Support Enforcement, which then forwarded any excess (beyond the arrearage) to the obligor. The obligor had the right to appeal.

1981—Chapter 402 (H.B. 937, codified at Article 88A, Section 59c(1) and (2)) provided that the Bureau and its clients were represented by the attorney general (AG) or an attorney under the AG's supervision, or by the local state's attorney. It also provided that the Bureau would provide support enforcement services to all those who could not afford private counsel and were below 50 percent of the median family income of the state (and that fees could be charged).

1983—Ch. 61 (Ex.Ord. 01.01.1983.02, codified at Articles 16, 27, 88A and 89C) renamed the Bureau of Support Enforcement the Child Support Enforcement Administration (CSEA), and moved it from the Income Maintenance Administration within the DHR to a separate administration within DHR. Ch. 505 (H.B. 1349) clarified the TRIP program, indicating that collection of support enforcement from tax refunds was second in priority only to state, county, and municipal taxes. Ch. 506 (H.B. 1087) (altering Art. 88A, Section 59e) provided that investigations requested by the obligor be made prior to deduction of intercepted funds, and that appeals be made after such deductions. Ch. 642 (H.B. 1052) altered Art 88A, Section 59c(2) to remove the below 50 percent of median income requirement, and implementation was scheduled for July 1, 1984.

1984—As part of an ongoing project of re-encoding Maryland law, Ch. 296 (H.B. 1) created the Family Law section of the Maryland Code; most child support provisions are at sections 10 and 12. Ch. 204 (H.B. 561, encoded as section 12-101 of the Family Law article) provided that support could be awarded from the time that a plea was filed. Ch. 400 (H.B. 313, encoded at section 12-101) provided that a court could include an order for health insurance in a support order (if the parent was covered by health insurance and the cost for the child was "reasonable").

1985—The Children and Youth Initiative, based on recommendations of the Governor's Task Force on Child Abuse and Neglect, included a provision for the enforcement of wage liens against obligors (S.B. 58/H.B. 618). Enacted as Ch. 329, it provided that a recipient of child support or enforcement agencies could request an earnings withholding order when the obligor was thirty days in arrears. It also provided funding for additional staff in the state child support enforcement administration and in local agencies for enforcement of this provision.

1987—Ch. 146 authorized the CSEA to approve child support services to nonresidents. Ch. 150 authorized the issuance of earnings withholding orders in contempt proceedings when the obligor is more than thirty days in arrears. Ch. 155 expanded the definition of income under the income withholding law to include commissions paid in connection with the obligor's employment. Ch. 316 gave the CSEA authority to request information and assistance from employers and labor unions in locating absent parents, and established that employers and labor unions could be held in contempt for refusal to obey a court order. Ch. 335 authorized the court in URESA proceedings to adjudicate the question of paternity.

1988—Ch. 338 (S.B. 691, codified as Family Law Section 12-104) provided that child support awards could not be retroactively modified prior to the date a motion was filed. Ch. 595 (S.B. 441, codified at Family Law Section 10-113) established an interception program for state lottery winnings in excess of $600, if the obligor was in arrears exceeding $150 and enforcement services had been requested through, or assigned to the CSEA.

1989—Ch. 2, enacted as an emergency measure, established the Maryland child support guidelines, which use the Income Shares Model. These guidelines were advisory only. (Even though federal law required that they be a rebuttable presumption by October 13, 1989. Maryland was the last state to adopt guidelines.) Ch. 546 provided that laboratory reports of blood tests could be introduced as evidence in paternity proceedings.

1990—Ch. 58 (S.B. 633, codified at Sections 10 and 12 of the Family Law Article) made the child support guidelines mandatory as a rebuttable presumption. The Secretary of DHR was required to review the guidelines and report findings and recommendations by January 1, 1993 and every four years thereafter (in compliance with the federal law).

1991—Ch. 36, requiring the filing of social security numbers for parents. Ch. 139 (H.B. 99) provided that the CSEA may collect fees, but such fees may not be deducted from a child support payment except under the federal and state income tax intercept programs. Ch. 37 (S.B. 56, codifed at Section 10-120 and 10-122 of the Family Law Article) enacted as an emergency measure (effective April 9, 1991) the federal requirements for earnings withholding, making all support orders entered through CSEA after April 9, 1991 subject to immediate earnings withholding, and all orders in which there is thirty days of arrears subject to immediate withholding (with a good cause exemption). Ch. 77 (S.B. 58, Family Law Section 10-121) altered the proportion of earnings withholding attributed to the arrears payment to between 10 and 25 percent.

1992—Ch. 169 transferred employees of the Domestic Relations Division of the Circuit Court Clerk's office for Baltimore City to the Child Support Enforcement Administration. Ch. 561 required the state CSEA and local enforcement offices to "promote and serve the best interests of the child in carrying out certain responsibilities."

1993—In response to the report of the Governor's Task Force on Family Law (October, 1992), more than sixty bills dealing in some way with child support or visitation were introduced. Legislation passed: H.B. 30, which broadens the authority of an equity court to grant visitation rights to grandparents. H.B. 381, which requires, rather than permits, a court to award expenses in enforcement proceedings for child support and alimony arrearages. H.B. 425/S.B. 332 establishes the Family Court. S.B. 350 makes grandparents responsible for financial support of child of their minor child if minor child has insufficient resources to support the grandchild, and requires obligor to perform community service under some circumstances S.B. 613 requires that the CSEA central registry interface with the Maryland Interagency Law Enforcement System (MILES).

1994—S.B. 312 passed, which required courts to issue default judgments adjudicating paternity in some circumstances, and establishes a rebuttable presumption of paternity in some circumstances. Also, S.B. 586, which transferred Cecil County's support division from the county state's attorney's office to the state Child Support Enforcement Administration.

Legislative History of Child Support Laws: State of Texas

1973—S.B. 168, Ch. 543, adopted Title 2 of the Family Code, including adoption of the Uniform Reciprocal Enforcement of Support Act. S.B. 708, Ch. 257, revised the penal code to make desertion or nonsupport of a wife by a husband, or a child by either parent, a misdemeanor; also made failure provide support for a period of sixty days a prima facie case of nonsupport (a rebuttable presumption). After initial misdeameanor conviction, subsequent convictions constitute a felony, with a sentence of ten days to two years.

S.B. 709, Ch. 572, required the state Department of Public Welfare (DPW) to "explore with the parent [applying for services] . . . the possibility of obtaining support . . . on behalf of the child . . . ." This support could be considered in calculating assistance. DPW was to provide notice to law enforcement officials regarding the desertion of the child by a parent. Assistance payments were not to be withheld if child support could not be collected. Collections were to go to the general operating fund of DPW.

1975—S.B. 943, Ch. 424, effective June 19, 1975, gave the state Department of Public Welfare the authority to operate the child support program required by federal law.

1977—H.B. 1152, Ch. 821, effective August 19, 1977, permitted judges of the District Courts and Domestic Relations Courts in four specified counties to establish child support office(s) for collection and disbursement of child support payments, and permitted the charge of a service fee not to exceed $1 per month, fees to be used for administrative costs of the child support office. H.B. 1271, Ch. 827, effective August 29, 1977, permitted courts to sentence defendants found in contempt for failure to pay child support or guilty of criminal nonsupport to serve their time on weekends or on off-work hours. Permitted but did not require defendant to inform employer to garnish wages for support.

1979—H.B. 468, Ch. 88, effective August 27, 1979, provided that application for AFDC services through the Texas Department of Human Resources constitutes an assignment of child support to the state. H.B. 1831, Ch. 787, also effective August 27, 1979, provided that attorneys employed by the Texas Department of Human Resources may represent the department in child support and paternity determination suits. DHR may also be represented by prosecuting attorneys or the attorney general in certain cases.

1981—H.B. 1538, Ch. 833, effective September 1, 1981, provided access to a jury trial upon the request of any party in a suit affecting the parent-child relationship. S.B. 105, Ch. 674, effective September 1, 1981, related to collection and enforcement of child support, permitting a sentence of probation contempt cases if the defendant makes regular payments and requiring the defendant to pay court costs, provided that delinquent child support debts be paid out of a deceased obligor's estate, and providing that paternity suits must be brought before the child is four years of age. Three separate bills dealt with authorization to charge fees for services by local child support offices in Wichita, Orange, and Smith counties.

1983—H.B. 2, dealt with provisions regarding enforcement of court ordered child support, method of payment, and possession and access to a child. H.B. 197 related to the period during which a suit may be brought to establish paternity. H.B. 229 permitted the acknowledgement of paternity on birth certificates. House Joint Resolution 1, which was on the November 8, 1983 ballot, allowed for the assignment of income for the enforcement of court-ordered child support payments. (A constitutional amendment was required to permit wage garnishment of court-ordered child support. It was passed by Texas voters.) S.B. 45, effective June 19, 1983, permitted the establishment of a domestic relations office in certain counties and the duties regarding court orders for child support. S.B. 872, effective September 1, 1983, altered Texas' URESA law by authorizing a deduction from child support payments for court costs. Several bills dealt with child support collection fees in individual counties.

1985—H.B. 1059, effective September 1, 1985, provided that the period for which periodic child support may be ordered is to the age of eighteen or to the completion of high school. S.B. 1175, Ch. 232, transferred child support to the Office of the Attorney General (OAG), and dealt with procedures to establish and enforce payment of child support, possession of and access to a child, establishing a state parent locator service, and provided for recognition and enforcement of orders from other states (the Model Interstate Income Withholding act).

1987—H.B. 617, effective September 1, 1987, permitted award of joint custody or sole custody. Joint custody is permitted whether or not both parents agree, but not permitted where there has been past or present neglect or abuse by one parent. Joint custody does not affect the authority to award child support. S.B. 1123, effective June 19, 1987, provided that voluntary legitimization of a child by biological father no longer requires the consent of the child's mother. Paternity suits may be brought by the mother, a man claiming to be the father, or any agency or person having standing to sue (including the child or child's guardian). The reason for this law was the case *In the Interest of Unnamed Baby McLean,* 725 S.W.2d. 696 (1987); the Texas Supreme Court ruled that the requirement that only fathers had to show that establishing paternity was in the best interest of the child violated the Equal Rights Amendment of the Texas Constitution.

1989—S.B. 67 revised child support provisions of the family code. The OAG may initiate actions to adjust, modify, or enforce child support orders and may review child support awards. Guidelines must be reviewed every four years, effective September 1, 1989. In all suits affecting the parent child relationship, court must require the provision of health insurance. S.B. 188, effective September 1, 1989, codified both guidelines and a standard possession order for visitation. If parents do not agree on visitation, the standard order applies. Existing orders may be modified if in the child's best interest. These guidelines superseded the guidelines that were issued by the Texas Supreme Court in 1987, and all existing local rules, and required the application of these new guidelines, based on a flat percentage of net resources of the non-custodial parent. The new guidelines may be a basis for modifying an existing order, but not if support has been more, or for the birth or adoption of another child, or based on change in either parent's financial resources due to the resources of a new spouse.

1991—S.B. 1335, Ch. 459, added a wage or salary presumption of minimum wage if there is no evidence regarding obligor's income, and added the requirement that a specific statement as to the reason for deviation from the guidelines must be included in the court order. H.B. 769, Ch. 467 provided for the accrual of interest on child support arrearages, even on prejudgment amounts; it also permits courts to order income withholding for child support arrearages. S.B. 186, Ch. 825, added overtime pay to the income to be considered in determining child support.

1993—S.B. 84 allowed enforcement of child support orders through withholding eligibility for state contracts, grants, and loans to delinquent obligors, authorizing the child support agency to request and receive information to enforce child support obligations, specified debt obligations and payment procedures for delinquent obligors, and facilitating the provision of medical support by requiring exchange of information between Medicaid and private employers, and requiring that medical support orders be treated as a change in family circumstances. S.B. 291, H.B. 792, expanded the role of the OAG in statewide enforcement and in locating and determining paternity. Required implementation of a voluntary Employer New-Hire Reporting Program. Copies of W-4s are sent to OAG; they are retained only if the employee had a child support obligation or debt.

1995—H.B. 655, effective April 20, 1995, completely revised Title 2 of the Family Code, and created a new Title 5 for matters related to suits affecting the parent-child relationship. Child support is now part of Title 5 of the Family Code. S.B. 793, Ch. 341, required the use of administrative processes where possible in child support proceedings, including in the establishment of paternity; also encourages the use of private contractors for child support collection functions where this is found to be cost-effective. H.B. 170, Ch. 597, permits payment of child support by electronic funds transfer. H.B. 1863, Ch. 655, which reforms the AFDC program, also provides for suspension of state issued licenses for failure to pay child support. H.B. 433, Ch. 751 contains a provision that makes parties who are more than thirty days in arrears on child support payments ineligible for state contracts and grants.

Note for Appendix A

1. This history provides details of the three major legislative initiatives, as well as reference to other federal laws that relate in whole or in part to child support enforcement. For a more detailed legislative history of federal child support law, see OCSE 1992a.

Appendix B

Child Support Administrators
Interviewed

List of Interviews Conducted

Federal U.S. Department of Health and Human Services

The Hon. David Gray Ross, Director, Office of Child Support Enforcement, Administration for Children and Families, April 22, 1994

Maryland Child Support Enforcement Administration

State Office Administrators
Meg Sollenberger, Director, May 25, 1993
Grace Clark, Director of Research, May 25, 1993
Joyce Stanton, Policy Division, May 25, 1993

County and Local Administrators
Lynda Botts, Director, Prince George's County Office of Child Support Enforcement, June 2, 1993
Marsha Blank, Director, Child Support Enforcement Division, Montgomery County Circuit Court, June 15, 1993
William Schmidt, Director, Child Support Division, Anne Arundel Circuit Court, July 7, 1993
Lynn Brewer, Director, and Michael Helms, Deputy Director, Child Support Division, Baltimore County Circuit Court, December 17, 1993
Louis Curry, Director, Baltimore City Child Support Office, June 28, 1994

Texas

*State Administrators, Child Support Division, Office of the
Attorney General*
Charlie Childress, Director, September 26, 1995
Sam Jackson, Special Assistant Attorney for Child Support, September
    29, 1995
David Vela, Deputy Director, Field Operations, October 5, 1995
Cecelia Burke, IV-D Division Director, October 5, 1995

Local Administrators
Emil Schattel, Area Manager, Unit 101, September 22, 1995
Steven Maines, Office Manager, Unit 121, September 22, 1995
R.K. Miller, Managing Attorney, Unit 102 (Lubbock County Office),
    September 22, 1995
Janis Vaughn, Special Counsel to the Area Manager, Unit 101, September
    22, 1995
Donna Morris, Office Manager, Unit 102, September 27, 1995
Earl Sneed, Managing Attorney, Unit 121, October 12, 1995

Appendix C

Methodology, Survey, and Results

This appendix provides more detailed information regarding the data collection methods and results of the court case samples and survey discussed in chapter 4, as well as a copy of the survey instrument itself.

Court Case Samples

Maryland

To analyze the effects of child support law in practice in Maryland, data on a sample of child support cases from Prince George's County was collected from court records. A listing was obtained for all child support cases in which a support order, temporary or permanent, was entered for the period from January 1, 1993 through August 1, 1993. From this list of 951 cases, a random sample of 315 cases was selected. Since child support cases in Prince George's County are classified into three different categories—those initiated as paternity cases, those initiated as support cases, and interstate cases—the sample was chosen to provide numbers of each set in approximate proportion to their frequency in the whole sample.

Data was collected on these cases with respect to a number of factors, including: basic case processing, the number of children, the date and amount of the support order and whether the child support guidelines were followed, income information for the parents when available, the method of support collection ordered, and whether medical support (health insurance) was ordered. Data was collected from court records in October and November of 1993; because many cases had been continued to January and February, follow up research on those cases was completed in March of 1994. Of the 315 cases on which data was collected, nine consisted of orders for arrears (retroactive support) only, and nine others were closed with no permanent order issued. In twenty-three cases, there was a temporary order, but no final order for support had been issued by the end of March. In five cases, the file could not be located or was missing information. This left a total of 267 cases that were complete—that is, a permanent child support order had been issued—as of the end of March 1994. Of these cases, 103 were AFDC cases, and 164 were non-AFDC cases. A case was classified as AFDC or non-AFDC according to the status of the custodian at the time of the permanent support order. Thus, there were six cases in the sample that were initiated as AFDC cases, but at the time of the order, the custodian was no longer on AFDC. These were classified as non-AFDC cases.

Texas

Because the method of court record maintenance is slightly different in Lubbock County, the cases were selected not on the basis of the entry of a support order (this information was not available in the computerized data base of cases), but by the date the case was originally filed with the court. Cases that were filed from January through March of 1995, and that had not been placed on inactive status at the time of data collection in October of 1995, were selected for the sample. Data was collected in October of 1995, and cases with incomplete files at that time were reviewed in December of 1995.

The sample included a total of 220 cases. In about half of the cases (108), ongoing support had been ordered at the time of the study. In order for the Maryland and Texas data to be comparable, the data reported in chapter 4 is on the 108 cases with orders for ongoing support at the time of the study. Of these cases, seventy-seven involved one child, twenty-three involved two children, three involved three children, one involved four children, and there were two cases each involving five and six children. The average number of children per case was 1.5.

The following information on cases that did not have a support order provides another view of the child support process and indicates some of the difficulties facing child support agencies in establishing support in some cases. In twenty-five cases, only retroactive support (arrears) was ordered, mostly due to parental reconciliation. A total of forty-two files contained cases that were incomplete at the time of the study. About half of these were due to inability to locate or serve papers to one or more parties, and most of the others involved paternity tests that were not yet complete. Twenty-seven cases had been dismissed for various reasons, ranging from previously existing cases establishing support for the child, to the exclusion of paternity by the paternity test, and including one case in which the obligor was being deported. In eighteen cases, no support was ordered, mostly due to an incarcerated obligor. These cases generally noted that support was to begin once the obligor was released from prison.

Survey Design and Methodology

From the set of court records in Prince George's County discussed above, cases were identified that consisted of a custodial mother residing in Maryland and a non-custodial father residing either in Maryland or in the nearby region for which there was a correct address in the record. This subset of cases, which included 230 women and 257 men, was included in the survey; they were also invited to participate in more individualized interviews through focus group meetings. Since Prince George's County is a suburban county of Washington, D.C., some members of the survey group had relocated either to the District of Columbia or to the northern Virginia suburbs of Washington. These parents were included since they could plausibly have attended the focus group meeting. Custodial parents in other interstate cases were not included, both for the obvious reason that they could not attend the meeting, and because in many cases their addresses were missing or incomplete. The surveys were mailed one week apart in March 1994. Respondents were asked to return the survey by the end of April. A reminder postcard was sent one week after each survey was mailed.

As anticipated, the response rate among female respondents was higher than the response rate among male respondents. Of 230 surveys sent to female custodians, twenty-seven were returned as incorrect addresses. Of the 203 remaining subjects, forty-seven returned the completed survey, with a resulting response rate of 23 percent. As requested, several respondents added specific comments to the survey form, including several who sent a separate letter along with the completed survey. Of the 257 surveys sent to male non-custodians, forty-one were returned as incorrect addresses. Of the 216 remaining subjects, twenty-nine returned the survey for a response rate of 13.4 percent.

Overall, the respondents to the survey were overwhelmingly African American: fifty-eight respondents or 77 percent of the total sample, thirty-eight women (81 percent of women) and twenty men (71 percent of men). African Americans constitute slightly more than 50 percent of the population of Prince George's County, so they are slightly overrepresented in this sample in relation to the population of the county. As the court records did not generally contain information about the race of parents or children, it is not possible to determine whether the respondents accurately reflect the entire sample. Most of the women respondents were single parents: thirty-five women, or 74.5 percent, lived in a household with children and no other adults present. However, thirteen of the men, or 46.5 percent, lived in households with children present; the remainder lived by themselves or with other adults. The average age of all respondents was 30.5 years; of women 30.4; and of men, 30.67. Most of the cases involved one child: fifty-nine, or 81 percent of valid cases. A valid case or valid response refers to the number of surveys in which the respondent answered the question, providing a measurable response. On the opinion questions, this refers to responses that actually offer an opinion (as opposed to responding "not applicable," or failing to answer the question).

Individualized Interviews

Included with each survey was an invitation to parents to participate in more individualized interviews. In Maryland, these interviews were conducted through two separate focus group meetings (one for custodial parents and one for non-custodial parents). The focus group meetings were held on Saturday mornings at a public library meeting room in an area central to the largest concentration of cases, in April and May of 1994. For each group, two leaders of the same gender as the respondents, one white and one African American, were selected and trained. In Texas, parents were invited to return a card volunteering for an individual interview. Parents who responded were interviewed in person and via telephone in December of 1995 and January of 1996.

A total of four male non-custodial parents were interviewed in Maryland and Texas. Eleven female custodial parents were interviewed, four at the focus group meeting in Maryland and seven in Texas. The results of these interviews are summarized in chapter 4. Some biographical details of individual cases have been changed to protect the confidentiality of respondents. The state of residence is also not indicated, to further protect confidentiality.

Survey Forms

The survey questionnaire that was used to solicit the information reported in chapter 4 is reproduced here. The first survey is the form sent to custodial parents. The second survey provides the wording of those questions that differed on the survey sent to non-custodial parents.

Maryland Child Support Survey
(Custodial Parents)

INFORMATION ABOUT YOU:

1. Age:_____ 2. Gender: _____Male _____Female

3. Race/Ethnicity:
__African American __Asian American __Hispanic
__Native American __White __Other_____

4. Present Household: *Circle the answer that best describes your present household.*

Self   Self + one child   Self + another adult

Self + another adult   Self + another adult
+ one child   + two children

Self + another adult   Self + two children
+ three children

Self + three children   Self + more than one adult

Other:_____

5. Do you and your child(ren)'s other parent have a visitation schedule?
__Yes __No   __Don't Know   __Doesn't Apply

6. Do you have any problems with the visitation schedule?
__Yes __No   __No Opinion   __Doesn't Apply

If you answered "yes", check any of the following that apply:
   __My child(ren)'s other parent does not follow the agreed upon schedule.
   __Sometimes I cannot follow the agreed upon schedule.
   __The schedule gives me too little time with my child(ren).
   __My child(ren)'s other parent lives too far away.
   __I don't like what happens when my child(ren) is/are with the other parent.
   __Other:_____

ABOUT THE CHILD SUPPORT PROCESS:

7. I felt the outcome of my child support hearing was fair to me.
__Strongly Agree __Agree __Agree Somewhat __Disagree
__Strongly Disagree __No Opinion __Not Applicable

8. I think the amount of child support awarded was fair.
__Strongly Agree __Agree __Agree Somewhat __Disagree
__Strongly Disagree __No Opinion __Not Applicable

9. I thought the judge/master was unfair to people in my situation.
__Strongly Agree __Agree __Agree Somewhat __Disagree
__Strongly Disagree __No Opinion __Not Applicable

10. The procedures followed in my case were explained to me.
__Strongly Agree __Agree __Agree Somewhat __Disagree
__Strongly Disagree __No Opinion __Not Applicable

11. I feel the child support system is fair to people in my situation.
__Strongly Agree __Agree __Agree Somewhat __Disagree
__Strongly Disagree __No Opinion __Not Applicable

12. The people in the child support agency were helpful.
__Strongly Agree __Agree __Agree Somewhat __Disagree
__Strongly Disagree __No Opinion __Not Applicable

13. If you received a child support award, was it made in accordance with the Maryland child support guidelines?
__Yes __No __Don't know __Doesn't Apply

14. How many children were included in the child support award?
__1 __2 __3 __4 or more

15. When you think about the time it took to receive a child support award, do you think it:
__Took too long __Took the right amount of time
__Happened too fast __No Opinion

Note: Answer question 16 only if you are currently receiving AFDC. If not, please proceed to question 17.

16. If you were awarded child support and **are currently receiving AFDC**, how regularly do you receive your bonus payments? *Check the statement that best describes what you usually receive.*
    __Does not apply
    __The full amount regularly each month

___A partial payment each month
___Irregular amounts at irregular intervals
___I haven't received a payment in more than three months.
___Don't know
___Other_____

Note: Answer question 17 only if you are not currently receiving AFDC. If not, please proceed to question 18.

17. If you were awarded child support and **are not currently receiving AFDC,** how regularly do you receive your payments? *Check the statement that best describes what you usually receive.*
___Does not apply
___The full amount regularly each month
___A partial payment each month
___Irregular amounts at irregular intervals
___I haven't received a payment in more than three months.
___Don't know
___Other_____

RECOMMENDATIONS FOR CHANGE:

Please indicate if you agree or disagree with the following proposed suggestions for changes in the child support system:

18. Parents who live separately from one another should be offered counseling and training to help them be better parents.
___Strongly Agree ___Agree ___Agree Somewhat ___Disagree
___Strongly Disagree ___No Opinion

19. The state should pay custodial parents a minimum child support payment whether or not the non-custodial parent pays child support.
___Strongly Agree ___Agree ___Agree Somewhat ___Disagree
___Strongly Disagree ___No Opinion

20. Custodial parents should be offered job training to help them support their children.
___Strongly Agree ___Agree ___Agree Somewhat ___Disagree
___Strongly Disagree ___No Opinion

21. Non-custodial parents should be offered job training to help them support their children.
___Strongly Agree ___Agree ___Agree Somewhat ___Disagree
___Strongly Disagree ___No Opinion

22. The state should help parents who are having problems with visitation.
__Strongly Agree   __Agree   __Agree Somewhat   __Disagree
__Strongly Disagree   __No Opinion

23. Child support should be handled by case workers rather than by judges and masters.
__Strongly Agree   __Agree   __Agree Somewhat   __Disagree
__Strongly Disagree   __No Opinion

24. The Maryland child support guidelines should be changed.
__Strongly Agree   __Agree   __Agree Somewhat   __Disagree
__Strongly Disagree   __No Opinion

  If you agree, how should they be changed? Check all that apply.
  __Guideline awards should be higher.
  __Guideline awards should be lower.
  __Guidelines should consider the income of a custodial parent's partner.
  __Guidelines should consider the income of a non-custodial parent's partner.
  __Child support awards should be reduced if the non-custodial parent has other children.
  __Guidelines should be based on after tax income.
  __Other:_____

25. If you were awarded child support, how much were you awarded? *Check the category that contains the total amount you were awarded in child support for all children.*
__Does not apply
__$1–100/month   __$101–200/month   __$201–300/month
__$301–400/month   __more than $400/month

26. Household income: *Check the category that contains the approximate yearly income to your household.*
__Less than $6,000   __$6,000–12,000/year
__$12,000–20,000/year   __$20,000–30,000/year
__$30,000–40,000/year   __More than $40,000/year

Thank you for your time!

Maryland Child Support Survey
Non-custodial Parents

Note: Questions 1–12, 18–24, and 26 were identical on the two surveys. Below are the questions that were different.

13. Was the child support award in your case made in accordance with the Maryland child support guidelines?
___Yes ___No   ___Don't Know   ___Doesn't Apply

14. How many children were included in the child support award?
___1 ___2 ___3 ___4 or more

15. When you think about the time it took to process your case, do you think it:
___Took too long   ___Took the right amount of time
___Happened too fast   ___No Opinion

16. If you are making child support payments, how difficult is it for you to make your payments each month? *Check the statement that best describes your ability to make your payment.*
___Does not apply
___I easily make the full payment each month.
___I make the full payment each month, but it's hard for me to do it.
___I pay something each month, even if it's not the whole amount.
___I occasionally miss monthly payments.
___I often have to miss payments.
___I haven't been able to pay in more than three months.
___Don't know.
___Other_____

25. If you were required to pay child support, how much were you required to pay? *Check the category that contains the total amount you pay in child support for all children.*
___Does not apply
___$1–100/month ___$101–200/month ___$201–300/month
___$301–400/month ___more than $400/month

References

Abramovitz, Mimi. 1988. *Regulating the Lives of Women: Social Welfare Policy from Colonial Times to the Present.* Boston: South End Press.

Amott, Teresa. 1990. "Black Women and AFDC: Making Entitlement Out of Necessity." In *Women, the State, and Welfare*, edited by Linda Gordon. Madison: University of Wisconsin.

Appleby, Joyce. 1992. *Liberalism and Republicanism in the Historical Imagination.* Cambridge: Harvard University Press.

Baca Zinn, Maxine. 1994. "Feminist Rethinking from Racial-Ethnic Families." In *Women of Color in U.S. Society*, edited by Bonnie Thornton Dill and Maxine Baca Zinn. Philadelphia: Temple University Press.

Bachman, Ronet. 1994. "Violence Against Women." Rockville, MD: Bureau of Justice Statistics.

Barrett, Michelle. 1988. *Women's Oppression Today.* London: Verso.

Barnow, Burt S., Laurie Bassi, Laudan Aron, and Abhay Pande. 1990. *Estimates of Expenditures on Children and Child Support Guidelines.* Washington: Lewin/ICF.

Ball, Jeffrey. 1991. *The Income Withholder's Role in Child Support.* Washington, D.C.: ABA Center on Children and the Law.

Ball, Jeffrey, and Virginia Sablan. 1990. *Effective Use of Liens in Child Support Cases.* Washington, D.C.: ABA Center on Children and the Law.

Bell, Roslyn. 1988. "Alimony and the Financially Dependent Spouse in Montgomery County, Maryland". *Family Law Quarterly* 22: 225.

Bellah, Robert, Richard Madsen, William M. Sullivan, Ann Swidler, and Steven M. Tipton. 1985. *Habits of the Heart.* New York: Harper & Row.

———. 1991. *The Good Society.* New York: Knopf.

Beller, Andrea H., and John W. Graham. 1993. *Small Change: The Economics of Child Support.* New Haven: Yale University Press.

Benn, Stanley I., and Gerald F. Gaus, eds. 1983. *Public and Private in Social Life.* New York: St. Martin's Press.

Bergmann, Barbara R., and Trudi Renwick. 1993. "A Budget-Based Definition of

Poverty, with an Application to Single-Parent Families," *Journal of Human Resources* 28 (Winter, 1993): 1.

Blankenhorn, David. 1995. *Fatherless America*. New York: Basic Books.

Bowles, Samuel, and Herbert Gintis. 1986. *Democracy and Capitalism: Property, Community, and the Contradictions of Modern Social Thought*. New York: Basic Books.

Brandt, Lillian. *Five Hundred Seventy-Four Deserters and Their Families* [1905], and Baldwin, William. *Family Desertion and Non-Support Laws* [1904]. 1972. New York: Arno Press.

Brown, Carol. 1981. "Mothers, Fathers, and Children: From Private to Public Patriarchy." In *Women and Revolution*, edited by Lydia Sargent. Boston: South End Press.

Bussiere, Elizabeth. 1993. "Rights vs. Needs: Gender Obstacles to Coalition-building in the Welfare Rights Movement, 1965–1975." Presented at the annual meeting of the American Political Science Association, September, 1993, Washington, D.C.

Burack, Cynthia. 1994. *The Problem of the Passions: Feminism, Psychoanalysis, and Social Theory*. New York: New York University Press.

Cassetty, Judith, ed. 1983. *The Parental Child Support Obligation: Research, Practice, and Social Policy*. Lexington, Mass.: D.C. Heath and Company.

Ceaser, James. 1990. *Liberal Democracy and Political Science*. Baltimore: Johns Hopkins.

Chambers, David L. 1979. *Making Fathers Pay: The Enforcement of Child Support*. Chicago: University of Chicago Press.

Chunn, Dorothy. 1992. *From Punishment to Doing Good: Family Courts and Socialized Justice in Ontario, 1880–1940*. Toronto: University of Toronto.

Cohen, Susan, and Mary Fainsod Katzenstein. 1988. "The War over the Family Is Not over the Family." In *Feminism, Children, and the New Families*, edited by Sanford Dornbusch and Myra Strober. New York: Guilford Press.

Collins, Patricia Hill. 1991. *Black Feminist Thought*. New York: Routledge.

Committee on Ways and Means, U.S. House of Representatives. 1993. *Overview of Entitlement Programs, 103rd Congress, 1st Session* ("Green Book"). Washington, D.C.: Government Printing Office.

Cook, Fay Lomax. 1992. *Support for the American Welfare State: the Views of Congress and Public*. New York: Columbia University Press.

Coontz, Stephanie. 1992. *The Way We Never Were: American Families and the Nostalgia Trap*. New York: Basic Books.

Cooper, Dennis C. 1985. *Interstate Child Support Collections Study*. Washington, D.C.: Office of Child Support Enforcement.

Cott, Nancy. 1977. *The Bonds of Womanhood: "Woman's Sphere" in New England, 1780–1835*. New Haven, Conn.: Yale University Press.

Czapanskiy, Karen. 1990. "Gender Bias in the Courts: Social Change Strategies," *Georgetown Journal of Legal Ethics* 4: 1–22.

Dahl, Robert. 1985. *A Preface to Economic Democracy*. Berkeley: University of California.

Danziger, Sheldon, Timothy M. Smeeding, and Lee Rainwater. 1995. "The Western Welfare State in the 1990s: Toward a New Model of Antipoverty Policy for Families with Children," Luxembourg Income Study Working Paper No. 128. Syracuse, NY: Syracuse University Press.

de los Rios, Patricia. 1994. "Louis Hartz: Political Theorist." PhD Diss. University of Maryland.

Dill, Bonnie Thornton. 1994. "Fictive Kin, Paper Sons, and *Compadrazgo*: Women of Color and the Struggle for Family Survival." In *Women of Color in U.S. Society*, edited by Bonnie Thornton Dill and Maxine Baca Zinn. Philadelphia: Temple University Press.

Dill, Bonnie Thornton and Maxine Baca Zinn. 1994. *Women of Color in U.S. Society*. Philadelphia: Temple University Press.

DiNitto, Diana M. 1995. *Social Welfare Policy: Politics and Public Policy*. Boston: Allyn and Bacon.

Dodson, Diane. 1994. "Children's Standard of Living under Child Support Guidelines: Women's Legal Defense Fund Report Card." In *Child Support Guidelines: The Next Generation*, edited by Margaret Campbell Haynes. Washington, D.C.: U.S. Department of Health and Human Services.

Ebb, Nancy. 1994. *Enforcing Child Support: Are States Doing the Job?* Washington D.C.: Children's Defense Fund.

Elkin, Stephen. 1987. *City and Regime in the American Republic*. Chicago: University of Chicago Press.

Ellwood, David. 1988. *Poor Support: Poverty in the American Family*. New York: Basic Books.

Elshtain, Jean Bethke. 1981. *Public Man, Private Woman*. Princeton: Princeton University Press.

———. 1994. "Single Motherhood: Response to Iris Marion Young," *Dissent*, 41, 2 (Spring 1994): 267–69.

Elshtain, Jean Behtke et al. 1991. "A Communitarian Position Paper on the Family," Washington, D.C.: The Communitarian Network.

Erickson, Nancy. 1992. "Obtaining Adequate Support for Children: Preventing Downward Deviations from the Presumptive Guidelines Amount," *Clearinghouse Review*, 26 (September 1992): 530–536.

Etzioni, Amitai. 1993. *The Spirit of Community*. New York: Crown.

Fader, John F. 1990. *Maryland Family Law*. Charlottesville, Va.: The Michie Co.

Figart, Deborah and June Lapidus. 1994. "Welfare Reform Should also mean Labor Market Reform: Comparable Worth as an Anti-Poverty Strategy," paper presented at the Fourth Women's Policy Research Conference, American University, Washington D.C., June 4, 1994.

Fineman, Martha Albertson. 1991. *The Illusion of Equality*. Chicago: University of Chicago Press.

Fishkin, James. 1983. *Justice, Equal Opportunity, and the Family*. New Haven: Yale University Press.

Folbre, Nancy. 1991a. "Women on Their Own: Global Patterns of Female Headship," In *The Women and International Development Annual,* edited by Rita S. Gallin and Anne Ferguson, Vol. 2 (1991). Boulder: Westview Press.

———. 1991b. "The Unproductive Housewife: Her Evolution in Nineteenth-Century Economic Thought," *Signs* 16 (Spring): 463–84.

———. 1994. *Who Pays for the Kids? Gender and the Structure of Constraint.* New York: Routledge.

Fraser, Nancy. 1989. *Unruly Practices: Power, Discourse, and Gender in Contemporary Social Theory.* Minneapolis: University of Minnesota Press.

Fraser, Nancy, and Linda Gordon. 1994. "A Genealogy of Dependency: Tracing a Keyword of the U.S. Welfare State," *Signs* 19 (Winter): 309–36.

Frazer, Elizabeth, and Nicola Lacey. 1993. *The Politics of Community: A Feminist Critique of the Liberal-Communitarian Debate.* Toronto: University of Toronto Press.

Friedman, Lawrence. 1973. *A History of American Law.* New York: Simon & Schuster.

Friedman, Marilyn. 1990. "Feminism and Modern Friendship: Dislocating the Community." In *Feminism and Political Theory,* edited by Cass Sunstein. Chicago: University of Chicago Press.

Furstenberg, Frank, and Andrew Cherlin. 1991. *Divided Families: What Happens to Children When Parents Part.* Cambridge: Harvard University Press.

Galston, William. 1991. *Liberal Purposes.* New York: Cambridge University Press.

Garfinkel, Irwin. 1992. *Assuring Child Support: An Extension of Social Security.* New York: Russell Sage.

Garfinkel, Irwin, Sara S. McLanahan, and Philip K. Robins, eds. 1992. *Child Support Assurance: Design Issues, Expected Impacts, and Political Barriers as Seen from Wisconsin.* Washington, D.C.: Urban Institute Press.

———. 1994. *Child Support and Child Well-Being.* Washington, D.C.: Urban Institute Press.

Giddings, Paula. 1984. *When and Where I Enter.* New York: Morrow.

Gilligan, Carol. 1982. *In A Different Voice.* Cambridge: Harvard University Press.

Glendon, Mary Ann. 1986. "Fixed Rules and Discretion in Contemporary Family Law and Succession Law." *Tulane Law Review* 60: 1165–197.

———. 1987. *Abortion and Divorce in Western Law.* Cambridge: Harvard University Press.

———. 1989. *The Transformation of Family Law.* Chicago: University of Chicago Press.

Goode, William J. 1993. *World Changes in Divorce Patterns.* New Haven: Yale University Press.

Gordon, Linda, ed. 1990a. *Women, the State, and Welfare.* Madison: University of Wisconsin Press.

Gordon, Linda. 1990b. "The New Feminist Scholarship on the Welfare State." In *Women, the State, and Welfare,* edited by Linda Gordon. Madison: University of Wisconsin.

Gordon, Linda. 1994. *Pitied But Not Entitled: Single Mothers and the History of Welfare 1890–1935.* New York: Free Press.

Grossberg, Michael. 1985. *Governing the Hearth: Law and the Family in Nineteenth-Century America.* Chapel Hill: University of North Carolina Press.

Hafen, Bruce. 1991. "Individualism and Autonomy in Family Law: The Waning of Belonging," *Brigham Young University Law Review* 1991: 1–42.

Harris, Deborah. 1988. "Child Support for Welfare Families: Family Policy Trapped in its Own Rhetoric," *Review of Law and Social Change* 16: 619–57.

Hartmann, Heidi, and Roberta Spalther-Roth. 1993a. "The Real Employment Opportunities of Women Participating in AFDC: What the Market Can Provide," Paper presented at "Women and Welfare Reform: Women's Poverty, Women's Opportunities, and Women's Welfare," sponsored by the Institute for Women's Policy Research, Washington, D.C., October 23, 1993.

Hartmann, Heidi, and Roberta Spalther-Roth. 1993b. "Dependence on Men, the Market, or the State: The Rhetoric and Reality of Welfare Reform," Washington, D.C.: Institute for Women's Policy Research.

Hartmann, Susan. 1982. *The Home Front and Beyond: American Women in the 1940s.* Boston: Twayne.

Hartz, Louis. 1955. *The Liberal Tradition in America: An Interpretation of American Political Thought since the Revolution.* New York: Harcourt, Brace.

Held, Virginia. 1993. *Feminist Morality: Transforming Culture, Society, and Politics.* Chicago: University of Chicago Press.

Hirsch, Amy E. 1988. "Income Deeming in the AFDC Program: Using Dual Track Family Law to Make Poor Women Poorer," *Review of Law and Social Change* 16: 713–40.

Hoff, Joan. 1991. *Law, Gender, and Injustice.* New York: New York University Press.

Holmes, Stephen. 1989. "The Permanent Structure of Antiliberal Thought", In *Liberalism and the Moral Life*, edited by Nancy Rosenblum. Cambridge: Harvard University Press.

———. 1995. *Passions and Constraint.* Chicago: University of Chicago Press.

Houlgate, Laurence D. 1988. *Family and State: The Philosophy of Family Law.* Totowa, N.J.: Rowman & Littlefield.

Hurtado, Aida. 1989. "Relating to Privilege: Seduction and Rejection in the Subordination of White Women and Women of Color," *Signs* 14 (Summer): 833–55.

Jacob, Herbert. 1988. *Silent Revolution: The Transformation of Divorce Law in the United States.* Chicago: University of Chicago Press.

Jones, Kathleen B. 1990. "Citizenship in a Woman-friendly Polity," *Signs* 15 (Summer): 781–812.

Kahn, Alfred J., and Sheila B. Kamerman, eds. 1988. *Child Support: From Debt Collection to Social Policy.* Newbury Park: Sage.

Katz, Michael B. 1989. *The Undeserving Poor: From the War on Poverty to the War on Welfare.* New York: Pantheon.

Kay, Herma Hill, and Steven Sugarman. 1991. *Divorce Reform at the Crossroads.* New Haven: Yale University Press.

Kerber, Linda. 1980. *Women of the Republic.* Chapel Hill: University of North Carolina Press.

Krause, Harry D. 1981. *Child Support in America: The Legal Perspective.* Charlottesville, VA: The Michie Company.

Kymlicka, William. 1990. *Contemporary Political Theory.* New York: Oxford University Press.

———. 1991. "Rethinking the Family," *Philosophy and Public Affairs* 20 (Winter): 77–97.

Ladd-Taylor, Molly. 1994. *Mother-Work: Women, Child Welfare, and the State, 1890–1930.* Urbana: University of Illinois Press.

Law, Sylvia. 1983. "Women, Work, Welfare, and the Preservation of Patriarchy," *University of Pennsylvania Law Review* 131 (May): 1249–1339.

———. 1988. "Homosexuality and the Social Meaning of Gender," *Wisconsin Law Review* 1988: 187–235.

Lehr, Valerie. 1994. "Rearticulating 'Family'." Paper delivered at Annual Meeting of the Western Political Science Association, March, 1994, Albuquerque, New Mexico.

Lindblom, Charles E. 1977. *Politics and Markets: The World's Political Economic Systems.* New York: Basic Books.

Littleton, Christine. 1987. "Reconstructing Sexual Equality," *California Law Review* 75: 1279.

Macedo, Stephen. 1990. *Liberal Virtues.* New York: Oxford University Press.

MacKinnon, Catharine. 1989. *Toward a Feminist Theory of the State.* Cambridge: Harvard University Press.

Mannix, Mary R., Henry A. Freedman, and Natarlin R. Best. 1987. "The Good Cause Exception to the AFDC Child Support Requirement," *Clearinghouse Review* 21: 339–46.

Marmor, Theodore, Jerry Mashaw, and Philip Harvey. 1990. *America's Misunderstood Welfare State.* New York: Basic Books.

Maryland Child Support Enforcement Administration. 1992. "Report to the General Assembly on Child Support Guidelines," Baltimore: Department of Human Resources.

Maryland Child Support Enforcement Administration. 1993. "Annual Statistical Report, FY 1992." Baltimore: Department of Human Resources.

———. 1994. "Annual Statistical Report, FY 1993." Baltimore: Department of Human Resources.

Maryland Governor's Task Force on Family Law. 1992. "Final Report," Annapolis: Office of the Governor.

Maryland Judicial Conference. 1990. "Report of the Special Joint Committee on Gender Bias in the Courts," *University of Baltimore Law Review* 20 (Fall): Ch. 3: Child Support.

Mason, Mary Ann. 1994. *From Father's Property to Children's Rights: The His-*

tory of Child Custody in the United States New York: Columbia University Press.

Mason, Mary, and Paula Roberts. 1989. *Improving the Quality of State IV-D Programs Through Litigation*. Chicago: Clearinghouse for Legal Services, Inc., No. 45125.

McKay, Mary McKernan. 1994. "The Link between Domestic Violence and Child Abuse: Assessment and Treatment Considerations," *Child Welfare*, 73: 29–39.

McLanahan, Sara and Gary Sandefur. 1994. *Growing Up With a Single Parent: What Hurts, What Helps*. Cambridge: Harvard University Press.

Mink, Gwendolyn. 1995. *The Wages of Motherhood: Inequality in the Welfare State, 1917–1942*. Ithaca, N.Y.: Cornell University Press.

Minow, Martha. 1990. *Making All the Difference: Inclusion, Exclusion, and American Law*. Ithaca: Cornell University Press.

———. 1991. "The Free Exercise of Families," *University of Illinois Law Review* 1991: 925–48.

Monson, Renee A. 1994. "Managing Mothers, Finding Fathers: Wisconsin's Mandatory Paternity Establishment Policy," Paper delivered at the Fourth Women's Policy Research Conference, June 3–4, 1994. Washington, D.C.: Institute for Women's Policy Research.

Murgatroyd, Linda. 1985. "The Production of People and Domestic Labour Revisited." In *Family and Economy in Modern Society*, edited by Paul Close and Rosemary Collins. London: Macmillan.

Murphy, Jane. 1991. "Eroding the Myth of Discretionary Justice in Family Law: The Child Support Experiment," *North Carolina Law Review* 70: 209–42.

Murphy, Jane C., and Barbara A. Babb. 1992. "Increasing Access to Justice for Maryland's Families," Report of the Maryland Governor's Advisory Council on Family Legal Needs of Low Income Persons, (March 1992).

National Commission on Children. 1991. *Beyond Rhetoric: A New American Agenda for Children and Families*. Washington, D.C: Government Printing Office.

Nedelsky, Jennifer. 1989. "Reconceiving Autonomy: Sources, Thoughts, and Possibilities," *Yale Journal of Law and Feminism* 1: 7–36.

———. 1990a. *Private Property and the Limits of American Constitutionalism*. Chicago: University of Chicago Press.

———. 1990b. "Law, Boundaries, and the Bounded Self," *Representations* 30 (Spring): 162–89.

Nelson, Barbara J. 1990. "The Origins of the Two-Channel Welfare State: Workmen's Compensation and Mother's Aid." In *Women, the State, and Welfare*, edited by Linda Gordon. Madison: University of Wisconsin Press.

Nicholson, Linda. 1986. *Gender and History: The Limits of Social Theory in the Age of the Family*. New York: Columbia University Press.

Office of Child Support Enforcement. 1990. *Paternity Establishment*. 3rd ed. Washington, D.C.: Department of Health and Human Services.

———. 1992a. *Essentials for Attorneys in Child Support Enforcement*, 2nd ed. Washington, D.C.: Department of Health and Human Services.

————. 1992b. *Fifteenth Annual Report to Congress*. Washington, D.C.: Department of Health and Human Services.

————. 1992c. *Program Results/Performance Measurements Audit, State of Texas*. Washington, D.C.: Department of Health and Human Services.

————. 1992d. *Program Results/Performance Measurements Audit, State of Maryland*. Washington, D.C.: Department of Health and Human Services.

————. 1993a. *Sixteenth Annual Report to Congress*. Washington, D.C.: Department of Health and Human Services.

————. 1993b. *State Plan Characteristics for Title IV-D Child Support Enforcement Programs* Washington, D.C.: Department of Health and Human Services.

————. 1993c. Proposed Rules. 45 CFR parts 302, 303, 304. *Federal Register* 58 (November 29): 62599–2616.

————. 1994a. *Seventeenth Annual Report to Congress*. Washington, D.C.: Department of Health and Human Services.

————. 1994b. *Preliminary Report for Fiscal Year 1993*. Washington, D.C.: Department of Health and Human Services.

————. 1995a. *Eighteenth Annual Report to Congress*. Washington, D.C.: Department of Health and Human Services.

————. 1995b. *Program Results/Performance Measurements Audit, State of Texas*. Washington, D.C.: Department of Health and Human Services.

Okin, Susan Moller. 1979. *Women in Western Political Thought*. Princeton: Princeton University Press.

————. 1989. *Justice, Gender, and the Family*. New York: Basic Books.

————. 1991. "Gender, the Public and the Private," in David Held, ed., *Political Theory Today*. Cambridge: Polity.

Olsen, Frances. 1983. "The Family and the Market: A Study of Ideology and Legal Reform", *Harvard Law Review* 96: 1497–1578.

Pateman, Carole. 1983. "Feminist Critiques of the Public/Private Dichotomy." In *Public and Private in Social Life*, edited by S. I. Benn and G. F. Gaus. New York: St. Martin's Press.

————. 1988a. "The Patriarchal Welfare State", In *Democracy and the Welfare State*, edited by Amy Gutmann. Princeton: Princeton University Press.

————. 1988b. *The Sexual Contract*. Stanford, Calif.: Stanford University Press.

Phillips, Roderick. 1991. *Untying the Knot: A Short History of Divorce*. Cambridge, England: Cambridge University Press.

Piven, Frances Fox and Richard A. Cloward. 1977. *Poor People's Movements: Why They Succeed, How They Fail*. New York: Vintage.

Polakow, Valerie. 1993. *Lives on the Edge: Single Mothers and their Children in the Other America*. Chicago: University of Chicago Press.

Quadango, Jill. 1988. "From Old Age Assistance to Supplemental Security Income: The Political Economy of Relief in the South 1935–1972." In *The Politics of Social Policy in the United States*, edited by Theda Skocpol, Margaret Weir, and Ann Shola Orloff. Princeton: Princeton University Press.

Regan, Milton C., Jr. 1993. *Family Law and the Pursuit of Intimacy*. New York: New York University Press.

Reeve, Tapping. 1862. *The Law of Baron and Femme*, 3rd ed. Albany: William Gould.

Roberts, Paula. 1991. *Turning Promises into Realities: A Guide to Implementing the Child Support Provisions of the Family Support Act of 1988*, 2nd ed. Washington, D.C.: Center for Law and Social Policy.

———. 1992a. "Cooperation in the Pursuit of Medical Support as an Eligibility Condition for AFDC and Medicaid," *Clearinghouse Review*, July 1992, 295–301.

———. 1992b. "An Idea Whose Time Has Come: Child Support Assurance," *Clearinghouse Review*, November 1992, 766–75.

———. 1992c. "Child Support Enforcement for Low Income Children," *District of Columbia Law Review*, 1 (Spring 1992): 143–56.

———. 1993. "Paternity Establishment: An Issue for the 90s," *Clearinghouse Review*, January 1993, 1019–29.

Rubin, Eva R. 1986. *The Supreme Court and the American Family: Ideology and Issues*. New York: Greenwood.

Ruddick, Sara. 1988. *Maternal Thinking: Towards a Politics of Peace*. Boston: Beacon.

Ryan, Alan. 1987. *Property*. Minneapolis: University of Minnesota Press.

Schneider, Carl. 1985. "Moral Discourse and the Transformation of American Family Law," *Michigan Law Review* 83:1803–79.

Schuele, Donna. 1989. "Origins and Development of the Law of Parental Child Support," *Journal of Family Law* 27: 807–41.

Select Committee on Children, Youth, and Families, U.S. House of Representatives. *Reclaiming the Tax Code for American Families*, hearing held April 15, 1991. Washington: Government Printing Office.

Singer, Jana B. 1989. "Divorce Reform and Gender Justice," *North Carolina Law Review* 67: 1103–21.

———. 1992. "The Privatization of Family Law", *Wisconsin Law Review* 1992: 1443–1567.

Skocpol, Theda, Margaret Weir, and Ann Shola Orloff, eds., 1988. *The Politics of Social Policy in the United States*. Princeton: Princeton University Press.

Skocpol, Theda. 1992. *Protecting Soldiers and Mothers: The Political Origins of Social Policy in the United States*. Cambridge: Harvard University Press.

Skowronek, Stephen. 1982. *Building A New American State: The Expansion of National Administrative Capacities, 1877–1920*. New York: Cambridge University Press.

Smart, Carol. 1989. *Feminism and the Power of Law*. London: Routledge.

Smith, Rogers. 1993. "Beyond Tocqueville, Myrdal, and Hartz: The Multiple Traditions in America," *American Political Science Review* 87: 549–566.

Sorenson, Annemette. 1992. "Estimating the Economic Consequences of Separation and Divorce: A Cautionary Tale from the United States," *Economic Consequences of Divorce: The International Perspective*, Lenore Weitzman and Mavis Maclean, eds. Oxford: Clarendon.

Stacey, Judith. 1990. *Brave New Families*. New York: Basic Books.

Stack, Carol. 1974. *All Our Kin: Strategies for Survival in a Black Community*. New York: Harper & Row.

Stamm, Lisa. 1991. "In Pursuit of Improved Child Support Enforcement," *University of Cinncinnati Law Review* 60 (Summer): 221–50.

Struening, Karen. 1996. "Feminist Challenges to the New Familialism: Lifestyle Experimentation and the Freedom of Intimate Association," *Hypatia* 11 (Winter): 135–54.

Subcommittee on Children, Family, Drugs, and Alcoholism, Committee on Labor and Human Resources, U.S. Senate. 1992. *Hearing on the Child Support Assurance Act of 1992* (S. 2343), June 4, 1992. Washington, D.C.: Government Printing Office.

Subcommittee on Crime and Criminal Justice of the Committee on the Judiciary, U.S. House of Representatives. 1992. *Hearing on H.R. 1241, "Criminal Penalty for flight to avoid payment of arrearages in child support,"* January 15, 1992. Washington, D.C.: Government Printing Office.

Subcommittee on Human Resources of the Committee on Ways and Means, U.S. House of Representatives. 1989. *The Child Support Enforcement Program: Policy and Practice*, (prepared by the Congressional Research Service), December 5, 1989. Washington, D.C.: Government Printing Office.

———. 1991. *Child Support Enforcement Report Card*, January 3, 1991. Washington, D.C.: Government Printing Office.

———. 1993a. *Written Comments on the Downey-Hyde Child Support Enforcement and Assurance Proposal*. Washington, D.C.: Government Printing Office.

———. 1993b. *Child Support Enforcement*, Hearing held June 10, 1993. Washington, D.C.: Government Printing Office.

———. 1995. *Child Support Enforcement Provisions Included in the Personal Responsibility Act as Part of the Contract with America*, Hearing held February 6, 1995. Washington, D.C.: Government Printing Office.

Subcommittee on Social Security and Family Policy, Committee on Finance, U.S. Senate. 1991. Hearing: *Child Support Enforcement*, September 16, 1991. Washington, D.C.: Government Printing Office.

Sunstein, Cass. 1993. *The Partial Constitution*. Cambridge: Harvard University Press.

tenBroek, Jacobus. 1964–65. "California's Dual System of Family Law: Its Origin, Development, and Present Status", Parts I, II, and III, *Stanford Law Review* 16 (March 1964): 257–317, 16 (July 1964): 900–81, 17 (April 1965): 614–82.

Texas Attorney General's Office. 1986. *Fiscal Year 1986 Summary of Accomplishments*. Austin: Office of the Attorney General.

———. 1991. *Texas Attorney General: The People's Lawyer. The Mattox Administration, 1983–1990*. Austin: Office of the Attorney General.

Texas House/Senate Joint Interim Committee on Child Support. 1988. *Final Report to the 71st Legislature*. Austin: Texas State Legislature.

Texas Office of the State Auditor. 1992. "Management Audit of the Texas Child Support Enforcement Program." Austin: Office of the State Auditor.

———. 1995. "An Audit Report on Selected Field Offices of the Attorney General's Child Support Division." Austin: Office of the State Auditor.

Tiffin, Susan. 1982. *In Whose Best Interest? Child Welfare Reform in the Progressive Era*. Westport, Conn.: Greenwood.

U.S. Bureau of the Census. 1991. Current Population Reports, Series P-60, No. 173, *Child Support and Alimony: 1989*. Washington, D.C.: U.S. Government Printing Office.

———. 1995. Current Population Reports, Series P-60, No. 187, *Child Support for Custodial Mothers and Fathers: 1991*. Washington, D.C.: U.S. Government Printing Office.

United States Commission on Interstate Child Support. 1992. *Supporting Our Children: A Blueprint for Reform*. Washington, D.C.: U.S. Government Printing Office.

Vernier, Chester G. 1932. *American Family Law* (5 vols.). Stanford: Stanford University Press.

Walzer, Michael. 1990. "The Communitarian Critique of Liberalism," *Political Theory* 18: 6–23.

Weitzman, Lenore. 1987. "Women and Children Last: The Social and Economic Consequences of Divorce Law Reform." In *Feminism, Children and the New Families*, edited by Sanford Dornbusch and Myra Strober. New York: Guilford Press.

Weitzman, Lenore. 1985. *The Divorce Revolution: The Unexpected Social and Economic Consequences for Women and Children in America*. New York: Free Press.

West, Robin. 1988. "Jurisprudence and Gender," *University of Chicago Law Review* 55: 1–72.

West, Robin. 1987. "The Difference in Women's Hedonic Lives," *Wisconsin Women's Law Journal* 3: 81–145.

Weston, Kath. 1991. *Families We Choose*. New York: Columbia University Press.

Wetchler, Sherry. 1992. "Child Support Awards: Public Preferences, Public Policy, and Government Behavior." PhD Diss. University of Maryland.

Williams, Joan. 1991."Deconstructing Gender." In *Feminist Legal Theory: Readings in Law and Gender*, edited by Katharine T. Bartlett and Rosanne Kennedy. Boulder: Westview.

Williams, Robert. 1985. *Development of Guidelines for Establishing and Updating Child Support Orders: Interim Report*. Denver: National Center for State Courts.

Williams, Wendy. 1982. "The Equality Crisis," *Women's Rights Law Reporter* 7: 175.

Wilson, James Q. 1993. *The Moral Sense*. New York: Free Press.

Wood, Gordon. 1969. *The Creation of the American Republic, 1776–1787*. New York: Norton.

Young, Iris Marion. 1995. "Mothers, Citizenship, and Independence: A Critique of Pure Family Values," *Ethics* 105 (April): 535–56.

Zingo, Martha T., and Kevin E. Early. 1994. *Nameless Persons: Legal Discrimination Against Non-Marital Children in the United States.* Westport: Praeger.

Index

About the Author

Jyl J. Josephson is an assistant professor in the political science department of Texas Tech University, where she teaches courses in modern and contemporary political theory and American politics and public policy. Her primary research interests include social welfare policy, feminist theory, and contemporary political thought.